T0265523

THE
MOTHERLOAD

THE
MOTHERLOAD

Episodes from the Brink
of Motherhood

Sarah Hoover

Simon Element

New York   Amsterdam/Antwerp   London   Toronto   Sydney   New Delhi

SIMON ELEMENT

An Imprint of Simon & Schuster, LLC
1230 Avenue of the Americas
New York, NY 10020

Copyright © 2025 by Bang Bang, LLC

First Simon Element hardcover edition January 2025

SIMON ELEMENT is a trademark of Simon & Schuster, LLC

For information about special discounts for bulk purchases,
please contact Simon & Schuster Special Sales at 1-866-506-1949
or business@simonandschuster.com.

The Simon & Schuster Speakers Bureau can bring authors to your
live event. For more information or to book an event, contact the
Simon & Schuster Speakers Bureau at 1-866-248-3049 or visit
our website at www.simonspeakers.com.

Interior design by Laura Levatino

Manufactured in the United States of America

10 9 8 7 6 5 4 3 2 1

Library of Congress Cataloging-in-Publication Data has been applied for.

ISBN 978-1-6680-1013-6
ISBN 978-1-6680-1015-0 (ebook)

Certain names and identifying characteristics have been changed.

To Guy Sachs, for changing everything.

Contents

THE
MOTHERLOAD

Edinburgh Postnatal Depression Scale

Name: _____   Address: _____

Your Date of Birth: _____   _____

Baby's Date of Birth: _____   Phone: _____

As you are pregnant or have recently had a baby, we would like to know how you are feeling. Please check the answer that comes closest to how you have felt **IN THE PAST 7 DAYS**, not just how you feel today.

Here is an example, already completed.

I have felt happy:
- ☐ Yes, all the time
- ☒ Yes, most of the time   This would mean: "I have felt happy most of the time" during the past week.
- ☐ No, not very often   Please complete the other questions in the same way.
- ☐ No, not at all

In the past 7 days:

1. I have been able to laugh and see the funny side of things
   - ☐ As much as I always could
   - ☐ Not quite so much now
   - ☐ Definitely not so much now
   - ☐ Not at all

2. I have looked forward with enjoyment to things
   - ☐ As much as I ever did
   - ☐ Rather less than I used to
   - ☐ Definitely less than I used to
   - ☐ Hardly at all

*3. I have blamed myself unnecessarily when things went wrong
   - ☐ Yes, most of the time
   - ☐ Yes, some of the time
   - ☐ Not very often
   - ☐ No, never

4. I have been anxious or worried for no good reason
   - ☐ No, not at all
   - ☐ Hardly ever
   - ☐ Yes, sometimes
   - ☐ Yes, very often

*5. I have felt scared or panicky for no very good reason
   - ☐ Yes, quite a lot
   - ☐ Yes, sometimes
   - ☐ No, not much
   - ☐ No, not at all

*6. Things have been getting on top of me
   - ☐ Yes, most of the time I haven't been able to cope at all
   - ☐ Yes, sometimes I haven't been coping as well as usual
   - ☐ No, most of the time I have coped quite well
   - ☐ No, I have been coping as well as ever

*7 I have been so unhappy that I have had difficulty sleeping
   - ☐ Yes, most of the time
   - ☐ Yes, sometimes
   - ☐ Not very often
   - ☐ No, not at all

*8 I have felt sad or miserable
   - ☐ Yes, most of the time
   - ☐ Yes, quite often
   - ☐ Not very often
   - ☐ No, not at all

*9 I have been so unhappy that I have been crying
   - ☐ Yes, most of the time
   - ☐ Yes, quite often
   - ☐ Only occasionally
   - ☐ No, never

*10 The thought of harming myself has occurred to me
   - ☐ Yes, quite often
   - ☐ Sometimes
   - ☐ Hardly ever
   - ☐ Never

Administered/Reviewed by _____   Date _____

[1] Source: Cox, J.L., Holden, J.M., and Sagovsky, R. 1987. Detection of postnatal depression: Development of the 10-item Edinburgh Postnatal Depression Scale.   *British Journal of Psychiatry* 150:782-786 .

[2] Source: K. L. Wisner, B. L. Parry, C. M. Piontek, Postpartum Depression N Engl J Med vol. 347, No 3, July 18, 2002, 194-199

1

Baby Drop

Los Angeles
August 2018

THE LAST LINE OF MY BABY SHOWER INVITATION SAID *no gifts unless it's drugs*. I'd never bought drugs myself, you know, aside from occasionally shoving a couple of bills into someone else's hands on their way out of a bar to go meet a coke dealer. But when I walked through the gate of the Chateau Marmont and saw the little bungalow we were renting–the dingy, midcentury house with long sliding glass doors that opened into a verdant yard–I couldn't resist scribbling my addendum below the RSVP instructions. It seemed like the perfect formula for a party to introduce my ten-month-old son to Los Angeles. I'd be in LA for a couple of weeks, staying at the hotel, and a diet of room service and edibles was my general game plan. Throwing a party would be the icing on that mess of a cake.

You should totally come! I texted some stranger I'd met earlier that day in the dressing room at Maxfield. *Bring a friend! Bring a friend with fake lips and access to pharmaceutical painkillers!*

A week prior, in sleep-deprived desperation, I'd made my husband, Tom, swear to get us out of New York, a place I found impossible to navigate with a tiny baby and his unwieldy stroller, something I'd never had to think about just ten months before. I'd begged him to take us somewhere west, somewhere I could just be quiet and warm, somewhere my postpartum brain, which felt like a tangled jumble, could settle.

I love the idea, but I can't make it for a few weeks, Tom said, stirring his coffee. He liked a wooden spoon so that he wouldn't hear it scrape the ceramic *chawan* he used as a mug. *I really have way too much going on at the office to leave right now. How about I come to you at the end of the month? Afterward, we can all go on that Bali trip together.*

I must have made a face then because his tone shifted. *Let me finish some stuff up here, and we'll go on an adventure, the three of us. You, me, and Guy.*

The very mention of a trip to Southeast Asia with a baby made my blood run cold. That sounded like a long stretch of time in an unknown environment with a kid. What if he cried? Got sick? Needed too much from me? I didn't want to think that far ahead, and when I pinched my eyes shut and tried to focus, the kitchen seemed to undulate slightly, as if a subway train were passing under my apartment. What I didn't understand then, as the room felt like it was closing in on me, was how deep I already was in the claws of an illness I could not name, half of my twisted thoughts and actions and reactions a consequence of everything inside me going wrong.

Wonderful, I said. *I can't wait.*

THE MORNING OF MY PARTY, I threw on a little dress embroidered with red mouths smoking cigarettes. Skipping barefoot around our enclosed backyard, I tied big, round balloons in primary colors on the tall gates, the bottom of my butt cheeks peeking out as I reached up to secure their strings. I'd shortened my dress so much that the tailor raised his eyebrows at me, but my dog, Napoleon, didn't seem to judge. He was following at my heels, sniffing the balloons suspiciously like they were strange alien life-forms floating in a breeze he couldn't feel. After I finished decorating, I walked him to the edge of the lawn to pee, kicking the ground softly while I waited for him to finish. Through the long sliding door, I could see our nanny, Sharon, as she changed the baby's diaper on her bed. Behind me, the high gate separated our bungalow from the pool and the main hotel. As I walked, I felt the grass slide strangely under my feet, so I nudged it again. Bending down to inspect it, I tugged on a few blades at the corner and realized it was laid out in one sheet like a big, lush, jade carpet. A pretend lawn. It was perfect.

James from in-room dining popped by to set up some cocktail tables and a bar, and I littered them with crayons, paper, cigarettes, and lighters. There'd be passed appetizers, lots of vodka, and a very casual door policy. And, of course, drugs.

I'D BEEN DRINKING WHITE WINE since noon when I got my long, disheveled, blonde hair blow-dried in my bedroom. While Napoleon growled softly at the blow-dryer, I sipped my Chardonnay from a teacup, trying to ignore the hairstylist's inadvertent insults. Sharon sat on the bed with the baby in her arms so that they could keep me company.

For someone with hair that's so frizzy and damaged, it blow-dries really well, she said. Sip. *Bark.* The dog had seen me through the worst parts of my early twenties. In return for his devotion, I'd spent the last decade bringing him everywhere, brushing his teeth nightly with poultry-flavored toothpaste, and insisting he sleep in my bed with his head on my floral-print pillowcases.

Have you ever thought about extensions? My girlfriend in Westlake does them for cheap. Have you ever heard about telogen effluvium? You should google it. You'll die.

I tried to take a deep breath, but it was hard to get air in. My rib cage felt too small for my lungs. I tried again and counted to twelve, my magic number. If I could just keep counting to twelve, I might have a shot at today being a good day.

You okay, baby doll? Sharon asked, the baby now asleep over her shoulder. She always played the slot machines on her phone while he napped.

Totally! I lied. I had to. Ever since I'd had this baby, I'd been lying constantly, too fixated on being a *good girl* to care that I was also being a bit of a con artist. But I couldn't tell her, or anyone, my ugly truth: so far, for me, motherhood had been an all-out fucking war. I felt nothing for this baby who'd come out of my body. I didn't want to change diapers and pretend I thought baby stuff was cute. I had no interest in sitting in Mommy-and-Me music classes or play groups where the squishy whelps drooled and stared at one another while all the mommies acted like it was all the most fun they'd ever had, gleefully proclaiming the magical love they felt for their offspring, which they avowed made all the boring parts worthwhile. Meanwhile, my baby, this baby, felt like a stranger to me, and I was gearing up for another afternoon of faking it. It wasn't that I'd hired a nanny that had kept me from some sort of maternal bonding. It wasn't that I'd thus avoided most of the poo-poo diapers and spit-up and nighttime crying and didn't fully understand the immensity of the situation I'd created. It was the simple, unspeakable reality that from the moment he was born, this baby sometimes meant as much to me as a stone-cold marble statue in the antiquities section of an art museum–aka something that I knew was valuable, but not so much to me. It didn't help that I found him so ugly, with all my worst traits: weird eyes and big ears, a mini replica of my own self-loathing.

So instead of admitting any of that, which felt like a Manson-family-level crime–which I'm not even sure I could have found the words for if I wanted to–I decorated and festooned until everything looked Stepford perfect, frozen in California nostalgia, lit by flat sun through hazy western dust.

Even ten months postpartum, my thighs rubbed together in a

way they never had in my life, and I still looked pregnant—a little puffy around the belly button—but the more wine I sipped, the less embarrassed that made me. I yawned, but I couldn't blame the booze for that: I hadn't slept more than two hours at a time since the baby was born, and not because I was performing the requisite maternal task of breastfeeding. I hadn't done that for one second of one day, and the thought of even trying had made a flash of something hot burn inside my ribs, my brow start to sweat, and my vision get wonky. With the luxury of Sharon working for us, I technically could have been sleeping through the night since the day I got home from the hospital. But my brain wouldn't let me.

Instead, every night, in my dreams, I watched the baby die. Night after night after night, I'd be jolted from sleep by some gruesome scene or other: he'd be shot by snipers, thrown onto the train tracks, burned up in a house fire. Or even dropped at the pool, his helpless little body making a horrible thud when it hit the ground—and I'd lie there, eventually opening Instagram to distract myself. I'd fall back asleep for a few minutes, and then *bam*, another grisly nightmare. I'd wake in the morning after interrupted, insufficient sleep, with faint traces of these dreams infiltrating my thoughts all day, making me feel shaky and nervous whenever I took my baby outside or down the stairs, or when I left him at home to go to work at the gallery. Even when I knew he was safe, I had little visions, cinematic blips of unspeakable things going wrong. And I didn't think that was so strange—wasn't motherhood a stew of worries? Didn't everyone always say that having a baby was like wearing your heart on the outside of your chest? My brain's sinister spasms, the tiny shudders of violence and horror it made me think of all day long, were mine to suffer alone and in silence.

There's a painting by Cecily Brown, one of my all-time favorites, and I pictured it often: it was one of those startling human creations that I was privy to experiencing in my art gallery job, singularly beautiful enough to stick in my brain. It's called *Black*

Painting I, a particularly literal and not very descriptive title, and it shows a loosely executed, writhing female form rendered in pale marzipan tones on a dusty-black background. What first appears to be shooting stars exploding above the erotically contorted torso reveal themselves, upon closer study, to be dicks: a hundred excited penises raining down from the Milky Way on the subject's dreamland. I would have loved to have sweet dreams like that in the months after I had Guy, and when I closed my eyes at night, I prayed for such a masturbatory fantasy. But my dreams were so horribly visceral. They lingered.

The thudding sound of Guy being dropped by the pool was so specific that I could feel a tingling at the back of my head, almost a burn, when I woke up with a gasp. I was never able to shake it. I'd see Tom tossing Guy in the air, like dads do, and hear his little giggle, his baby arms reaching toward a cerulean sky, and then *smack*, hear his soft, tiny body landing on the concrete. Late at night, I'd replay this scene, picturing the spot where his head hit, if it was on the pool gutter or just the ground; I'd imagine if it bled, if he died. Even though no part of me wanted anything like this to ever happen to any child, let alone my own, I suppose I wanted to test myself—to gauge how I'd feel if it ever came true. To try to fend off the likelihood of it happening by fixating on it.

BY FOUR O'CLOCK, friends and their friends and their significant others started showing up to my shindig. They pushed their little gifts into my palm, mixing their own drinks at the bar. I let people hold the baby even if they hadn't washed their hands first, and he went silently from lap to lap. I don't think he'd ever seen so many people. I held him briefly for a picture and sent it right off to my friend to photoshop. I didn't look right holding him, I thought; it looked like I'd borrowed him as a joke—*Ha ha, imagine if I was really so stupid as to think I could be good at having a baby*—and my dress was bunched up weirdly where he clung to my hip, exposing a leg that didn't even look like it belonged to my body.

By midnight, I'd changed, put on a silk chemise over a bikini, trying to make my new curves work in my favor, piling up my hair on my head to avoid the smell from all the people smoking in my backyard.

Don't put cigarettes out in the grass, I kept telling everyone. *It could catch on fire! Los Angeles is in a drought!* And they all thought I was making some sort of dumb joke, giggling at me and ashing wherever they wanted. I don't know why I hadn't thought of that sober, when I'd put packs and lighters all over the place, but suddenly it seemed urgent, and then, just as suddenly, I stopped caring, so I went down to the pool with someone I'd met just then—someone's girlfriend—and got in up to my thighs while she dove under in her clothes. I let the silk of my hem drift in the water. I stared at it, hoping the chlorine wouldn't dye it, watching torn leaves and drowned bugs float in its wake. Suddenly the hotel pool phone rang, echoing across the water in the black night and jangling my brain enough that I went to pick it up.

Ms. Hoover? The owner of the hotel would love to come up to your bungalow. We know you're having guests in tonight, but he has someone he'd like to show the property to. I said that was fine and went back up to make sure no one had lit the ground on fire.

ONE PERSON HANDED ME A VAPE PEN, and some guy handed me a tiny pebble of what looked like shit. *It's mushroom tar; just trust me*, he said, and I did them both. By the time the owner walked in, I hardly recognized him.

Thanks for having us, he said. I watched his eyes look around the living room and wondered if he noticed that I'd taken down the painting above the fireplace. I hadn't liked it, but, should he ask me about this, my inebriated, fuzzy brain couldn't think of an excuse that was polite. *I'm just showing my friends here the space. They might check in next month.*

Tom is coming soon, I told them, doing my best to be sober and welcoming. *We'll have you back for cocktails, and you can see the place when it's less of a mess. And meet my baby! He's asleep.* They smiled, and I hoped I'd gotten away with it. I hoped I seemed stable.

Let me tell you a story about this bungalow, the owner said, becoming the immediate center of the party. *John Belushi died here, and once, in the middle of the night, I was sleeping in that bedroom back there—*he pointed all the way down the hallway, to the room I was sleeping in—*I swear I saw his ghost. I couldn't move, I was so damn scared. I was literally frozen in place. I haven't stayed here since*, he said proudly.

People were staring at him with rapt attention, and I couldn't help myself.

That's called sleep paralysis, I said. *Ghosts don't exist.* Everyone continued to look at him, as if I wasn't totally right. It was as if they couldn't hear me. *If ghosts existed, then God would exist, and if God existed, He wouldn't let me waste my life away in this puddle of misery and bullshit. I've never even seen a John Belushi movie*, I kept going, more to myself, standing at the back of the crowd.

Everyone was pretending to be amazed by the ghost story, looking mesmerized by the owner. Or maybe I hadn't spoken at all. Maybe I was just thinking so loudly that it seemed like I had.

And then the guests all seemed to leave my party at once, letting the tall door to our gate slam loudly. I could hear them laughing as they walked down the steps toward the pool and the towering, alabaster palace of the main hotel. I ordered a movie on the living room television, something innocuous and rom-com-y, and wandered around putting half-empty glasses into a bus bin that one of the servers had brought up for me. I stuck it outside so I wouldn't have to smell the tequila when I woke up, and as I walked to collect the balloons that I had placed so carefully, I noticed the expanse of grass sparkled with dew, and the grid lights of the city below us fanning out like endless airplane-landing strips. Birds were chirping. I'd been up for so long that the dark edge of night was tinted, and I figured the sun was soon rising. The drapes were drawn across the sliding door of my baby's room, and I knew he was safe and comfortable, fed, and alive, and lucky.

I showered to get the smoke out of my hair and climbed into my crisp, white hotel sheets, watching a daddy longlegs crawl across the ceiling, from corner to corner. I'd left all the doors open during the party; I probably had all sorts of creatures in here. I wondered if everyone was at home talking about how crazy I'd acted with the owner, how many drugs I'd done. I didn't know if it was obvious to anyone that I wasn't myself. I didn't know if I should be embarrassed. I didn't quite know what was reality and what was only in my head. And then I was asleep.

THE NEXT MORNING, I went down to the pool, hungover and stupid, settling myself in and staring at the lemon and orange trees at the water's edge. *Maybe if I could always live in a warm place where random trees grow delicious fruits, and find a way for this to be my life forever, I'd be happy?* I thought about the baby up in the room with Sharon, crawling around until I came up there for the mandated thirty minutes of playtime I forced myself to participate in a few times a day. My heart sank.

How dare I let myself be this miserable when I was so deeply fortunate? *He is loved and beautifully cared for, even if not by me*, I thought, wondering yet again if one day I'd feel guilty about any of this. I wondered what I'd be doing without Sharon. And I also wondered what was wrong with me that I felt so tortured. I couldn't even think that much about my situation—I couldn't even analyze it—without starting to panic.

If you had looked across the pool at that moment, you would have seen a tired, tan, blonde girl in a cheerleader pony, skinny but with a little belly, sitting underneath the giant billboard, always Gucci, that hovered over the pool and the Sunset Strip below. French families on vacation and old Angeleno men ordered rosé and pranced around like they deserved this life of leisure. It was cinematic and probably would have been kinda glamorous had I not been ugly crying behind my color-coordinated, heart-shaped glasses. I took out my phone and started typing a text to my best work friend, Petunia.

I'm so sad I don't know what to do. And then, realizing I'd have to explain myself with words I didn't have when she replied with something like *oh no bb what's wrong,* I deleted it letter by letter. I couldn't tell anyone how I felt for fear that they'd think I was being ridiculous. *Stop partying for a few days! It's probably the drugs,* my best friend since college, Augusta, would say. But I didn't want to stop partying; it was the only time I felt close to normal.

All I could manage was to sit, staring at that lemon tree over the pool, drinking a steady supply of Earl Grey iced teas with a shit ton of simple syrup. This would soon become my everyday workflow. Sure, there'd be half-hour breaks to order Caesar salads—*Extra croutons, please; this mom gut isn't going anywhere, so I might as well get my money's worth*—or swim with my baby. And I made sure to call my therapist from a pool chair to complain about everything from my sex life to my husband to how Britney Spears's lyrics were insidiously rapey, something I did twice weekly no matter who was around to listen.

About two weeks after the party, as I was writing in my journal one morning, Tom showed up at the pool, looking sexy and confident in his Ray-Bans.

Surprise, baby, he said and smiled, like his presence was a gift. *I came early,* he added softly, bending down for a kiss.

I squinted through the foggy anger I felt burning under my ribs and willed myself to fake it.

You're here! I squealed, snapping my journal shut and standing up quickly to meet his mouth. He had airplane breath, and it made me a little nauseous.

Guy is up in the bungalow if you want to bring him down for a swim. I pointed up the hill behind the pool. *He loves the water. He's been coming in with me every day, and you won't believe how cute it is.*

I was confused by what was spilling out of my mouth, like I was trying to convince my husband how well I'd been performing as a mother, when he could easily ask Sharon for the truth; when he'd see it for himself now that he was here. He went to get the baby and change into a swimsuit, and I flopped onto my stomach and opened another book. I admit that I did feel some sense of relief, like maybe I wouldn't need to put any effort into pretending to be a happy mommy now that my husband was here. Maybe I could just sleep and stare at the trees and let Tom pick up the slack, and maybe Sharon wouldn't notice that I couldn't even manage to do the bare minimum.

Tom came back down, Guy in his arms, and put him on the lounge chair next to mine, under an umbrella. *Does he need sunblock?* Tom asked.

Absolutely, I said, rolling back over to help. As I turned to face Guy, Tom walked away, leaving my little baby alone. And then I heard it. I didn't see him fall; my turn was too slow. But I knew intimately the sound of a baby's head hitting the ground. I'd been hearing that sound in my nightmares for months.

There was a pause. No one made any noise at all. I swear the birds stopped chirping, and everyone in the pool stopped swimming and slipped under the still water without even taking a breath.

I wondered if I was hallucinating, imagining this thing I'd

dreamed so many times: the crack of a little skull against cement. But then Guy started wailing, so I knew it was real. I knew he was alive, at least, that was good. But I knew that Tom had done it, just like my subconscious had feared and predicted; he'd dropped my little creature at the pool, he'd hurt him, possibly maiming him, maybe forever.

I felt all the blood in my body rush to my head so fast that the power of it made me dizzy. I grabbed Guy from the ground while his little fists shook in front of his red face. Tears streamed from his eyes. He was so scared he could hardly get the sobs out, and I rushed him behind some potted palms to soothe him. Tom followed soon after.

Is he okay? he asked, the words tumbling out quickly. The baby was screaming, and our conversation took on a frenetic tone. *I mean, I didn't even step away for two seconds!*

You and your weak-ass excuses, I said, my voice shaking in a half sob. *If you had any natural intelligence, you would know not to leave a baby on a high surface. You keep one hand on a baby. You have two hands so you can keep one on him!* My voice was getting higher and higher, and I could feel myself losing it, as the anxiety I'd been attempting to quell overtook me. *All the times I told you that, I knew you weren't listening. You always doubt my instincts. You never believe in me.* I wasn't sure I had instincts, or that I even believed in myself, but I couldn't stop my fury.

I held Guy close and rocked him, stabilizing my shaking hands with the balancing force of a rage so intense that it somehow focused me. Unbothered by the audience, I continued: *Of all the fucked-up, negligent, lazy-ass shit. Do you know how hard I worked to make this baby? I'm already battling so much, and I can't battle you too!*

Tom stared at me, blinking.

Oh, now you have nothing to say? Mr. Entitlement, Mr. Artist, with his own unique way of doing things, is silent?

Guy was still wailing, and I spun around, running him up to Sharon so that we could both cry in peace, not caring if Tom followed, which he did.

Sharon, it wasn't my fault, he said urgently as we both stepped into the bungalow. *He just rolled off the chair, but it was totally an accident. Should we go to urgent care?* She ignored him and shushed Guy until he calmed down.

You are a nightmare of a husband! I said in a voice so intense that it was practically an octave deeper than normal. *I hate you and I wish you would die.*

IT WAS THIS EMOTIONAL LANDSCAPE—this unscalable Everest of confused feelings and rocky desperation; this bottomless, agonizing worry about my child but simultaneous inability to feel anything resembling love for him; this rage over Tom's seeming lack of accountability; and this endless hatred of myself—that set me up perfectly to go off the deep end in the weeks and months that followed.

In my defense, birth and motherhood did not match up to the narrative I'd been fed, and it felt like a nasty trick. And while my mental breakdown was embarrassing at times, especially considering how it exposed me as a puerile and spoiled little fool, it also showed how pernicious it is to sell tales of motherhood being so distinctly wonderful and feminine: *the very essence of womanhood!* It wasn't all totally my fault, you know?

I'd been misled.

2

Balthazar

New York
2009

THE FIRST TIME TOM CALLED, I was at the gallery, sitting at my wooden desk, which we called the *Long Row*. All of us assistants shared an open-plan office with one desk, maybe twenty-five feet long, down the middle of the room, windowless chambers behind us housing our bosses.

I knew who he was when I took the call, of course. People told stories about him at the office. Little myths. I'd even read about him in my contemporary art history class at NYU. Plus, he was kind of what I call "New York famous," so I'd often heard his name. He was mentioned in tacky gossip columns like Page Six. People name-dropped him at parties. A girl he'd dated was on the cover of this downtown band's album. He guaranteed the leases of young film-makers and painters who couldn't afford their own studios, gave whole circles of sculptors and ceramicists their first gigs. He put on performance art shows that turned into street parties, which we all went to, clasping warm beers from the corner deli and people-watching. He'd once plastered the inside of taxi cabs with stickers that read *Kill All Artists*, and everyone talked about it. Stuff like that.

In other words, he wasn't real-world famous, so I had no idea what he looked like, but he was everything I wasn't: Established.

Influential. He was one of the very few people in the history of the world who had made it as an artist—that is, made enough money to live on solely from making their art.

It was a pretty small roster, and for girls like me and Petunia, who had studied art history in school, who followed the *New York Times* and *New Yorker* art reviews, read artist biographies the minute they were published, argued over drinks about who was a genius and who was derivative, spent Thursday nights going to gallery openings in Chelsea, and worshipped art and the art world, he was mythological. There was a scene around him: he had acolytes, collectors of his work, interesting friends, disciples. His writing had been published, and other people had written about him. There were entire books, heavy and beautiful, devoted to his sculptures. I had read all those books. All that had been written about me at that point were a few mawkish sentiments inside the front cover of my high school yearbook. All I'd written was sitting in my collection of private journals next to my bed.

Is there any chance you or someone in the research depart-ment can help me edit my Wikipedia? he asked. His voice sounded warm. I started googling him to see if I could find his picture. *The info they have on there about me is crap, especially the description of the last show I did with the gallery.*

On the screen, an image emerged of a man with thick hair, in a dark-navy linen jacket, which I would later learn was a copy of a vintage French work smock that Prada had made for him. He was wearing old Levi's that seemed faded by hard work and also a tie—one day I'd know it was his grandfather's—clipped into place with a piece of silver engraved with the word *Debaser*.

Of course, Mr. Sachs, I can help you with that. I saw your work—the Chanel Guillotine (Breakfast Nook), *which I loved, by the way—at the Pompidou museum a few years ago when I studied abroad. I took my mom to see it when she came to visit. I told her what you said, that it was "an examination of France's two most notorious exports," and she laughed.*

At that, I cringed, wondering how a sentence about my mom popped, unbidden, out of my mouth.

I'm really into the International Situationists? I added. *So, I could maybe contextualize you within that movement, talk about your work more as a response to capitalist ideas of ownership?* I hoped that made me sound competent, even though my high school debate coach told me to never end sentences with a question mark. She said it was something girls always did to undermine themselves. Why weren't my brain and my mouth connecting? *Don't you worry*, I continued, trying to make up for my nervous chatter by putting some confidence into my voice, *I'll make you sound as cool and smart as you are.* I looked down the Long Row to see if anyone was listening, but they were all typing away, heads down.

Oh, so you think I'm cool, he shot back. Somehow, I could hear the smile in his voice, a sound I would later come to know very well, and I grabbed my cell phone, texting Petunia, one seat away.

I'm on with Tom Sachs, and I swear he likes me. She smiled at her phone as it pinged.

Well, let's not go crazy; I said I'll make you "sound" cool. Maybe a little handsome, too.

I wondered if I'd get fired if someone was listening. I decided to ignore that concern as we volleyed back and forth.

Excuse me, but I am extremely handsome.

Oh yah? I'll believe it when I see it.

Well, come out to dinner with me, and you will.

My brain screeched to a halt. I couldn't even think for a few seconds; there was just black in there. I was in free fall. Biting my thumbnail, I decided to go for it.

Okay, okay, I'll think on that one, I said. Out of the corner of my eye, I could see Petunia studying me as she texted. I didn't have to look at my phone to know she was in relationship-coach mode.

Enough playtime for one day. I'll email your office with a new Wikipedia draft, I said.

After I hung up, I just sat there, a little unnerved to find myself flirting at work, and I let my mind wander, imagining dating him. It seemed unfathomable yet so fantastical that it could almost happen, like something you'd only visualize at the end of a very long shower, where you'd used up all the hot water thinking about possible iterations of your future.

A boyfriend hadn't been a goal for me when I'd started working in the art world at twenty-two and still in grad school. I just wanted to *live*. I had friends—so many friends—to hang with whenever I wanted. I had Petunia, next to me all day at work in her proper silk high-necked dresses and shiny little ballet flats. She lived in Greenpoint, which is a neighborhood in Brooklyn, with her boyfriend, who was a fine art framer. They had a big, shaggy rescue dog, Byron, who'd pull her hungover ass to the bakery in the mornings on her skateboard so she could bring donuts into work for me from Peter Pan, my favorite cruller in the city.

And there was Augusta, an immaculately tasteful Mississippian I'd met studying abroad in Paris. We were the only two blondes in a sea of smoking brunettes one night at the French equivalent of a dive bar in the Marais, and I could tell she was American immediately because of how big she was laughing, like one of those sparkling, glittering Fourth of July fireworks going off whenever her perfect little mouth opened.

I'd message the two of them, plus other friends from college, other friends from work, friends from home who had moved to NYC, friends I met at bars, friends from my summer internships, friends of friends who wanted to go out on the nights other friends didn't, friends who then became friends with one another. I wanted to eat New York alive with all of them. I wanted to laugh and drink and pose for sexy pictures and dance on tables, walk down deserted streets in Chinatown after midnight, forget my coat at home in January while wearing cheap vintage minidresses with no tights, and people-watch and gossip and devour my way through town so ravenously that I'd never be bored enough to sleep. I wanted everyone to like everyone else and crave one another's company the way I did. I wanted everything, all day–even work, even the mundane assistant tasks such as doing expense reports and budgets–to be fun as hell and I wanted it all to feel *cool*, like it was stuff you couldn't do in other cities.

Socialism starts with going out every night, said the late, great Warholian Glenn O'Brien. In that sense, I guess we could say I wanted to start a revolution, a coup against loneliness, an insurgency in support of fun and indulgence, for no other reason than it was absolutely the most vibrant I'd ever felt.

For years, I threw myself into the middle of it. I went to all the Thursday-night openings in Chelsea, trudging from gallery to gallery, from cheap white wine glass to cheap white wine glass, looking at all the art but mostly the artists. I scraped together money to buy the lowest-rung tickets to the junior parties held after all the major museum galas so that I could be in the museums at night, feeling glitzy, even though I wore the same thing to every single one: a sparkly black dress I'd bought at a vintage store in Paris on that study-abroad trip where I'd first learned about Tom's art.

The assistants, registrars, art handlers, and front desk staff from all the different galleries and museums would go out together after work. If a dingy dive bar had existed in downtown Manhattan in the 1950s, '60s, or '70s and was still around, it most likely had been a home away from home to some group of artists–or at least a source of income for them before they made it big. So, we'd find any hole-in-the-wall mentioned in an artist's biography–say, the White Horse Tavern in Jackson Pollock's–and try to soak up whatever was left of that avant-garde energy. We'd drink and spread art-world lore. Stories like the time Richard Serra's show of monumental steel sculptures was supposed to open on September 11, but the cranes were diverted to Ground Zero, or like how my favorite female painter had been forbidden by doctors to paint with acrylics while pregnant and breastfeeding, and so had been forced to take a two-year break to have a family—an inherent glass ceiling I couldn't reconcile. With drunk, impassioned tears in our eyes, we'd defend a painter we loved or denounce one we saw as being unduly influenced by predecessors, devoid of any original inspiration. We threw around gossip, like who was currently fucking whom, and any other intel that made us feel part of the food chain, where artists were always at the top.

And the artists always delivered. There was an artist couple in New York who lived without electricity, lit their town house only by candlelight, dressed like it was the Victorian era, and rode horses to work across the Brooklyn Bridge. I saw artists show up to parties nursing babies not their own and leave their breasts out during dinner. They railed lines of coke at the table at incredibly lavish events, such as one curated by a female performance artist who had installed a huge table of barbecued ribs in the middle of a loft space with a mechanized robotic fountain arm traveling back and forth over it, drizzling BBQ sauce and honey onto the meat. They put out their cigarettes in rooftop swimming pools and got into fights over *ideas* and talked about books and movies and museum shows instead of people.

The artists were the cool kids. They were untouchable. They were what I moved to New York to be, or at least to be around. If I wanted a lovely life, I could have had a much bigger house and an easier commute back in Indiana. But I wanted excitement, and culture, and to work surrounded by strange and interesting people. I did not want to go to Abercrombie & Fitch at the mall and then the local swim club for dinner.

SO WHEN TOM KEPT CALLING, I kept picking up. An older friend had told me that when she first moved to New York in the mid nineties, she'd seen him walking up the Bowery, barefoot, in army fatigues cut short, with a giant head of curls and a T-shirt printed with *Nuke the Swiss*, a sticker he plastered on every telephone pole south of Houston Street.

But when I talked to him—when anyone talked to him, it seemed from my reconnaissance—he was normal and kind and the opposite of art-world pretension. He felt like a safe spot in a crazy world, and I realized I didn't really know him, but I knew that my instincts told me he wasn't one of the bad guys. Over the next few months, a mix of flirting and work turned into real conversation, and eventually we formed a funny friendship. Finally, over take-out salads at the Long Row, Petunia asked what I was waiting for. *Why don't you just say yes to a date, you lunatic? He* likes *you. And he talks like he has a big dick.*

That's not actually a selling point, P. Big dicks kind of freak me out. I think I'm going to start a fan club for men with micropenises. No joke, I whispered, in case anyone was listening. *How do I find a boyfriend with a tiny dick?* She rolled her eyes at me.

Okay, well, he likes you, which is more than I can say for any of the other guys you think you're dating.

She had a point. The last man I'd gone out with had been secretly engaged, the one before that had basically taken me aside at a bar and told me to stop telling people we were seeing each other because it was making it hard for him to pick up girls. *So you don't want to meet my mom?* I'd said, and I swear it was a joke, but he'd looked panicked enough that it embarrassed me.

I dunno, I said to P. *People might think I'm trying to ride his coattails, even though I'm not sure where they'd even get me. Like I'm trying to skip a grade in school just to hang with the older kids.* I bit into a green bean and thought about how sick I was of all the delivery food in our neighborhood.

Stop caring what people think! I don't care what anyone thinks, and look how far it's gotten me! She looked to her right, at another assistant, also eating a shitty salad-bar lunch, and then down at her worn-in "work flats." We both laughed. *Ask Augusta what she thinks*, Petunia continued. *She's smarter than either of us.*

Augusta always had nice boyfriends, a pretty little apartment filled with her mom's surplus of antique furniture, a coveted internship, and a cousin coming to visit from down south who would take her to fancy dinners and foot the bill. She prioritized things such as marriage, and she loved babies, instinctively. We trusted her opinion about dating.

Petunia texted her on our group chat. *Should Sarah go out to dinner with a cool older artist whose work we love and who seems extremely nice? She's worried about the optics—eye roll. So annoying, needs mothering.* Our heads together, we watched the phone for a reply.

She's had a leg up all over town since she moved here, and suddenly optics are important? I'm sorry, am I back in the Mississippi delta? Is her daddy gonna answer the door when she gets picked up with his shotgun in hand? Go on the damn date! You can borrow a dress! Augusta had four older brothers, and she was always offering to loan out a dress, like it might come back to her with a sister inside it. *If it gets weird, we can always crash,* she added, which made me feel stronger.

WHEN I OPENED THE BEAUTIFUL wooden doors to Balthazar, the French brasserie in SoHo, and walked inside past the human-sized bouquet of peonies, I wasn't nervous. It sounds crazy, but the night already felt right. The hostess seated the two of us at a red leather booth large enough to accommodate four or five people, but it was just for me and Tom. She knew him by name and kissed both his cheeks.

Tom ordered a bottle of champagne and started asking questions about things we'd never talked about before, and it wasn't awkward the way a first date can be. There were no odd pauses or moments where we had to fish for conversation, and the only thing that made me feel anxious was when he looked right at me. He had huge brown eyes and a full head of big, soft curls. Something in me wanted to know what it smelled like to be close to his cheeks.

I told him about growing up in Indiana, about tornado season. I described standing outside in my dad's arms, watching lightning crackle across flat farmland, surreal skies behind shoulder-high corn. I told him how the clouds would be purple and green, like strange bruises, and it would get quiet, no birds chirping or squirrels shaking the trees. We'd wait for the storm to get so big that we'd have to go down to the basement. One time, I was in my mom's station wagon, bringing my little brother home from preschool, and we had to pull off onto the side of the road because we could see a twister tearing through the cornfields.

After tornado season would come the hottest, most humid summers you could ever imagine. Which meant that we had the best tomatoes, corn, and peaches on earth.

Better than Italy? he wanted to know. I rolled my eyes. The champagne bubbles had hit my brain, and I was feeling myself.

Yes, you fucking snob. Have you ever heard of a Decker melon? They're from Decker, Indiana. Down by my grandparents, close to Kentucky. They taste like fancy candy, and they're about twenty bucks at Dean & Deluca. He watched me talk like there was no one else in the room. I told him about stopping at farm stands in the summer on the way home from this giant cement pool, spring-fed with freezing-cold water. It was called the Riviera Club, but no one knew what the Riviera was—that it was a reference to a fancy area of France—so we just called it the Rivi. *Best grilled cheese I'll ever have. The gold standard to which all grilled cheeses are held.*

He said he wanted to visit. I said maybe he'd like the Indianapolis 500, telling him, *My family has had the same seats for, like, ninety years.*

The waitress handed us big bistro menus, and I asked him what he thought we should get–I had so much more to tell him that I didn't care what I ate. He said he'd order all his favorites, and I said that would be great. When he finished, he remembered what we'd been talking about, which threw me off guard. I was accustomed to men talking about themselves or not really listening to anything I said.

Is it like the Formula 1 race in Monaco?

Okay, no, and, clearly, you've not spent much time in the Midwest. The Indy 500 is faster, cooler, and way more fun, I explained. *You couldn't handle it. The first time I went to the Indianapolis 500, I was five. I could handle it, though, because I was just born like that.* I tossed my hair over my shoulder, and he laughed.

Usually, people didn't ask any questions or want to know anything about my life in Indiana. They figured I was small-town rich, from one of the few families in the middle of nowhere that could afford to send their offspring on some sort of Rumspringa to New York to find a husband.

And they were right. I *was* on the typical track. Private school, private college, job in the art world–which could have been the fashion world, or publishing. I'd meet a man in finance, also from somewhere midwestern, and we'd move close to home after our first baby.

But Tom soaked in everything I was saying. Sometimes he'd pull out a little yellow notebook with a soft cover, and a five-color pen from the plastic protector in his breast pocket and write down something. *I'll look that up,* he'd say. Or *I don't want to forget this.*

He told me all about his own family: how he'd lived in Bogota, Colombia, for his dad's corporate job when he was a kid. His mom had a stillbirth, and the baby was buried in the Jewish cemetery there. They'd settled in Westport, Connecticut, "the bohemian Greenwich," by the time he was seven. Tom's parents dropped acid in the backyard with their friends and made him repeat both kindergarten and ninth grade, which would presage his getting kicked out of both college and architecture school. One of Tom's greatest influences was his aunt Alma, a psychotherapist who performed LSD therapy when it was still legal out of the guest wing of her full-floor apartment in the El Dorado, a storied building on Manhattan's Upper West Side. She told him to read Ralph Ellison when he started making sculptures of stuff his parents couldn't afford, like a film camera, and he thought his homemade versions would be second best.

I found Tom adorably nerdy when he snorted, the way he rolled his eyes and guffawed at my joke about Jane Jacobs, the activist and urban planner I'd obsessed over for all of senior year in college, then hot when he took off his sweater and I saw his biceps while he was telling me about drug use during the Third Reich and why the existentialism inherent in living at the edge of Western civilization produced Hollywood, the Conceptual art movement, Scientology, *and* the Jet Propulsion Laboratory. I was amazed by him, not just because he was smart and well read and fun but also because he was what I'd hoped for when I moved to New York. He talked about ideas—not people, not gossip, not stuff. He wanted to hear about my master's thesis and how I loved Foucault, how reading about the panopticon in his book *Discipline and Punish* changed the way I saw school and work and everything else. Tom trafficked in paradoxes: *Creativity is the enemy* and *One plus one equals a million.* I learned later that these were his signature phrases that he applied to everything, from his art to advertisements.

The space program is the greatest art project of the twentieth century, he told me, dipping his fry into the au poivre sauce. *But* Grand Theft Auto *is the greatest art project of the twenty-first.* His eyes and his smile were impish as he said it, and I thought I'd never met someone brilliant like this: every facet of him shimmering with excitement and enthusiasm and goodness toward what could be learned in life and shared with other humans.

After a seafood tower and a bottle of champagne, and another bottle of red wine, Tom looked at me sheepishly. I thought I'd said something wrong for a second, that maybe I blew it.

I forgot my wallet, he said, fumbling in the pockets of his jeans. I couldn't tell if he was joking. *And if you want to walk with me to my studio a block away, I can get it and come back and pay.* I figured he was trying to get me to go to his studio with him so he could kiss me.

I'd rather not go to the second location just yet, I said, sinking into the cracked banquette. I felt myself deflate at the idea that this guy I thought was so nice was lying to me with some weird wallet story instead of just making a move, but I put my emergency credit card down before I could do any more analysis. I heard Tom say to the waiter, *I'll take all this to go,* gesturing to the steaks we'd been too excited to eat.

What a weirdo, I thought. *Taking the food I can't afford, and I'll now have to ruin my month to pay for.*

I knew I had the safety net of my parents, and that separated me from most people, but their credit card, kept in the last pocket of my wallet, was for real emergencies, and I wasn't sure fanciful dinners with rogue artists qualified. Even with their help, I'd run out of money by payday regularly, and every month was a different scramble. Sometimes I'd use old gift cards to pay for dinner; sometimes I'd take NyQuil and go to bed without any. Sometimes I'd overdraw my account, and I'd eat green apples and saltines, which I kept on top of my fridge. It was a very delicate balancing act: if I bought even one extra thing–a manicure or a thrift store dress–I'd have to make up for it with a few missed or compromised meals. I don't think I ever went to the dentist or doctor for things like routine checkups, knowing that would have put me over the financial edge.

I had no shame about this. Except for Augusta, most of my friends were living the same way. I knew I had nothing to complain or worry about—but still, Tom was leaving me with a bill I couldn't afford, and I was not quite sure of the polite way to handle it or if it meant anything. Was I horrible at feminism if I had assumed he would pay? Should I have never accepted an invite if I couldn't split the bill halfway, like a proper grown-up? I wondered if it was a sign that he didn't like me or care.

We went out into the humid air and made awkward goodbyes, not touching. The street was empty, and we saw a huge rat crawling across a trash bag. Tom insisted on waiting for a taxi with me, telling me about a time in the nineties in Chinatown when he walked outside his studio and there were hundreds of rats walking down the middle of the avenue like they were marching to protest something.

I don't think you could make it without my help against all those rats, he said. *They seemed pretty coordinated. It was a troop surge, Gunnery Sergeant Hartman-style.* I made a joke about him being brave and manly, which fell a little flat as he helped me into a cab.

The next day at work, the front desk buzzed me around lunchtime.

There's a messenger here for you? said Rosa, one of the front desk girls. She had one of the hardest jobs, I think, dealing with the public all day long and manning the phones. *He's from Tom Sachs's studio?* Heads popped up at the seats around me. Petunia made eye contact with me and wiggled her eyebrows, so I widened my eyes at her to make her stop, then peeled my thighs off my chair and ran downstairs to the front of the gallery.

A guy my age stood, holding his fixed-gear bike in the massive, polished concrete entrance, twenty-foot-tall glass doors behind him. His helmet looked almost rustic in contrast with the smooth, minimalist entrance desk, helmed by two young women dressed in all black. They pretended to type emails while keeping one eye on this dude. In his bike basket was a big white bag that read "Mc-

Donald's," scrawled in Sharpie. He handed it to me, and I rushed out a breathless *Thank you!* as I tore the bag open.

Inside were a dozen steak sandwiches and two folded hundred-dollar bills. The sandwiches were wrapped in ersatz McDonald's packaging, and there was a note that read *I hope you enjoy the leftovers. I used my grandma's sandwich recipe.*

OVER THE NEXT FEW WEEKS, Tom and I drove to New Jersey and went indoor skydiving. Then I took him to a nearby mall and ordered all my favorite junk food at a Cheesecake Factory, where he'd never been. We went to Connecticut and took driving lessons at the Chip Barber Racing School and then practiced donuts in his old Jeep in a nearby parking lot. We pulled off on the side of the highway to make out on our way home, my stomach flip-flopping out of my body. One night, after dinner, he took me to the big graveyard near JFK Airport. He led me to a crypt with the door cracked open. Inside, a cellist played Bach's *Goldberg Variations* while a bartender made cocktails.

We went to Philip Johnson's Glass House for a small dinner, and Tom showed me through the archives, talking to me about the paintings and what they all meant to him. He flipped over the Frank Gehry-designed chair in Philip's library and said, *I knew it! This is a prototype; I made it with my own hands when I worked for Frank after I failed out of architecture school.* The way he said it was almost like a kid–so earnest and excited. Later, he took me for a tour of his studio, a space in Chinatown where he'd worked since the nineties, even living in the lofted bedroom area when he first came to New York. Back then, Chinatown was still the machine district. *This neighborhood is how we beat the Nazis*, he told me, unlocking the roll-down gate. *We out-manufactured them thanks to the factories that were in buildings like these.* He opened his door and punched off the alarm, and I stepped into a long, dimly lit space. The ceilings were double height, but the walls weren't quite wide enough apart for it to be considered a loft, and there were no columns in the middle, like the big, industrial SoHo spaces I was used to seeing turned into chic apartments. I could make out strange, lumpy shapes–tables and chairs, I thought–darker than the space between them.

This was, at one point a really long time ago, a workspace of Thomas Edison, Tom said. *Can you feel the ghosts?*

He flipped a light switch, and a cat scampered out of the way. Then the shapes became a jumble of old-fashioned-looking machinery, which he told me were welding tools. Behind him stood a wall of wooden cabinets, like a turn-of-the-century doctor's office or maybe an old library. Each little drawer was carefully labeled on its face, *washers* and *logjam* and *14 pan* and other words I didn't know, and everything was so perfectly organized but also confusing, and I wondered if this is what it was like to be in his brain.

When I glanced up at the old tin ceiling, I saw a surfboard he'd made in the nineties with an unauthorized Chanel logo on it, long before any fashion brands made nonclothing items and branded them. On a very high shelf there was a nativity scene made out of what looked like papier-mâché, but the Jesus figure was Bart Simpson, and Mary was a Hello Kitty. I remembered from art history class that he'd been protested by the Catholic League for that work. I followed him through a hallway lined with thick books–*My research library; it's organized by subject*–and then we continued to a room of shelves and deep, labeled bins, boxes of Bibles and baby dolls and Barbie legs and skateboard wheels and suture kits in alphabetical order, one after another–until we got to the wooden stairs down to a cavernous basement where the woodworking happened.

This is my sacred space, he said solemnly. *It's the place where I'm the most me. If being an artist were illegal and punishable by death, I would die for the feeling I have when I am in here making my work.*

Maybe someone else would hear this and think it was strange, or a red flag of some sort, but I found it inspirational—and sort of hot that he had such passion. Maybe one day he'd have that sort of fervor for me. I could see outlines on the walls where paintings had once hung, and half-finished paintings were mounted around them, like a palimpsest of an entire career. I thought about how making art was some sort of magic, like alchemy, where the right person could look at their own story, the sadness and the joy and the fucked-up parts of their life, and see a way to make it so interesting and beautiful that it would make other people *think.* Art could hold people in its thrall and change people's minds. I couldn't imagine having that kind of power.

OVER THE NEXT COUPLE OF WEEKS, Tom played me the Pixies, and I gave him a full tutorial on Rihanna and Beyoncé. I made him watch YouTube videos of the latter singing the national anthem so that we could compare them critically to the famous Whitney Houston version. He sent me flowers at the office—huge, lush arrangements that smelled incredible and made Petunia come over and whisper, *Oh my gosh, he's obsessed with you! Get knocked up and let me tell everyone all the slutty shit you've done when I get wasted at your baby shower!* When Augusta saw pictures of the bouquets, she offered to dry and press them for me.

He gave me a copy of *Endurance: Shackleton's Incredible Voyage* and marked the pages where the polar explorer was forced to sacrifice his dogs for food so I could skip them, because he knew I would be triggered, which I found especially romantic. I didn't want our late-night phone calls and dinners and conversations and jokes to end. At the time, I didn't have a handle on my own value. I thought my only currency was the potential for sex. I was scared the sex wouldn't be exciting enough in the end for Tom to come back for more, and I knew how sad I'd feel. I thought of every part of myself I was ashamed of and imagined him seeing it all and never picking up my call again.

The first time he saw me naked, I'd been lying out in a park in Tribeca with my girlfriends, day drinking, and he happened to text me. *I'll walk past your studio on my way home and say hi*, I replied. It was a blazing-hot day, and by the time I crossed the fifteen blocks to get to him, I was sticky and smelled like gin and the grass I'd been lying in.

You were drunk, and you smelled like my grandma, he joked later, tenderness in his voice. *But you were so incredible looking with all your hair, and your tan, and your clothes fell off—just slipped off. You showed up in a bikini and a little sundress, and you were so wet when I touched you. I could tell you'd been thinking about me the whole walk.*

I used the gin as an excuse that day. I did things I would normally be too nervous to do, like perch on his lap and put his hands on my breasts and strip naked in sunlight, even though I was embarrassed by so many little flaws, like the chicken pox scars from childhood near my crotch and pale stretch marks on one butt cheek—faint tiger stripes that almost shine in the light, like they've been shellacked. He had such good lips, like the kind of lips a girl wishes for, pillowy and puffy. When I was in high school, guys called them *dick-sucking lips*, and now practically everyone has a fake version of them—filler from the dermatologist. When Tom pressed them to my forehead in public, and I felt the soft puff of a kiss against my hair, I practically cried. I was so happy.

ONE NIGHT IN SEPTEMBER, he took me to this tiny Jamaican sushi spot on West Fourth Street and asked me if I wanted to spend the night.

I'll make you peanut butter toast in the morning, he offered, *and we can spend the whole weekend together, too, if you still like me.* I didn't know if he was joking, but the acknowledgment of a possible shared insecurity about liking each other afterward made me feel a little more secure in our fledgling relationship. *I'll "do brunch," or whatever it is that you young people claim to enjoy,* he continued.

That really won't be necessary, Grandpa Sachs, I said, hoping that I seemed confident. *I don't "do brunch." I prefer to order large quantities of takeout and eat it in bed.* I imagined us sharing delivery bagels and watching movies or reading books next to each other on Sunday. *I'll come over, but I'm a package deal.* I played with my hair and looked up at him. *I have to run home first and get my dog, Napoleon. I don't like to leave him alone overnight.*

Tom raised his eyebrows. *That's cool. I've never had a dog, but I love them.*

Glad to know you find dogs tolerable, you murderous psychopath. In that case, you won't mind that Napoleon sleeps with us in bed.

As Napoleon and I walked into Tom's bachelor pad, a one-bedroom duplex on West Ninth Street with a bathtub on the roof, I thought about how when my dog's namesake, Napoléon Bonaparte, was two weeks from uniting with his beloved Josephine, he wrote to her asking her not to bathe. Similarly, my Napoleon had a curious and horny sense of smell and had been known to topple seemingly sturdy trash cans to get to my used tampons. He'd swallow them whole and wait until we were in public to puke them up, sometimes days later.

As soon as I walked in the door, Tom leaned in to kiss me. We went at it like in movies, two open mouths on top of each other and a lot of tongue action, big strokes with heavy muscles. I feigned needing to pee so I could make sure all the spit swapping hadn't done something insane to my makeup, like leaving me with a ring of lip gloss around my mouth or some strange circle where he'd worn off my concealer.

I looked at myself in the mirror on the back of the powder room door as I pulled my undies down to pee, so it wasn't until I was wiping that I noticed bright red blood in the bowl. I wondered if it was a sign, like maybe God *did* exist, and she *was* a woman, if she'd sent my period right as I was about to sleep with this new man. Maybe it meant he wasn't as nice as he seemed, and She was trying to warn me. I rifled through my purse for my emergency tampon and shoved it up there as far as it would go.

I had no idea what to say to Tom, and I was embarrassed I'd made such a thing out of sleeping over when I wasn't even going to be able to go through with the sex we were supposed to be having. And I was probably going to ruin his sheets, since I had only that one tampon. He came toward me and started kissing me again, his hands snaking down my legs.

I pulled his hands up to my waist but kept kissing him back. The hands crept back down. I pulled them back up.

Want to go upstairs? he asked.

Okay, I said. I sat on his bed. I heard a truck zoom down the street outside, rattling the walls a little bit. He laid me down on my back and pressed on top of me, and I moved his hands up to my waist.

What's wrong? he whispered.

Nothing's wrong. I just don't want to. I tried to distract him by sounding sexy, like a kitten saying no.

I'm confused, though, he whispered. *Why don't you want me to touch you? Did I do something wrong? Or read this situation wrong? I got tested, just so you know.* He told me that as if it were an indication of his commitment to me, when all it did was provoke my insecurity. Why, exactly, did he need to get tested? What, exactly, had he been doing in between all these dates we'd been on?

His hands were not huge, but they were confident. He put them on my hips in the right place. He looked directly at me. I could see his eyes glisten in the dark.

Sarah, do you have your period? he asked. I turned my face into a pillow, croaking a response into the pile of down. Tom heard it anyway. *It's not something I care about,* he said. *Sheets are washable, and I'll take your tampon out with my teeth if you want.* I laughed.

This is what an adult life looked like, I thought. This man was a grown-up. I had to be honest with him.

Please don't, I said. *But how would you feel about running to the deli to get me some Super Plus tampons? I have a wide-set vagina and a heavy flow.* I waited a beat and added, *It's a quote from* Mean Girls, *Father Time, don't panic.*

But aside from this instance, I would not be honest with him about my body or myself for another ten years. It would take much more introspection to unravel the information and memories stored in my cells.

In the meantime, I let myself roll around in Tom's clean sheets, in his beautiful little bedroom, windows on two sides and wide-planked wood floors, in his warm arms; I told myself my nerves were from excitement. And I did, truly, feel a thrill when he touched me; I felt my insides flip over, and it was like my brain and my eyesight and my whole body just sort of buzzed.

Was that you coming? he asked.

I think, I lied, blushing in the dark, a little too nervous to express myself honestly. What did I know then about intimacy or the way the mica of resentment can build up in a marriage over time? I couldn't tell him about my past and how sex made me feel empty. How penises scared me. I didn't really understand their mechanics; how I felt they carved out my insides, physically emptying me, leaving me lying there in discomfort, legs trembling in a mix of fear and the mild pain of someone else being inside my body; a precursor to the potential emotional roller coaster of violence and rejection that was to come. Maybe if I had shared all of this from day one, the trajectory of our relationship and how he cared for me would have looked different. But who among us has ever been completely honest in the first phase of a great love? I didn't have the confidence, and beneath all of my glowing thoughts about Tom remained the tiny itch of insecurity that said, *This could all go away.* Every minute he wanted me was proof I was doing something right, proof he still liked me, and I was relieved.

My relief was short-lived, though. I squeezed my eyes tight and hoped I was imagining it when I heard that familiar choking noise coming from somewhere in the dark. As I felt Napoleon crawl up to the head of the bed, Tom turned over and switched on a light, and before I could do anything, my dog puked up a tampon right onto my naked chest. I could feel bile drip down my ribs and watched Napoleon lick his lips, satisfied.

Oh my God, Tom said next to me. *Oh my God!* And then he started to laugh, and then I started to laugh. Tears were coming out of my eyes, and I could feel my hot cheeks as he ran to get a washcloth from the bathroom.

Napoleon is such a little horn ball! Tom said. *That was epic!*

I knew then. I knew when he laughed at my dog puking up a used tampon onto my naked breasts that we'd be together for a long time.

AFTER THAT FIRST NIGHT, we were just a couple. I had Chinese food with his parents, and they took us to an Off-Broadway play. He took Petunia out for pasta, and they exchanged dirty jokes. Augusta brought him to a lecture on Meissen china at the Frick, and they left midway through for martinis at the Carlyle Hotel because she said the lecture was *dry and stuck in the past* (like it was ever going to be anything else). We would sit in bed on weekends, our legs under the comforter, heads against a pile of pillows, and he'd draw with pencil and paper next to me, holding his clipboard and slurping coffee, while I wrote in my journal and took breaks to tell him stories or try to make him laugh.

Sometimes after we had sex, I'd feel overwhelmed with emotion, and I'd turn my head away from him in the dark to cry very quietly. I thought maybe it was because I loved him so much and felt so relieved to be with him, but they didn't feel quite like happy tears. And when he finally did notice, touching my face to kiss me and feeling it wet, he said very simply and sweetly, *You don't have to explain it to me if you don't feel comfortable, but you should look into that*, which I'd never even thought to do.

ONE NIGHT BEFORE BED, propped up on opposite elbows facing each other, he told me that if I were a flower, I'd be an orchid.

I'd be a giant pink peony! The fuchsia ones! Orchids are what Tom Ford keeps in his dressing room to prune before bed at night as a meditation. I'm a hot-pink ball of lush vaginal metaphors. This was the kind of sickening romantic conversation we had, sincerely, while staring into each other's eyes in bed.

No, really, he said, draping an arm around my waist. *Orchids bloom over and over. Just when you think they're done, another strange little flower starts to grow. They're temperamental, but the most special, and they're always changing. That's you, you know. You're going to have many lives, all in one life.* Tom was being serious, and I felt reverence toward his prophecy. He was so much wiser than me. *You're going to find your calling, and it's not some gallery job. You're going to find ways to change the world, and I'll be here waiting and cheering you on*, he finished, staring right into me. I loved him so much I couldn't believe it, like a fizzy explosion in my whole body every time I looked at him or smelled him or heard his name or even thought his name.

Tom woke up every morning, stumbled outside, and peed into a copper urinal under his Japanese maple tree. I lived in my cookie-cutter rental studio, subsidized by my dad, a sublease I'd found in a high-rise development filled with low-level traders and wannabe investment bankers with B-school tastes. I didn't own anything; I didn't have a headboard or chairs or wineglasses.

Did you ever have that feeling when you were learning something, and it was like your brain was on fire? Tom asked me once, while making me some late-night peanut butter toast. I knew just what he meant. I remembered how it felt the first time I heard Philip Glass's music when I was thirteen, and I remember how it felt the first time I walked into the Guggenheim Museum, when the banister was coated in Vaseline for Matthew Barney's *The Cremaster Cycle*, and the first time I saw Picasso's *Guernica* painting in person, when I cried. It felt like little explosions going off in my brain. He told me that was his favorite feeling, and he was always chasing it, but that he'd never had it in school or as a kid. The first time he ever felt it was when he took a welding class in college. *I was a complete loser before I learned that I could make art*, he explained. *I failed at everything. I was bullied. I had nothing going for me. Learning how to make art saved my life.*

I told him I couldn't draw a stick figure. *I have no idea what it's like to be able to create something*, I admitted. *But I feel some version of that when we're talking. Like I'm unfolding into something better.*

He said he felt something special with me, too. *Inside every person is the ability to be an artist; you just have to tap into whatever your version of art is*, he added. *And then you'll feel like you're unfolding even more.*

And when I was at a party by myself, feeling alone in my existence, I would think back to being in Tom's bed, under the white comforter, and imagine how I got to go back to it later that night, and I'd be able to breathe easy. I'd come home and run up the stairs, and he'd be there reading. His body was always very warm.

I'd lean into him and tell him all the ridiculous things I'd heard people say, and he'd make me laugh about it, propped up on his side, one hand at my waist.

I went to the most insane house tonight. Some South American collector I'd never heard of before, but my boss said it would be good if I could go. I counted fifteen Picassos on one single wall.

Were they good ones? he asked. He tapped my butt softly as I stepped out of my black dress, and it pooled on the floor at my feet. *Late*, I said. People were snobby about late Picasso, but I liked pretty much any Picasso.

It was wild, though. Everyone was smoking, and I was just, like, who lets people smoke around their Picassos? But the wine was amazing, and the servers were pouring it like it came out of a box. I started to tell this collector's wife about something funny that happened to me once at the Hôtel du Cap because she was using an ashtray from there—my one and only story about that place—but she'd turned back to the table, and no one acknowledged me. Tom had followed me into the bathroom and was watching me go about my oral hygiene regimen, which has five steps and is a nonnegotiable for me in order to fall asleep. *It's just not that hard to be polite to someone, even if you don't think they're important*, I said, spitting toothpaste into the sink.

You're allowed to be more of a bitch, you know, Tom said. *Don't take that shit.*

Back in his room, we climbed into the bed, and I lifted Napoleon up onto his pillow. Tom wrapped his arms around me very tight and reached down to pull one of my legs over his and kissed me. *You are a nice person, and you treat everyone nice. Besides that, the only thing that matters is your own internal standards of excellence. Join me on the dark side, baby. Let's conquer the universe.*

I wasn't quite sure what he meant, but I knew that he listened to my stories and liked my opinions. I knew that he wanted me at the table. I knew that he made me feel safe.

. . .

FOR CHRISTMAS THAT FIRST YEAR, he gave me a keychain, the silver-plated heart dangling from it engraved with our names and a little Hello Kitty, in Tom's shaky handwriting. *It's the key to my apartment*, he explained. His eyes sparkled at me, and they were so big and open. I gave him a pair of vintage cuff links because he didn't own any. He told me I upgraded him. Then we got dressed together and went to his friend's holiday party at her loft in Greenwich Village. She'd kept it in her divorce, and it was very big. There was a vast library in the middle of it that contained her rare books collection.

The party was elaborate. There were Christmas-tree-shaped towers of shrimp cocktail, and stone crabs in big silver bowls, little dishes of old-fashioned Christmas candies, and colorful cigarettes everywhere, which people were smoking in clusters inside, giving the room a haze. An assistant poured a big magnum of champagne into crystal coupes and handed them to us as we walked in, with a beautiful little linen napkin that had the hostess's initials on it embroidered in red and pink.

By that point in our relationship, I knew that Tom stayed close with all his exes. He told me it was important to him, that they were all good people whom he liked. I couldn't really argue with that, though glancing over as a text from a woman's name popped up sometimes tested the limits of my meager confidence. This woman wasn't an ex, but I knew we'd be seeing a few at the party. They were all established in their careers and very pretty, and when I tallied up the imaginary score I kept in my brain for so many infantile years, the only point I could come up with that I had on any of them was my youth. I was proud of my outfit because I'd been smart and used my birthday money that summer to buy a black minidress, low in the back, which showed a lot of skin but in a sort of demure way, like if Audrey Hepburn had liked minidresses.

The air outside had made my cheeks very pink, and I knew I

looked fresh-faced when I walked into the party. I let my vintage coat fall open so that my legs were visible, and Tom took it to coat check for me, which exposed the low back of my dress.

An ex of Tom's came up to him for an air kiss and gave me one too, but I knew she wouldn't talk to me much or really have anything to say besides something about the weather or traffic, so I smiled and tried to be friendly, eventually turning to scan the room. I pulled out my phone and pretended to be in the middle of something important when I heard her voice drop lower.

Why were you at the Mercer with Christine last night? That was weird, she said to Tom.

Oh, yeah, he replied very quickly. *I just stopped into the lobby to say hi to her.*

Last night? Last night Tom told me he couldn't make it to a dinner with friends I'd invited him to; that it just wasn't a good night to leave the studio early. My mind started racing with all the things he'd said, and I must have looked disgruntled, or maybe confused, because he took a few steps toward me and put his arm around me.

Should we sneak out and go to dinner? he whispered in my ear. I could feel myself blush because I had never specifically demanded he not see other people, and I had no evidence that his meeting with this mysterious Christine was sexual or romantic, but then why hadn't he told me about it? And why had he lied and said he was too busy for me if he wasn't too busy for her? All my earlier confidence slipped away as I imagined Christine's perfect features and her easygoing demeanor. Little demonic voices started up in my head. *This would not happen to you if you were more beautiful*, the main voice whispered. I felt my happiness drain out of me slowly, like I was bleeding to death from a tiny pinprick in the sole of my foot–barely noticeable, not even a trickle.

I can do this, I thought. *I can tolerate little pains to be with this man that I absolutely worship. I can pretend I don't care.*

And I let him take my hand and lead me to dinner.

3

Love and Marriage

2012

IN THE SIXTH GRADE, they made us take a Safe Sitter course in order to graduate middle school. Part of the curriculum entailed carrying around a doll twenty-four hours a day as some sort of litmus test for adulthood. I could not have cared less about my doll, or about babysitting, and I never read a single installment of *The Baby-Sitters Club*. Instead, I used to relish telling people, *I don't really like babies.* I liked watching their faces fall when I said it. It made me feel different from all my girlfriends, who gingerly took their practice baby dolls home from class and changed their diapers and rocked them to sleep, as if the toy infants had real emotions and needed to be loved. These girls couldn't wait to get their Safe Sitter certificates so that they could babysit, and not because they were excited for the money. They played house during recess, cradling their plastic children, and they watched kids' cartoons, reciting lines from them to one another like inside jokes. In the face of this saccharine display, rebuking my future maternal role, even if on some level it was an act, made me feel like a cooler kind of girl.

But it was also the truth. I never wanted a baby. I never daydreamed about baby names or my future life as a mom with a family of four. I never imagined myself nursing my baby or cuddling an infant. When my little brother came home from the hospital, I felt no instinct to adore him. Babies seemed chaotic and unpredictable, like they might cry or break or pee or puke all over me at any second. I put becoming a mother in the same box as becoming a banker or a circus performer: a vocation I might be conscripted to perform in some far-off future but didn't have to worry about anytime soon.

And how could I have known what I wanted, anyway? My mother's style of parenting wasn't emblematic of mommyhood. When a stay-at-home mother of three would pass our car in the pickup line at school, my mom would shake her head and say, *That woman has a master's in English, and all she gets to do with it is help her kids with their homework.* Her palpable disapproval hung in the air like a fog and filled me with a feeling I could not name. I was the kid with the homework who would have loved extra help, but also, I knew there was something wrong with this picture: being a woman in a car, saddled with kids who needed, needed, needed. Didn't everyone deserve to have a life solely their own?

WHEN I MET TOM, I was twenty-two, and we got married when I was but a wee twenty-eight, which I have to say is one of the most annoying ages I've ever been. I was rife with insecurity, having no detailed vision for my future, no calling to fulfill or idea of who I really was. I thought I knew so much about myself, and, in retrospect, I knew almost nothing, of course. Now, when I look back, I wonder if that's just the pattern of life that repeats ad nauseam until it's over. I felt so worldly and experienced for finding a mate, someone who loved me and believed in me even if I was his junior. When the two of us met, I'd been just an assistant, but by the time we'd been together for a few years, I'd managed to corral a couple of clients who'd walked in off the street just to look at art but eventually started buying things from me, probably because I smiled a lot, knew my shit, and was never late. My midwestern polite- ness appealed to the kind of wealthy guy who was happily married back home in Ohio but ventured to New York once a year and just genuinely loved pretty paintings and wanted someone nice to deal with when he was in the mood to buy some. Once I was generating profit for the gallery, I started getting bigger projects and working directly with artists, which felt like the pot of gold at the end of the rainbow. I got to do everything from arranging their travel itiner- aries to proposing their work to major museums, and no matter what they asked of me, I felt grateful to do it. I was surrounded by the kind of people I admired the most—smart and wildly inspired and dedicated to their work—and I was trusted to facilitate their creative dreams. What more could I have wanted?

I moved off the Long Row and away from Petunia, to a desk of my own. Petunia got her own office, too. I'd have to buzz her new phone and whisper into it instead of turning my Eames chair 15 degrees to speak to her. When I wasn't marching through my to-do list or running every move by her, I'd take breaks to call my mom to chat. We spoke three or four times a day, usually for under two minutes at a time, but we were in touch constantly.

THE MORE SERIOUS MY RELATIONSHIP WITH TOM BECAME, the more the conversations with my mom revolved around him: our little fights, surprises he made for me, dates he took me on, art shows we saw, what we talked about at night with our heads on the pillow. In wintertime, the galleries would be freezing cold, their twenty-foot ceilings a challenge for traditional methods of climate control. We all kept heaters under our desks, which posed a serious fire hazard in buildings that often stored a hundred mil- lion dollars' worth of art.

One Tuesday morning, deep in a conversation about my future, I remember asking my mother, *Do I even want to have babies?*

while I shuffled my feet in my black leather boots, wrapping a scarf around my arms. *Shouldn't I know this after three years of being with someone?*

I don't know, she answered, her voice a little distant. She usually called me from her speakerphone while driving. *But I think when you get to my age, or even older, you'd be really lonely if you didn't have a baby.* She sounded very serious, and I stopped scanning my emails to listen. *I think you'd look at your whole life, and you'd say to yourself, "What did I do all of this for?"* I stayed quiet for a beat, the gravity of her question weighing on me.

This was the most prescriptive my mother ever was with me. Her assertion that humans revolved around the family unit surprised me a little, as I'd never felt she was having that much fun being my mom. What resonated, however, was that creating a biological legacy would pay off someday, far, far from now, when I needed someone to prove all my life's efforts had been meaningful, and, more importantly, to drive me to my colorist when I needed my gray hairs covered up.

BETWEEN MY WORK AND TOM'S, which often overlapped, there was always an art opening, or an artist's talk, or a cocktail party, or a gala to attend, and they all felt glittery and fun and new. Instead of days and weeks, I counted our time together in art fairs, dinner parties, and work trips abroad.

In Tokyo, we went to the French ambassador's residence to see his Prouvé collection; outside of Paris, to a young art dealer's family chateau, where she was turning the vineyards into fields of weed and a sculpture park. We had Japanese food on tatami mats with an Icelandic curator, and we sat in dining rooms tinted gold by the Gustav Klimt paintings on the walls, sipping soup served in china passed down for generations. We ate roasted chicken topped with spiced Tunisian paste in a fashion designer's Parisian kitchen while we listened to a French philosopher describe his doctoral thesis between burning mouthfuls. We were often on a plane, sometimes to Paris or Marrakech or Venice but also to places like Des Moines, to visit clients of mine, or Minneapolis, to see an important regional museum. And while it energized and entertained me to spend all my days and nights around people–discussing and commenting and critiquing–Tom and I were almost never alone.

In the rare moments when it was just the two of us at home, the topic of starting a family never came up. We'd drink coffee and relax on our roof in the garden we cultivated year-round. I'd watch Tom–still naked from his outdoor shower–prune his Japanese maple tree and evergreens. He installed a grill, and we bought a long wooden farm table from our friend who had an antiques store on Fifth Street.

One crisp September night, the fourth year we were dating, I made my mom's Bolognese recipe for dinner. Tom invited our neighbors, a striking photographer and her filmmaker husband, people he'd known for years who'd become my friends, too. An earlier owner had built a fireplace into the brick wall of our terrace, and I watched Tom as he blew on kindling to ignite the Duraflame as I poured red wine into thin-stemmed glasses.

So, when are you having babies? the photographer asked me. She had jet-black hair down to the small of her back, like an exquisitely intellectual Morticia Addams, and she dressed like she was in a religious cult, in clothes sewed for her by a seamstress. On anyone else, they would have been terribly unfashionable, but she was so tall and lanky and mysterious that she made everything look interesting–as if she were the subject of a Diane Arbus photograph. I thought she was one of the most beautiful people I'd ever seen.

I'm so bourgeois, I admitted, scooting my folding bistro chair a little closer to our fire. *But I want to get married and have a wedding and all of that.* I peeked up at the photographer sheepishly because I knew she'd been with her husband for a dozen years, and they'd never had a wedding. *I guess I want kids because I love my siblings so much, and I want that for myself, but it feels very . . . eventual. I can't even really imagine it.*

That's because you're so young, she answered matter-of-factly. She sipped her wine, her long hair folding in her elbow crease as she lifted her glass. A chill breeze skittered the Japanese maple leaves at our feet.

You still have awe for Tom, she said. *You still have awe in general. We don't have awe anymore; we're too old.* She laughed and clinked glasses with me. *To your awe!*

She was right in the sense that, at the time, I did put Tom on a pedestal. He was older than I was, he made more money than I did, he'd moved to New York and started a life here while I was still in grade school. He had a very developed network. I revered that he was an artist; I thought it was brave that he put himself on display like that and made his own rules. I watched him wake up every morning and make drawings before he even had coffee, and then at night I listened as he explained how he'd taken one little detail of one of those sketches and made it into something three-dimensional. He hadn't had a boss of any sort in decades. We took vacations when and where he wanted, which was perfect, because I hadn't been to enough places to know what might appeal. We went away for weekends with his friends to spots such as a charming beach bungalow in the Rockaways, on the same street where Judy Garland once lived. We ate at the restaurants he liked, places I went only when my parents came to town, the sort of venues I normally had to call weeks ahead to get a reservation. He paid for everything, including my dinners out with my friends, which I often went to without him, knowing he'd rather work late.

MEANWHILE, I scheduled my life around when Tom was free, even though he never altered his schedule to accommodate mine. I lived in his apartment. He gave me cash for taxis when I was late to work. He covered my doctors' fees so that I could go to the good ones he saw, who often didn't accept my mediocre insurance. When his ex-girlfriends or former flings came to town, he made sure to introduce us but didn't correct them when they'd pretend I wasn't there after the first few minutes of pleasantries. He made room for me in his life, and he was generous, but his work always took precedence, and he didn't especially alter his behaviors from his pre-Sarah existence. On some level, I knew this was how artists were–real artists, that is–they were married to their art. Tom said that if being an artist were illegal and punishable by death, he'd do it anyway, after all, and I saw from how hard he worked that he meant that. I knew where I fell on the priority list. But when I spotted him texting a woman from his past or watched him smile big and make extra eye contact with some fabulous woman at a party while I was at the bar, it knocked my confidence in a different way. And I worried that if I said too much about his exes, if I complained in a way that made it hard for me to fit into his life, I'd fall to the wayside.

By our fourth Christmas, Tom stopped suggesting vacation destinations or whisking me to romantic, faraway places.

I'd rather stay here and work, he said, studying a to-do list he'd made in his small yellow notebook as we sat at our wooden dining table, a hand-me-down antique from my mom that had moved into Tom's house with me, one of the few objects in the whole place that was mine. *The week between Christmas and New Year's is what I call Lonely Week, because everyone else is gone. I get so much done. We can go away another time.* I glanced over at his list, and it was long, but something about his hesitancy hurt my feelings.

Don't you want to recharge, though? I asked. *Soothe our tired souls in salt water? Find inspiration in nature or . . . at a swim-up bar?* I had an office job–I couldn't just go away "another time." There were rules.

Recharge? He sounded incredulous. *I don't need to recharge. The reward for good work is more work. There's nowhere I'm as happy as when I'm alone in my studio, working.* The words cut me a little bit. They made me think I wasn't beautiful, smart, or electrifying enough to be his muse. And while a muse, by definition, was a passive role, a position I didn't want to be in, I did long to captivate him. I wanted him to *want* to join any vacation I could dream of, just to be near me. I wanted to inspire passion in him the same way his art did. Was I really less interesting than a blank canvas or a stack of plywood?

I started to perceive our potential marriage as the proof I needed that Tom really loved me, that he chose me, and that I was enough. Yes, it was my little power trip, a small corner I could control in the grand design of our relationship. The more I thought about our future, the more obsessed with a wedding I became. There were plenty of things Tom controlled in our relationship, but when it came to marriage, I decided I wanted to call the shots. I became intractable on this one point. I was going to get what I fucking wanted, even if it was just this one time.

ONE MORNING, IN OUR FIFTH YEAR TOGETHER, our condom broke. We talked about what we were going to do, and later that day, Tom messengered a box of Plan B and a CVS bag full of candy to my office.

I got it for you so you wouldn't have to deal with the pharmacist, he said. *I've had abortions with girlfriends before, and I never want to do that again,* he added. I pressed my desk phone to my ear as I unfolded the instructions. His voice was strong, but not unhappy. *The next pregnancy I'm involved in, I want to end with a baby.*

I could tell he was smiling as he said that part, and something about the warmth of his voice made me happy, too; the idea that he was thinking about our future, and it included that word: *baby*. I popped the pill into my mouth easily, not thinking twice. *I've always wanted kids*, he added. *They are the greatest art project a human can possibly create.* I laughed because he was always saying things like that, showing me how everything could be a creative act. Then I heard the toilet flush, and I could tell he'd been peeing throughout our entire conversation.

THAT NIGHT, while possibly shedding our first zygote as we walked home from dinner, seemed like the right time to pounce. As he asked me if the Plan B had made me crampy, I came out and said it:

Before I have kids, I want to have a wedding and be married. With a diamond ring and all of that. I linked my arm through his and put my head on his shoulder. I could smell the skin of his neck. He stopped in his tracks, and I thought he was about to turn and say, *How common. Artists don't participate in conventional institutions like marriage.* But really a giant cockroach was scrambling across his path, and he didn't want me to see it. He took his free arm and steered me away from the pile of garbage on the sidewalk's edge, the cornucopia in which rodents and insects were undoubtedly feeding and copulating. *Don't look*, he said.

We walked by a tree that a friend had once told me was the oldest in Manhattan. Its leaves cast dappled light onto the pavement under the orb of a streetlamp.

You should have that if that's what you want, he continued, turning me into Washington Square Park. *But you should know that real marriage isn't a rock I buy, a ten-minute ceremony, or some giant party paid for by your parents. It's living together for a very long time. It's falling out of love and figuring it out. It's being stuck no matter what. It's all that shit. What you're describing is just expensive stuff plus a piece of paper.*

Well, it's what I want, that's all I'm telling you, I replied, trying to keep it playful, even though his soliloquy bothered me. It wasn't what I wanted to hear, but I didn't want to come off as defensive. I also didn't care if he was right or wrong—I just knew I wanted to get married. Maybe that was my midwestern cultural conditioning or a predilection for state-sanctioned stability rearing its head, but I wanted the ceremony. I wanted a public declaration that we belonged to each other. I wanted to tell the world how much I loved him while all our friends sat there in fancy clothes. He didn't have to change; that's not what I was saying. He didn't have to leave the studio early and come home every night for a seated three-course dinner. He didn't have to move to the suburbs and buy a station wagon and start wearing dad jeans. I didn't want to take his last name and insist people call me by it. But even though I knew it was a fallacy, I wanted him for myself, and, at the time, I was naive enough to believe that marriage would corral him into loving me the way I wanted to be loved.

Real marriage is sticking around even if you're bored or you want to murder the other person. It's making babies. That's the actual definition of a lifetime commitment, he said. And even though he'd never been married, he said it with the conviction of someone who'd experienced a lot more life than I had.

I watched as a hyper German shepherd chased a ball, his owner engrossed by something on his phone. I couldn't let my point go. *I hear you, but one thing at a time. I'm not even thirty.* We were quiet as we finished our short walk home, too consumed by our individual projections to imagine the course reality would take.

BUT EVENTUALLY WE DID GET MARRIED. And we did want to murder each other sometimes, though it was fun to throw a party, and get a pretty dress, and tell everyone I knew how much I loved Tom. But in other ways, our nuptials didn't mean much beyond that. I was still myself at work and out in the world, and I was still sort of accidentally in Tom's shadow at home. My blind adoration, the kind that had allowed me to embed myself in his life without asking that he do the same in return, did fade slowly over time, but our marriage certificate did nothing to quell my burgeoning resentment that his work was the most important thing in his life, more important than I would ever be. And while I loved my work, and respected the art world and what I did within it, I would have given up everything for him at the drop of a hat.

SOMETIMES AT NIGHT, when he was in the shower, I'd look at his cell phone. I'd watched him punch in his code often enough that eventually I could mimic his fingers and get the thing open. God, I wasted so much time looking at his text messages and emails, the deleted folders and the drafts, his photo library, the messages on his Instagram—analyzing every interaction with a woman, wondering how I did and didn't compare to *her*. Right before our wedding, I saw a conversation with an ex-fling who was passing through New York.

I'll be in the city next week, she said, using all the most flirtatious emojis, adding the exact dates. *Baby,* he replied, which was what he called me, *I have to travel—can't get out of it. Take you to dinner next time.* What he didn't say was: *I am marrying the girl of my dreams, my best friend, the one I spend hours in bed with, the one who calms me when I spiral and takes my call at any time of day to work through office problems or logistics; the one who advises me whenever I need it, who makes sure we have fresh milk and coffee even though she doesn't drink it. The one who makes dinner plans with my parents, keeps our soap refilled, helps me pack for trips.*

It killed me that he didn't say any of that. I felt hot with shame. The worst part was that I, mired in the insecurity of my twenty-something-year-old brain, was too scared to confront him and talk it through. I feared, for no particular reason aside from the narratives I wrote in my own head and the ways that I saw men treat other women around me, that he could use this invasion of his privacy against me. I feared that I'd start a fight, and it would snowball, and snowball, and snowball, the flakes sticking to one another in a deadly mass, and I'd end up alone, crying under a big white comforter with no one to hug me. I didn't want to be without him. Of course, our relationship had its pitfalls, but so much of it was so good–better than I ever could have imagined–and the fear of rocking the boat chipped away at my courage. I felt I had no option but to stew silently. What was I going to do, leave him? Too afraid to take action, I let my nosiness become an addiction I couldn't abandon, the same way some people pick their cuticles. I was constantly searching for ways he was disloyal to me.

SOON AFTER OUR WEDDING, I found myself in an old restaurant on the Quai Voltaire in Paris, a glossed wooden jewel box that feels somewhat like you're in the captain's quarters of the kind of ship that might see pirates and mermaids. The place acts as a sort of clubhouse for sophisticated expats. It's one of the few spots one might go in the City of Light, hear English at every table, and not be bothered by it. Plus, they serve pommes puree, and mashed sweet potatoes, *and* French fries with their steaks.

I was at one end of a long table, and Tom was at the other, next to an older French actress I didn't recognize. As soon as someone raised a glass to toast our marriage, the actress singled me out.

You know who you look like? she asked. All the glimmering, bejeweled heads at the table swiveled toward me. I swear she was faking her accent, or at least making it sound extra French. She lit a long cigarette, inhaling, and fanning the match delicately with one hand. *You look exactly like that girl, that girl in the Ingres painting.* She exhaled her smoke. Jean-Auguste-Dominique Ingres was a nineteenth-century French painter of the Neoclassical movement who was known for painting exotic, racist scenes of the Far East. He was also known, in art history circles, for being terrible at painting hands. Man or woman, child or adult, the fingers always looked like deformed alien sausages. *You know the one*, the actress said, sipping daintily on a glass of white wine between drags. *She's your twin! Madame Moitessier!* I could feel my eyes widen in surprise, and the smiles on everyone's faces froze, like bewildered masks.

Madame Inès Moitessier was not what anyone would call pretty by modern standards. She was an older woman who had begged Ingres to make her portrait, and he'd said no to the commission for something like ten years before finally giving in. I was blonde, with a messy head of hair that hit the crease of my elbow even after a trim, and that woman was brunette, her hair coiffed smoothly, pulled back tightly. I was tall and slim, with narrow hips and small breasts—I'd been told more than once, scornfully, that I had the body of a boy—she was thick and curved. I had faint acne scars on my cheeks and a few pockmarks from the worst of my teenage zits, where her smoothly painted face was like marzipan. All we had in common, I figured, was that neither of us was beautiful.

Oh, I found her! Tom said, his face lit up by his phone screen. He flashed the image of the zaftig brunette around the table. I could practically see the mental gymnastics of all of their brains, the wheels turning to figure out how to redirect the convo. Tom started nodding, his head bobbing up and down like he was performing "agreement" for the back of an opera house. *You're right*, he said, locking eyes with the actress in a way that I swear seemed seductive. *This looks exactly like Sarah. You're so perceptive.* I willed my jaw to stay closed as my brain scrambled to process his confirmation of her insult. Maybe all ugly girls looked alike to them?

Later that night, back under the embroidered canopy of our Louis XIV hotel bed, instead of confronting him, instead of having to explain the subtleties of this sort of girl-on-girl warfare, I rolled over and pretended to fall asleep. I was afraid that if I started a fight, Tom might say what I feared deep down: I was too unattractive to have the power of a woman who couldn't be insulted, and he'd rather indulge that actress than protect me. This fear etched away at my mind like an awl: that my ugliness would be my downfall and that if I said or did the wrong thing, Tom would leave me for a prettier, easier woman.

Ignoring the small humiliations of our union became my survival plan, like a ballerina dealing with blisters and calluses in service of my art. I'm not saying I got pregnant to make our relationship better or to change Tom. It wasn't like that. It wasn't that deliberate. There was always a reason to wait, to keep using whatever kind of birth control, to plan our lives without infants and diapers. We talked about it, of course, because we talked about everything. But we didn't make any concrete schedules or a plan to "start trying." We didn't track my ovulation. We didn't pick out names or talk about summer camp. One year passed, and then another and another.

YOU KNOW HOW EXPENSIVE PRIVATE SCHOOL IS, RIGHT? I asked Tom one night in our kitchen, a room so small he'd had his Lacanche stove custom-made to be four inches narrower than its narrowest model, which he'd further tailored by adding bronze knobs he'd designed himself and commissioned from a foundry. He'd never gotten around to engraving the temperatures on them, though, so when we cooked, we had to wing it. We were eating peanut butter toast cut into small squares.

I have no idea how much it is, he replied, crunching through a piece of crust. *But I'll make more paintings if I need to. I'll work even more. Shouldn't we send our kids to public school anyway? Does that shit really matter?* He had crumbs stuck to his lip, and I let them stay there.

We'd never talked about public versus private school before, and I knew that, at least in New York, everything about where you sent your kids to school involved a ton of stress, and money and connections and all sorts of things I didn't quite have a grasp on because it didn't work like that back home in Indiana. But Tom made everything sound so uncomplicated. And while I knew having babies wasn't easy–everyone always said you'd never sleep again, never have sex again, that you'd be unable to vacation or go to a movie or a restaurant until your kid turned five–I didn't know what any of that actually meant. I didn't know what a baby would really do to my emotional life, my marriage, my adrenal glands, my brain, my body, my dreamscapes, my breasts, my vagina, and my ability to think and function. And his nonchalance was so soothing. I guess I figured my husband grokked something that I didn't. That anything meaningful was hard, and easy was boring, and life was about family, and family equaled offspring. Plus, I wasn't blind to the fact that we could use his money to pay our way out of many of the nuisances that accompany child-rearing to the point that having a baby would maybe, possibly, be worthwhile, or perhaps tolerable, or even fun.

All I knew was that I loved Tom. Even if I was no longer totally in *awe* of him, even if he chose his work over me, I was committed to him–both because of the time I'd invested and the potential I saw in our partnership. As time went on, we both seemed to fade into our individual work and social lives more than evolving into a joint one. It wasn't what I had expected, but it wasn't entirely unwelcome, either. And the next time our condom broke, the torn latex sack glistening limply as Tom walked it to the trash, neither of us said a word about Plan B.

4

Pregnant

New York
January–October 2017

I TEXTED MY MOM A PHOTO of my positive pregnancy test while I sat on the toilet, my feet cold on the white marble floor. The bathroom was so small that I could touch the sink with my hand from where I sat, and if I stuck my legs out, my foot could open the shower door. Seven years earlier, I'd been so impressed with Tom's apartment, despite its diminutive size. I'd noticed how curated every detail was, like the oak-paneled living room with its hidden cabinets and drawers.

And while it had awed me that Tom was so tasteful, I'd come to detest all these carefully chosen elements, since none of them felt like mine and, secondly, the layout of the bathroom meant that if I was taking a shower and he was taking a shit, I had no choice but to stare at him. Now a single accidental night of no birth control had gotten me pregnant, the faint crosshairs of a positive test appearing while I was home alone, as I almost always was, on a late-January Sunday.

The minute I saw the second blue line emerge, I felt both surprise that it had really happened and a confirmation of something I'd suspected. I'd felt a little off the last few days, more dreamy than normal, and when I'd gotten Botox earlier in the week–and,

I'll admit it, a hint of filler—which almost always left me with a bruise, I'd emerged unscathed.

I mean, I could have picked up the phone and called Tom, but I honestly didn't know if I was supposed to be excited. So, I texted my mother, hoping she'd text me back, and we could leave it at that, and in seven months or so, I'd wake up with an adorable, basketball-sized bump, and then two months after that, my water would break in a taxi home from a romantic date with Tom, and we'd rush to the hospital in a panic, I'd get an epidural, and be holding a gorgeous baby within ten minutes of checking in.

But, of course, none of that happened.

Is that test for real? my mom asked, breathless on the phone. I stood up from the toilet, naked, and got back into bed. I was scared, briefly, to acknowledge her question, like it implied I was an adult, moving on with my own life, and that it would hurt her feelings or something, or separate us.

Mom, it's fucking real. I'm pregnant. I said it like I was guilty, covering my head with my comforter even though she couldn't see me.

Does Tom know? I could envision the face she was making: a wide, open-mouth smile, excited eyes. I wished I could meet her enthusiasm, but I felt destabilized. I'd taken mushrooms a few weeks ago. I'd done a bump of coke the other night—not my coke, of course, someone else's, but, still, *coke.* I'd ordered a two a.m. grilled cheese just ten hours ago and was now looking at its crust on my bedside table, wrapped in deli paper. How could someone who acted this immature be pregnant?

I literally just took the test and sent you the picture. I don't know what to do now. My voice was flat compared to hers.

How do you feel? she asked, and I closed my eyes against the cold winter sunlight in my bedroom, burrowing deeper under my covers.

I'm not sure. Kind of jittery, like I have this giant news inside me, but I'm not supposed to tell anyone, and it doesn't really mean anything yet. I wondered to myself when this would get fun.

Oh shoot, I'm getting a call on the other line, she said.

WHEN TOM CAME HOME, I was waiting, smiling, holding the test in my hands at the door to our apartment as it opened. I think I was hoping that if he got really excited, it would push me to get really excited too, so I stood there, still naked, displaying the plastic wand, wanting his reaction to be over the top and romantic.

Is this real? he asked, grinning but not openly weeping. There were no shrieks of glee; he didn't sweep me off my feet and carry me to bed and offer to bring me tea and do whatever it took to make me comfortable. *When can we tell people?* he wondered out loud, taking off his coat and shoes and putting his keys on the counter.

I made a doctor's appointment for tomorrow to confirm it, but I want to wait as long as possible, I said. *So don't tell your parents yet or anything.* When my sister, Deechie, found out she was pregnant, we were on a family vacation in Denmark, and we told everyone we met, even though she was not twelve weeks yet. We were just so elated. We thought that getting pregnant was all you had to do. My dad had ordered champagne, and we toasted–even her. A family friend had said, *You should tell anyone you'll need support from in the case that something goes wrong*, which made perfect sense to all of us, ecstatic with her news, so certain that things would turn out perfectly.

I thought about what it would feel like to have my turn at telling people I was pregnant, to say those words out loud, now that I was knocked up. *It's never really true, though*, I reminded myself. *It can be taken from you at any moment.*

• • •

TOM CAME WITH ME TO EVERY APPOINTMENT. We liked that my ob-gyn's office seemed old-fashioned, with floral wallpaper and comfortable couches. The waiting room overlooked Central Park. I was so early in my pregnancy at this first appointment that we needed an internal sonogram, not the over-the-belly kind that you get later when the fetus is bigger, so a nurse took us into a small exam room and told me to get undressed.

This is certainly good news! the doctor said when she walked in, all smiles. She was young with neat brown hair clipped back with a barrette. *I love to hear one of my girls had a positive test.* I smiled back, feeling like I'd done something right, like my test had proven I could be initiated into her clan. That old desperate desire to be good at being a *good girl* bubbled up into my brain like someone had hit the power on the Jacuzzi.

I had my feet in stirrups and was leaning back in my gown, not a paper one; she used laundered pink cotton gowns each time, a small luxury that did not go unnoticed by me. Tom was sitting on a little stool, and they introduced themselves to each other.

You're probably only seven or eight weeks, but sometimes I can get a heartbeat if we are lucky, she said, lubing the sonogram probe with a thick coat of gel and sliding it inside my body. It didn't hurt, but I don't think I'll ever be able to reconcile that I'm supposed to allow medical instruments and penises inside this same cavity, and just turn off the different emotions that each provokes.

It's complicated that a site of female pleasure can also be the site of immense discomfort and pain and trauma, something I would have loved to discuss out loud with someone, but the doctor was totally quiet as she worked, which I hated. I wanted her to talk the entire time, fill every silence so that I didn't have to wonder if something was wrong. She moved the probe around, which still didn't hurt, but I could feel it in a low-grade way in my abdomen, and she turned a knob on the screen in front of us. Suddenly the rhythmic squish of a heartbeat filled the room with sound as a little round blob twitched on the screen.

The doctor laughed. *There we go*, she said. I stared at the clump of cells while Tom took a video on his phone.

I wasn't sure what to feel as the fuzzy, pixilated image on the screen fluttered. I knew from what I'd read online that my clump didn't actually have a heart. It had tissue that would *become* a heart in a few weeks, and that tissue had the ability to flicker. The machine the doctor was using to produce a picture for me mimicked the sound of a heartbeat at the same velocity that the flickering happened. It was sort of cool that we were watching something alive inside my body, but it was almost as if I knew too much to fall into the trap of letting it make me sentimental. Except that as I turned my head to look back at Tom, I felt tears I hadn't even known were coming leaking slowly from my open eyes.

It's so sweet that you're so excited, the doctor said to me, pulling out the probe. *Get dressed and come find me in my office so we can talk.* I wiped my face with the tissues she gave me, and then wiped all the gel off the inside of my legs so I could put my clothes back on. I didn't know why I was crying, but it wasn't happiness or excitement, I didn't think. I hadn't winced or frowned, nor felt my face crumple. My eyes had just started making droplets, and they'd dribbled out without sound or warning.

Tom didn't say anything as we filed into the doctor's office, a small room with a big wooden desk covered in photographs of her kids, but I didn't really need comfort because it wasn't that I was sad, either. As we sat, the doctor finished writing on a small notepad and handed me a lined sheet of paper with her name at the top.

Here's your calendar of all the tests and things you need to know leading up to your due date, she said. *I guess the most important thing to know is that after July ends, you can't travel, and you're due in early October.* I was watching her intently as she indicated different lines with her pen, explaining what the tests were for.

Why are you crying? she suddenly looked up and asked, more surprised than concerned. I reached for my face, thinking that maybe I was dribbling tears again, but then I realized she was looking at Tom, who had his head in his hands and was making little whelp noises.

Baby, what's wrong? Instinctively, I reached out to touch him. It was as if he had gotten terrible news by text or something, like someone had died. He could barely stop whimpering to speak. He didn't open his eyes or untwist his face, but he did pick it up out of his hands so we could see his distress.

I'm . . . I'm just really overwhelmed. Tom drew a very deep and shaky breath. *So, if we wanted to go to Spain in August, we couldn't? Is that what you're saying?* His face contorted again as a muffled sob came out. I was too annoyed to hear what else he said.

I mean, you can do anything you want, she replied, with a little bit of an attitude that I appreciated. It made me feel like she and I were in one corner and Tom in another–not ideal, but at least I had someone with me. *But unless you want your wife to have a baby in Spain, with a doctor you don't know, in a hospital that is Spanish speaking, and be stuck in Spain for a month after, you should not go to Spain in August.*

Tom wiped his eyes and did not seem to have any more questions. We moved on to cover the payment structure and all the rest of the logistics the doctor thought we needed to know for now, and then got in a taxi to go home.

What was that? I asked him, thumbing through the stack of paperwork the doctor's office had given me. *We don't even have plans to go to Spain in August. Is that really what you were upset about?* I almost had to laugh at the guy–he was really upset about a hypothetical vacation while I was growing someone's bones and brain next to my bladder?

It's just really overwhelming, he kept repeating. In some way, I felt for him, I really did. I understood what he was going through, and I found his emotions kind of pure and funny, but . . . *I also* felt overwhelmed–something that he did not seem to get. And on top of how overloaded I was, I felt very alone. I couldn't tell many people my news yet–my doctor had warned me to wait until at least twelve weeks–and anyone I did tell was so happy for me that it felt criminal to do anything but match their excitement.

All babies are blessings, Augusta said. By now, she had two of her own, little boys who looked just like her but with bright, blond hair, almost towhead. She had a hardworking, equally-as-southern husband who made her very happy, even though I had the feeling they scheduled BDSM sex on a shared calendar that also included meetings at their church.

Two days later, Petunia, of course, gave me her own version of things:

Just you wait, she whispered to me at my desk at the end of the workday, cracking open a beer while I finished my emails. There was a whole horde of us who'd never even thought about leaving the gallery, with all its perks and prestige. Instead, we'd developed some comfortable habits, and one was end-of-day beers at somebody's desk. *My sister's done this twice. You're going to start feeling like shit soon.* I stopped typing for a minute and looked at her in disbelief.

P, I'm hanging on by a thread here. Not everyone gets that crazy morning sickness your sister had.

Okay, but I'm warning you. It's going to suck. She sipped her beer. I didn't believe her. I thought her sister must be an anomaly. Everyone I knew had always seemed so grateful to be pregnant.

The reality kicked in a week or so later when I woke up with such strong nausea that I didn't think I'd be able to function. *Morning sickness* was a fallacy, my symptoms persisting at all hours of day and night, for nineteen straight weeks of my pregnancy. Puking made it worse, not better, and there were three whole days where the smell of water itself would make me start to throw up. The very thought of meat, lettuce, or garbage would provoke peristalsis so intense that I couldn't have lunch with a girlfriend or dinner in a restaurant–but I could have sat there, I could have done my makeup and put on a nice dress and had somewhere to be and someone to talk to, if watching people eat hadn't also made me puke.

I cried openly at my next doctor's appointment. *My quality of life is absolutely zero*, I told her, watching the little, growing fetus twitch on the screen. *I feel so sick, all the time. All I can eat is the inside of bagels, and it's terrible. I don't want to puke in trash cans on the way to work anymore.*

She didn't even look at me. She just moved the sonogram wand around my puffy belly, measuring things and logging numbers into her computer.

The thing about becoming a mom is that you're nothing but a house for your baby for ten months, she said, keeping her eyes on her work. *That's your only job, and it can mean a little discomfort. I just don't like to give first-time moms anti-nausea meds. But if you don't feel better in the next couple of weeks, I'll consider it.* I looked at Tom, panicked, and I could tell he didn't know what to say because he just stared at both of us.

Just try one more week, babe, he suggested at last. *If the doctor doesn't think the meds are a good idea, I mean, we trust her, you know?* He handed me my pants and top off the chair where I'd folded them. They were brands I'd normally buy, but two sizes up, my ass having ballooned in a way I couldn't believe when I looked in the mirror. I had assumed I was imagining things until a guy I knew from the art world said, *I knew you were pregnant! I could tell because your ass was getting so fat. Looks great.*

I knew Tom was right, but I wondered how bad it would be if I took an edible, just once, just to have one day off from the nausea and eat one meal, and texted Petunia to start researching as I was pulling on my clothes.

You're going to have a lot more symptoms, the doctor said, notepad in hand. *The nausea means things are working–the right hormones are in your body! So be grateful. And keep me updated but try to stay positive. You're making a baby!*

I fundamentally disagreed with the kind of ascetic denial of my body and its pleasure that she seemed to claim was required to be a good mother, but that didn't stop the symptoms, which–she was right–were plentiful. Next came what's called *round ligament pain*, a side effect of the stomach muscles and tendons loosening and stretching. I felt like the muscles near my hips were going to snap at the sides, pull right off the bones, the pain just dull enough that it kept me up at night, a little worried that this meant my body was changing irreparably. Then there was the acne all around my chin and neck, on my chest, under my boobs. The shame of feeling so ugly and pocked was reminiscent of my high school embarrassment: that realization that someone is looking at you closely, staring at your overgrown features on a face that hasn't caught up, at your pubescent, frizzy hair, your speckled forehead–noticing all your flaws while you speak.

Then came swollen ankles, sciatica so painful I once had to crawl from a taxi to my front door, heartburn so bad I was taking double the daily recommended dosage of Tums. Sure, my hair grew fast, but even my *leg* hair was thicker, the hair under my arms like a pelt of fur. I can't speak for my other parts, as I could no longer see them beneath a round belly with a dark stripe down the middle. Each hard-to-accept development was replaced every couple of weeks by two more.

The most beautiful time in a woman's life!

The body makes too much blood to be contained in order to supply a fetus with everything it needs, so there were the weeks of spontaneous daily nosebleeds, gums bleeding when I brushed, cuticles bleeding during my manicures. I was like a giant, blood-filled, monstrous balloon, ready to pop with any prick.

I can't forget to mention the overflowing breasts with salami-sized nipples, for which I blamed the near-constant and escalating catcalls I got on the street almost everywhere I went. I tried to cover up those boobs, but it was virtually impossible, and I looked at them as culpable for the unwanted attention, which seemed even greater than what any woman normally faces. Once my belly popped and I was clearly pregnant, I couldn't walk one block without a *Hey, mamma!* followed by a whistle. Strange men would approach me in line at the grocery store and ask me when I was due, which implied they were looking at my body, noticing me.

Meanwhile, Tom was busy at work. In fact, I wasn't sure if he was interested in my new self at all. For a man who had dedicated his life to learning and to an obsession with science, and who professed to love women, it didn't feel like he was able to marry those interests with an eagerness to know more about what I was going through. He didn't ask how I was feeling nearly often enough. He didn't ask what I was thinking or if I was afraid—at least not that I remember. He didn't check in on me during the day. He didn't wonder if he could bring me anything. He didn't buy me books about pregnancy, offer to take a birthing class together—not that I asked. He didn't compliment my new body or share my fixation on its changes. Or at least not as much as I wanted him to and not in the ways that felt right to me.

Add to all that the pressure I'd always felt—made up in my head or absorbed from the pop culture ether or both—that I simply *had* to be nonchalant about my own emotional needs in order to be desirable. There was no way I was going to be able to suddenly demand a new version of our marriage that felt adequate to my growing realization of my needs. Womanhood, in my estimation, was death by a thousand cuts. It was trying to have a career yet feeling huge pressure to make dinner for your kids every single

night; it was feeling sick and depressed to death while perpetuating the human species and having your very *doctor* tell you to be
grateful for feeling that way. How could I suddenly let my husband
know that I wanted constant and attentive babysitting and, fur-
thermore, that I didn't like how he had friendships with his exes
or texted silly messages flirtatiously? What would I even say? That
it had cut me for years and I'd never spoken up and now I was a
withered, emotional mess? That it didn't used to bother me, but
now I was in a hormonal slump? We had developed a relationship
based on being two independent adults with their own lives who
came together when they chose to, and suddenly my needs were
different: I wanted someone who could read my mind and understand my predicament and hold my hand. Maybe he'd always been
this absent, and I'd never noticed? But more likely, I reasoned, he
was distancing himself from me on purpose. And while, in retrospect, a mentally well person would have asked him what was
going on, would have clearly stated her feelings and demanded
agreed-to boundaries and collaboration, I stewed alone, listening
to the voice in my head that told me I did not deserve better, and
I would spend the rest of my life feeling exactly this unimportant
and unloved.

Those thoughts left me in a lonely and sad daze. I spent my
free time wandering around SoHo, window-shopping, sipping
iced teas and lemonades, and trying not to sweat. I'd always been
someone who felt things strongly, but now if I saw a TV show in
which a character died, I would cry uncontrollably for hours, as
if I knew the person. In an effort to keep my head above water,
I tried to pour myself into work, visiting the studio of an artist
I managed who would be having his first show that fall, checking in on his progress and coordinating press visits, photography,
framing, shipping, the production of a catalogue for the show, and
the travel arrangements we needed for his installation and opening, for which I was determined to fly to LA. I worked out faith-

fully every morning, trying to keep the edema at bay, and roamed farmers markets for fresh berries and watermelon, which I craved madly, eating pints of blueberries by the fistful and crunching through fleshy chunks of red melon.

ONE PARTICULARLY SAD AFTERNOON IN JUNE, I decided to call Tom at work. It had started raining while I was on one of my walks— not just a normal rainstorm but a heavy summer downpour with big gray thunderheads rolling over the skyscrapers. I'd liked the droplets at first because they'd cooled off my hot, hormonal skin, but once I saw lightning in the distance, I headed home. When I got there, I wasn't sure what to do with myself, cooped up inside, unable to eat, all alone.

The night before, when the baby was kicking, and it was visible from the outside—actual tiny human body parts pressing their way out of my body—I squealed, *Oh my God, Tom, look! This is crazy!* I was propped against pillows in bed, watching what I could have sworn was the clear imprint of a foot trying to stamp its way out between my ribs.

I'm reading, he replied, turned on his side, so I grabbed his arm.

Come on, babe, just look, I said, pulling on him to pay attention. A shape rolled across my belly, straining the skin from within.

It's like Alien! Tom said, laughing. Then he turned back over and yawned, and I felt my heart sink so low that it left a vacuum of space in my chest, a deep hole that sadness rushed into like dark flood-water. He picked up his book and opened it as I sucked in a sob.

If you think my body's disgusting, you can just say it, I said. My voice was hoarse and deep, and I stared at my belly because I couldn't bear to look at him. I felt Tom's head swivel toward me, and I pressed my hands over my eyes. *If you hate pregnant women so much, maybe you shouldn't have injected me with your vile seed.* My voice cracked, and I let myself weep out loud–an ugly, wounded-animal sound. I knew I sounded unhinged. I knew the intensity of what I was feeling wasn't right or normal or standard for me, but I still *felt* it, and I couldn't control whatever was surging through me. I couldn't stop the swell of emotion even as I understood that it was strange.

Sarah! What? You look so beautiful! Tom said, panicky and hushed. *I'm not even sure what I said wrong, but I'm sorry,* he continued, trying to wrap his arms around me. I was too big for him to really hold; he just sort of smashed my body into his side, and I tried to let it go, even though I felt a sadness settling right into my chest–a sort of trembling mound of depression that I couldn't see ever dispelling.

SARAH? Tom said now, picking up his landline.

What time will you be home, my love? I asked. *Maybe when it stops raining, we could go sit outside somewhere and people-watch and talk?* I offered, drying myself off with paper towels in the kitchen. I threw out the wet paper towels and poured myself a glass of water. At this point in my pregnancy, if I didn't hydrate, I got horrible headaches that took days to go away.

I don't have time to do that today, Tom said. I could tell by his voice that he was doing two things at once. He was talking intensely, as if he was focused on something, but the focus wasn't me. *I'm sorry, babe. It's just that I'm finally on a roll here. You know how hard it is for me to get into my flow . . .* Something in the way he trailed off broke me, and I was overcome with another wave of heaviness. I had done everything to be his partner, and now I was growing this creature–his spawn–in my body. Nourishing it with my blood. My eyelid pulsed.

Once the baby comes, are you going to set a new schedule? I tried to control my voice, but it was starting to crack.

We gotta figure that out, honey. And we will. It's just–I can't leave work early right now.

TOM, I sobbed, letting it out. *I'm not– Earlier today I saw a dead bee on our windowsill, and I cried because it was probably lonely when it died. Then I tried to eat some toast, and I almost puked. And then–*I hiccuped–*a man in a suit on Spring Street told me I had nice titties. I feel like I'm in an elevator, and it's like the cables have snapped, and I'm careening down from the top floor, and you're not even listening to me, and I know it.* The words came out hot and heavy as I paced around our small kitchen. I sobbed like a newborn, choking on my own despair so much that it quieted me for a few seconds, until I could let out another proper wail. His lack of urgency was enraging. I wanted him to rush home to me.

I'll–I'll come home for dinner, he said. *I'll rush.* I looked at the time on the microwave clock. It was already late.

By the time he arrived at our apartment, I wasn't hungry at all. I was too tired and emotionally spent to eat and didn't even have it in me to ask what had taken him so long, the interval between his call and arrival clearly longer than necessary for the short commute. I knew then that I couldn't count on Tom for anything–for absolutely anything–and I was totally alone.

Later that night, I looked at his phone when he was in the shower. I saw he'd rung my mom. His texts to her read *Call me back. Sarah is so depressed. I don't know what to do.* All I wanted was for him to spend some time with me, ask me how I was feeling, to never even look at another woman, to belong to me 100 percent in every way. And instead of doing that, which seemed easy enough, he'd made me someone else's problem.

I flipped through the rest of the texts on his phone as I heard him humming to himself in the bathroom. There was one to an ex-girlfriend, someone I actually liked, which read, *Hey, sexy, come visit me at the studio sometime, same address as always.*

My stomach dropped, and my cheeks grew warm, a reminder

that these exchanges made me feel embarrassed for myself. I was, in a way, conditioned to being a second-class citizen in relationships. My mother had always emphasized her career over my company and the duties of motherhood: it wasn't the fact that she was a *working mother* that messed with my head but the feeling that she *preferred* work to being a mother. And then the entire world trained me to believe my worth was limited by virtue of the fact that I was a woman operating in a world revolving around men. These texts were just like catcalls on the street or having to placate pushy guys in a bar: they stung, and they made the voices in my head say things like *You don't deserve better* and *If you were a more beautiful pregnant woman, this wouldn't happen*, or, worst of all, *Don't complain, because he will leave you, and then you'll be alone.*

Anyway, I could guess what he'd tell me if I brought up the messages. *I was just being friendly, it didn't mean anything, she knows I'm married, I love you, I chose you.* Every woman I knew, practically, dealt with the same sort of small infidelities in their relationships, complaining from time to time over wine about a girl from the office who emailed their husbands with inside jokes or sent texts that read a bit too flirty. The outlook across the board seemed to be that this was just what men did with technology in the modern age. So, what was I to do, divorce the man over silly, meaningless words? Then I'd have no one. I noticed he'd sent this message the night before at ten o'clock, which was when we were getting ready to go to sleep. Maybe that's what had kept him too distracted to care about our baby moving inside my body. I put back his phone carefully and rested on my side of the bed, stewing on what I perceived as my husband's disinterest. He could send flirty texts behind my back for all I cared, but I wanted more wonder from him. I needed his enthusiasm to buoy me—I couldn't conjure it on my own.

I had too much to deal with. I had bigger fish to fry. Tom had been unsure about hiring someone to help take care of our baby, but I'd sold it to him by explaining it would mean we could both go back to work faster. And while no one I knew in Indiana had even used the term *baby nurse*, I'd spent the last six months being asked who mine was the minute I told anyone I was pregnant. Before they asked *When are you due?* I usually heard *Do you need a baby nurse recommendation?* followed by suggestions for preschools that were harder to get into than Harvard.

I'm just not comfortable with someone living in our house, Tom complained when I told him it was possible to pay a baby nurse to live in; that, in fact, in some NYC circles, it was common. *My parents never had that*, he'd rationalized over breakfast when I said that a mom I really trusted, with well-behaved and well-adjusted children, had given me a list of baby nurses to call about their availability.

You've been in therapy for thirty years talking about how those same parents raised you, I said. *Don't you think it might have saved you some anguish if there'd been an extra set of hands to assist with your care?* He slurped his black coffee, mimicking the exact noise his dad made at breakfast.

My mom used to tell me she hated me, Tom once said matter-of-factly. *She came to my therapist with me once to talk about it, but she told him she didn't remember any of what I was saying*.

One time, over martinis, my own mother confided that she hadn't really started liking me until I was about twenty-two, so I got what he meant. This was why I thought it was so essential to have help: we could protect our child from all our flaws by limiting his exposure to them.

It's a fortune, isn't it? Tom continued. *Doesn't it seem a ridiculous way to spend money?* He started packing up his morning drawings into his workbag, and I could tell I was losing the battle.

But if we don't have help, you'll have to be home with me, and you won't be able to work, and we will actively lose money, I countered. *At least this way we have a shot at breaking even. Isn't spending money to give someone a job and help make parenting more of a delight the whole* point *of working hard?* He looked at me. Neither of us seemed to be all that steeped in joy, but I could tell he knew what I meant.

Later that day, I interviewed a series of perfectly acceptable, responsible-sounding women. I liked them, though some of them made me think of the phys ed teachers at my high school who were always yelling at me to run faster, their opinions on breastfeeding schedules and nap times like a sport I didn't actually want to play. Finally, I ended up on FaceTime with Sharon, who swore like a sailor and made me laugh about ten times in the first five minutes of our interview, where I sometimes felt like she was interviewing *me* to see if she wanted to work for *us*. She had four grown-up kids of her own and wanted to one day return to Trinidad, where she was from, to run a pig farm—not because she loved pigs but because she loved bacon, a passion I understood. She took no shit, I could tell. I loved her. For the first time in my marriage, I made a decision without consulting Tom and paid her deposit that day. The idea that she would be working for us, taking care of the baby and making sure it didn't die, kept me from many a panic attack, my mind pinballing between a host of nightmarish scenarios that all seemed imminently possible.

I agonized constantly about falling. *One fall,* my older friend with three kids said. *It could all be over.* The thought paralyzed me. How else could I fuck this all up? I worried about placental abruption and preeclampsia. I worried about the umbilical cord strangling the baby. Breech birth. Bleeding out on the table. But then I wondered: How sad would I be? A thought that made me feel immediately, disgustingly guilty and awful. I knew people who would give anything for my problems.

• • •

THE ARTIST ALICE NEEL, my favorite twentieth-century portraitist, made a painting in 1930 called *Degenerate Madonna*. A distorted, ghostly mother sits cross-legged in the center, her skin veiny and pale. One infant perches on her lap, and another is seen in profile in the background, floating off into a forest of bare trees. The painting always stuck in my mind: the mother depicted as a shell of herself, the children haunted and strange. I was not surprised to learn that Neel created the work after the death of her firstborn, a one-year-old little girl lost to diphtheria.

Neel would go on to lose another child to kidnapping and then suicide. She suffered a miscarriage in 1937 that preceded a stay in a psychiatric ward and her own suicide attempt–but she also had two other children, who, as adults, described her absent parenting, her neglect. That part both surprised and resonated with me. How could she experience such loss and continue to disrespect the fragility of what she had? I was never sure if the mother in her painting was tortured by the children who died or the ones who didn't. And I was not sure how close to or how far I felt from Neel's degraded maternal figure.

But I also lived in abject fear of losing my baby, remembering the shock I'd felt seven months before, when my mom called me on the day my sister was due with her first child, expecting to hear news that he'd arrived. Instead, my mother's voice had been tearful.

Oh, Sarah, the worst thing has happened. I thought she would tell me that Deechie had to have surgery, something surmountable that with perspective would seem like a blip. I was sitting at my desk, thumbing the cord of my office phone as I waited for her news to come out.

He's dead. The baby's dead. He was born dead. We don't know why, but his heart stopped. For no reason.

Immediately, I thought back to the moment my sister had told me she was pregnant. My little sister, barely a year younger than me, always more beautiful, with incredible, shiny, thick brunette hair that hung in heavy curtains around her face. I'd been so jealous of her as a kid. I'd wanted her name, I'd wanted her face, I'd wanted her quietness, the way she wasn't too much for people. I thought about how she followed all her passions, learned about all the weird and niche things she wanted to so unapologetically: horses and Buddhism and regenerative agricultural practices and artisanal butter making. I thought about her radiance on her wedding day. She'd looked like a midcentury Italian beauty, a virginal Juliet, beaming and content. She'd wanted a small wedding at home, raspberries from my parents' garden, and champagne from my dad's cellar for dessert. I'd fought with the wedding photographer, needing everything to be perfect for her, annoyed by his lateness. And then, two years later, we were on that family trip to Denmark, and when I'd come down to the hotel bar on the first night for drinks, she'd blurted it out: *I'm pregnant! I can't have a cocktail!* And we'd all cried.

Eight months after that moment, the baby was dead. I rushed to the airport to get on the first plane to Indianapolis with a seat available, and before I'd even made it into a taxi, I'd had to call my mom back to check if I was dreaming or if it was true. Nothing felt real, so I'd texted the news to myself to be sure I wasn't imagining things or having some sort of nervous breakdown.

The baby died, and we don't know why, I texted to my own phone, and had to keep looking at it. I called Tom and told him I was leaving for a few days. *You don't have to come, but Deechie's baby died. We don't know why.* He cried, I didn't. He said he'd meet me in Indianapolis; I told him not to. I felt immediately calm, almost like I was stoned, watching a movie about a baby dying, incapable of conjuring secondhand emotion for a character that wasn't real. And I started making lists of everything we needed to do: cancel the baby announcements, cancel the postpartum doula, call the funeral home. Did my sister want us to take her nursery apart or leave it up for when she got home? Did she want to see it another time, even though she wasn't bringing home its intended inhabitant?

Every morning when I woke up, for months, I'd remind myself that the baby we'd all been expecting hadn't made it, but I couldn't believe it had really happened. I hadn't cried much, even when I'd held his little body, still warm, in the hospital, or even at the funeral, with the tiny casket. Tom had flown in to hold my hand.

You really didn't have to be here, I said. It wasn't that I didn't find it tragic and inexplicable and unfair, this idea that a baby could die, with no cause; it wasn't that I truly thought it was an unremarkable situation or that I didn't need support from my husband to get through it–it was that I couldn't seem to will my emotional core to react to the news.

I think you're in shock or something, babe, Tom told me as he unpacked his overnight bag. *This is really, really sad.* I'd looked at him, knowing he was likely right. Yet I still felt nothing.

However, at every one of my own ob-gyn appointments, I found myself crying endless, cold, calm tears. They leaked out of my eyes until I saw the heartbeat flash on the screen and heard my doctor say, *There's our baby!* As if my body had emotions that my brain wasn't feeling, or maybe vice versa. Some secret, hidden part of me knew to be worried and knew to cry. So, every time I pulled down my underwear to pee, many times a day, I searched vigilantly for blood, terrified of all the things that *could* go wrong. Spooked by the idea that I could somehow jinx everything, I refused all offers of a baby shower.

It was like I was living in a frozen universe, trapped between a glacier of past sadness and an iceberg of potential future pain, and trying to avoid both. The thought of expressing this to anyone, of doing anything that could possibly be perceived as complaining, seemed beyond egregious, by the way. My fetus was growing and thriving, and I could afford to pay for medical care. I could have gone to therapy, I could have asked for professional help or meds, and that alone was an advantage not available the world over, and of course I knew it. But when I thought about sitting on a couch and saying any of this out loud, it made me feel like a stupid mess of a person, like a failure of a *good girl*. I was raised not to complain, not to tell strangers my private problems. Wasn't therapy just another way to be self-indulgent? The more I ruminated on it, the more I hated myself for thinking I had jack shit to complain about. I had a great job. I was surrounded by art and artists. I was healthy. I had a husband who could say the same for himself. And maybe, if I just held on long enough and focused on the positive, this period of disorganized, superstitious thinking would pass.

ONE NIGHT I WENT TO A WEDDING DINNER and was seated with a woman who had recently had twins. The affair was in Brooklyn, and it looked it: long tables with candles and minimalist floral arrangements all in white. The bride wore a short dress and had a sharp, French haircut, dark brown with strong bangs, like Madeline from the children's books. She worked in an art gallery, and her new husband was an artist, and everyone there was someone I knew one degree removed. I felt very comfortable asking my tablemate about her pregnancy.

Well, they cut my pussy to my asshole, she said as she sipped her wine. *A woman has to come to my house every week with these glass tubes, and we do pussy physical therapy.* She signaled for a waiter to pour her another glass.

Oh my God. Is that, like, a twin thing? I'm sure I sounded terrified. I shoved a piece of bread into my mouth.

No, that's a birth thing, honey. Google episiotomy. *My babies together weighed less than most single babies do. Labor is just fucking brutal.*

I put my hand on my bump and rubbed it up and down, like I

was apologizing to the little fetus in there for having to witness all of this.

I hear you, I said. *But how do I make it less brutal? Should I get a doula? Would that help? Or should I schedule a C-section and avoid the pussy-ripping thing altogether?* I stared into her face as if I could absorb all the wisdom in her brain if I looked hard enough.

My only recommendation to you would be to do everything you can to get the baby out fast. Let them take it out of your mouth if they want to. Just get it over with. And make sure you have plenty of help when you get home. Babies are much easier to deal with when they're inside your body. She glanced down at my belly. *I'm warning you*—she paused, and I leaned toward her as best I could lean with my big ass in back and baby bump between us—*things do not get better from here.*

5

Mother Wound

Indiana
1990s

EXCEPT FOR A FEW PARTS DOWN SOUTH, Indiana is supremely flat. Around Indianapolis, where I grew up, the farmland stretches for acres, and if you're driving—and you are always driving in Indiana—you can see miles upon miles of corn and soybeans, not a dip or a rise in sight, only fences and wooden barns and farmhouses, and the occasional cluster of wind turbines. You can drive east to west across the entire state, and never lose your stomach going up or down a single hill.

One of my earliest memories is being in my dad's arms, watching neon lightning crackling against an immense expanse of sky, not a tiny bit afraid of its power; I knew that when I was outdoors with my dad, I didn't have to be scared of anything. He would stand on our porch and hoot like an owl until the one that lived in our backyard hooted back. He'd look at the insects in the air and be able to tell me what fish were biting and where on account of the size and genus. He'd cup his ears and tell me where a squirrel was in the trees, and bring home quail from his bird-hunting trips, which my mom would roast for weekend dinner parties, warning her guests about swallowing buckshot.

Sometimes my mom would pick me up early from kindergarten and take me to this one chain restaurant at the mall and we'd have a "ladies' lunch," but the place closed eventually after a friend of my parents' found a severed rat tail in her Caesar salad and reported it to the board of health. After that, if my mom came and got me from school, we'd go home and sit in our kitchen at the Formica built-in banquette, and I'd practice my letters with her until my dad came home from work at six o'clock sharp. My little brother and sister and I would watch his car pull into the driveway and exclaim in unison, *Daddy's home! Daddy's home!* until he came clacking into the house in his dress shoes, loosening his tie and unbuttoning his suit jacket. He'd bring with him any missing ingredients—usually coffee beans for the morning or lettuce picked up from one of the farm stands dotting the back roads—and then we'd tuck ourselves in at the dinner table, where acceptable conversation topics included the news and court cases and politics.

We had to put our napkins in our laps and say *Please* and *Thank you*, and we had to clear our plates and ask to be excused. We used our forks and knives the right way and chewed with our mouths closed. We wrote thank-you notes. We called our parents' friends *ma'am* and *sir*. We got summer jobs as soon as we were old enough and used our paychecks to buy after-school snacks or miniskirts on sale at the knockoff Urban Outfitters. We didn't talk about money or religion, and we got lectures about hard work and discipline. We supported the local civic theater and went to high school basketball games and had spring picnics in the gardens belonging to the tiny private university a short bike ride away.

All of it looked like some sort of American fantasy: a handmade quilt of married parents maintaining well-mannered families, children without any hint of messiness or anxiety or loneliness. If you didn't know any better, you'd think in a place this polite, this flat and open and wide, nothing bad would ever happen; there'd be no place to hide secrets. But if you scratched the surface, you'd see why *Close Encounters of the Third Kind* and *Children of the Corn* and that television show *Cops* were all set in places like Indiana.

"America's First Serial Killer," H. H. Holmes, murdered the last of his more than two hundred suspected victims in Indianapolis in 1894. D. C. Stephenson, grand dragon of the Ku Klux Klan, was born in Evansville. (So was my father.) At one time, almost 30 percent of men in Indiana were members of the KKK, and every single government official was either a member or approved by the organization. Depression-era gangster John Dillinger was from Mooresville. Jim Jones was from Crete. Michael Jackson was born in Gary.

I went to high school with the daughter of a serial killer. The bodies of his victims were discovered, raped and buried, on their family farm when I was a sophomore, which was more curious to me than terrifying. Not one but two kids I grew up with had fathers who went to prison for child pornography, each in an unrelated case. The headmaster of my school committed suicide in his house on campus. There were several teacher-student sex scandals, but nothing much changed or happened after the news subsided. Bad things happened to children, *very* bad things happened to girls, but absolutely no one I knew was in therapy, which didn't seem strange to me, or even notable, because I barely even knew the practice existed. I didn't even learn the word *therapy* until my middle school sex ed class, during which our gym teacher put on the movie *What About Bob?*, some out-of-date dramedy about Bill Murray's outlandish phobias, and told us not much more than the fact that obsessive-compulsive disorder and anorexia nervosa both required professional help to cure. There was no normalization of mental health treatment as part of everyday self-care. In fact, for years, I lumped therapy with learning about periods and semen: something shameful that made boys smirk.

EVEN THOUGH MY MOTHER was a sex crimes prosecutor when I was little, my own attitude toward sex was mostly that if you thought about it, wanted to do it, or liked it, you should definitely *not* tell your mom–even mine, who worked in the second sex crimes unit established in the whole country; who, instead of wearing Laura Ashley frocks like all the other moms, donned leggings and cropped jean jackets, used curse words, and made wicked jokes. Instead of wrestling her big blonde curls into straight submission in the style that was popular among the other ladies in the mall, she dyed her tresses auburn and let them layer softly around her face, and didn't own a blow-dryer. And, at least in the early years, unlike most women around me, she eschewed anything fussy when it came to her appearance, as if rejecting the overtly feminine would make it easier for her to infiltrate the boys' club of lawyers, judges, and cops to whom she initially had to prove herself.

When I was in middle school, she'd point out the sites of her past cases from the front seat of our family station wagon, nodding toward grassy knolls near the interstate and patches of farmland in the middle of newly sprouted neighborhoods.

I had a case a few years ago about a prostitute who was raped and murdered behind that bar over there, she once told me, gesturing to a shitty downtown watering hole that looked as if no one had been inside in years. The sign on the door read *Open*, but the boarded-up windows and peeling facade indicated otherwise. In any other context, if my mom mentioned sex, I'd gag and cover my ears until she stopped. When she talked about her various cases, though, it was with such a sad reverence that I mostly just listened, imagining the ghosts of terrified women flitting across our windshield.

How can you be raped if that's your job? I'd asked from the back seat. I watched the decrepit storefronts go by as we drove north, their crumbling elevations slowly turning into more stately homes with yards and fences.

Oh, sweetheart, she'd said with her familiar twang and a sigh. *What do they even teach you at that silly school? It doesn't matter what her job was*, she continued, a gentle persuasiveness in her voice. She was staring straight ahead, and I could see her in the rearview mirror, her eyes on the road. *If you don't want to do it*—I appreciated her not saying the word *sex*—*that's rape. Got it? If you were a professional football player, that wouldn't mean it was okay for someone to tackle you anytime, anywhere, right?* I don't remember how I responded, but it was probably something bitchy and pubescent about how she didn't know anything about sports.

THESE STORIES WERE ALWAYS PART OF MY LIFE, but when I was six, my mother left the prosecutor's office. *Can Mommy tell you a secret?* she asked me one afternoon in the solarium of my grandparents' nondescript, squat, stone midcentury three-bedroom house, a short drive from ours. The room had lots of windows overlooking the backyard. I could see dust particles floating in the light, hovering over Grandma Frieda's collection of waxy-green houseplants.

I nodded at my mom, who stood off to my side while I sat on a chintz-covered couch. *Mommy's going to open a restaurant*, she faux-whispered. I could hear my grandfather's Mozart bellowing from the living room at a decibel level more appropriate for Metallica.

As my mother elaborated about her project, I could tell she was so excited, like she could barely contain her proud smile. *Remember how sick I was when I was pregnant with your little brother?* I'm sure I nodded. *But do you remember how much weight I gained? I gained thirteen pounds with you, fourteen pounds with your sister, and seventy pounds with your brother. It was unholy.* This probably meant nothing to me at six, though at sixteen I would have rolled my eyes and said something cruel under my breath. *The doctor, God bless him, told me I was probably not eating well enough, and I should try the salads at McDonald's.* McDonald's! I nodded at her, my eyes big, unsure where this was going. I'd never had McDonald's; she'd always forbidden it, as well as the Velveeta shells and cheese I saw on TV commercials and begged for–I wanted to squeeze the packet into the steamy pasta and watch it melt with every ounce of my tiny body. Her words got faster. *McDonald's was the best that short-sighted, artery-clogged, aged man could come up with. And we live by all these farms.* She gestured out the window. *Why don't restaurants just serve produce grown here, on these farms?* She laughed a little bit. *I'm going to start a restaurant that does that.* I remember I could feel the energy in the air between us, like it was crackling from her fingertips, from her smile.

What I couldn't see behind that smile was a woman to whom the bank would give a business loan only with my dad's name on the paperwork. I didn't see an inspiring restaurateur whose contractor had refused to install a dishwasher because he'd said she'd never be successful and didn't want her to waste the money, or a lonely woman whose girlfriends had told her that if she worked, people would think my father couldn't provide properly for his family. I didn't see an entrepreneur who wouldn't take no for an answer, or a young, hardworking prosecutor whose boss said *You're nothing but a cream puff* when she gave him her notice, as if she were too weak to find success doing anything but working for a man. I didn't know that when she named her restaurant, she chose a riff on the French word for *cream puff* as a fuck-you. I didn't think to myself, *Maybe being super sick while pregnant plus working for men was so awful that she had to go out and do something for herself, on her own terms.*

By high school, when my mom's restaurant had become a restaurant group and then her whole business expanded exponentially, I felt the easy coziness of our relationship slip away. It was like our stars had rotated toward different orbits. Hers was its own elliptical, and it often crossed with mine, but there were more and more moments where I felt like I was hurtling away, at light speed, from the fullness of her presence. I couldn't see how utterly alone she must have felt as a woman building a business, how frustrating the demands of parenthood must have been. I knew only that she seemed to have a whole separate and secret work life that made her happy, and didn't seem to love every single aspect of being a mom. I knew it from the lackadaisical way she approached certain mothering tasks. I knew it from how she snapped at me, from how she seemed to resent my needs, from the way she muttered *God-damn it* every time one of us accidentally made a mess or needed something from her, from the ways she was so different from the perfect examples of suburban wifedom all around us. It was as if she thought that if she waded too far into the obligations of motherhood, the sea of it would overtake her, the strong tides would keep her from emerging on the half shell with her identity intact—so she didn't do many of those things that the mothers around us did. She didn't send out family cards at Christmas, or have us wear matching outfits to holiday dinner, or order our yearbooks or frame our school photos, or watch my dance recitals, or hang out with the other moms in the other room at birthday parties.

Instead, she seemed to waffle in and out of the suburban adherence to norms. She closed her restaurants at three so that she could pick us up from school, but instead of cheerful conversation about our days on the way home, she'd blast Annie Lennox and the Beastie Boys, turn on *The Simpsons* the minute we got into the kitchen, then silently cook a full dinner. She often said that the most important thing a family could do was eat together at a table every night, and she loved cooking—she'd turned it into a career. But then why did she seem so unhappy with all of us there with her while she made our meal, night after night? We were forbidden from using the kitchen ourselves, and I swore I could sense how little she wanted to interact with me as she cooked, and cooked and cooked, risotto and roasted chickens and potatoes au gratin, pies and cookies and vinaigrettes on repeat.

• • •

AND WHILE THE HABITS OF MIDWESTERN POLITENESS meant that difficult topics were not discussed openly and honestly, that manners were prioritized, and that girls had better be *good*, my mother had her own ideas about shit, and sometimes that did not cohere with Indiana norms nor with mothering according to Indiana's definition. In fact, she encouraged me to ignore parts of the Hoosier culture that didn't make sense to her. When my high school cheerleading coach caught me skipping practice and sidelined me at the homecoming game, my mom laughed. When I told her I planned to write my phone number on the butt of my spankies and do a round-off during halftime anyway, she told me to go for it. She'd been the one to take me to the tailor to have my uniform shortened two extra inches at the beginning of the season, and when I got in trouble for that, too, she encouraged me to write an essay about the inherent sexism of dress codes. She made endless complaints to my school when a male teacher called my group of friends *the coffee klatch of Aunt Blabbies*, which I had interpreted as a joke.

That's a man trying to tell you that you talk too much, baby girl, she'd explained. *And no one asked his opinion.*

And then, somewhere along the line, I became aware of her insecurities and the way they skewed her worldview. I'd listen to her call herself fat, waiting for my dad to tell her she was beautiful. She didn't bother to dress like anyone else, wear makeup like anyone else, style her hair like anyone else, or spend her days like anyone else, and she was still unhappy with herself. The message was clear to me: To be the kind of woman I saw all around me was going to disappoint my mother. To be a woman at all was risky. There were things about life that were way fucking better than being a suburban mom, like having a job outside the home that you loved. And in my early teen years, as I tried on all the ways there were to be a girl, my mother's disdain for a certain type of small-town femininity drove me into myself and away from her at the same time.

When I was in seventh grade, my mom forgot to send in the payment for an after-school ballet class, which I found out when I was turned away at the door, the teacher telling me gently that I could use the office phone to have someone come over with a check or take me home. Later, when my mom finally arrived, though I'd called and called our home phone to reach her, she seemed bewildered by my need for her.

Goddamn it, I was in the middle of cooking! she snapped, gliding up in her car as if I'd just stepped outside, though I'd spent two hours waiting for her. I'd put my gym clothes over my ballet uniform to stay warm. *I'll call the teacher tomorrow*, she said, cranking up the radio with an exasperated sigh, adding, *They cashed my check!*

That ballet class never came up again, but my anger at her lingered after every infraction, burning in my chest whenever she made up an excuse for the ways she didn't prioritize me, forgot my needs, or let me down. It was an endless list of tiny things, like promising she'd drop off lunch for me at school–her idea–and then not showing up, keeping me waiting at the school entrance, hungry, while all the other kids were finishing their trays of gray meat products; or never being on time to pick me up, leaving me locked out of my own house, sometimes for hours, when I got a ride home with a friend's mom.

One year, when I asked her what to wear to the holiday pageant, she reached into my dresser and pulled out a stretchy pink outfit I'd just worn to school. *How about this?* she said, suspiciously averting her eyes from mine. When I got to the auditorium, I heard a kid in my class whisper, *You look nice*, and I gave an automatic *Thank you. Not you*, he said. *You wore that yesterday. Didn't you know you're supposed to dress up?* He pulled at his bow tie and laughed with the girl next to me, while I felt my cheeks turn red and my eyes prickle with tears.

No one would have felt sorry for me had I complained about such tiny lapses in care, nor would I have betrayed my mother by talking about them. I was fed, loved, sheltered, educated. My mom was home every night, fisting the chicken and slamming it into the oven, Madonna blaring. But her indignant responses to my needs, the hot and cold nature of a mom who at times could be sweet to me and at other times seemed to despise the job of mothering—to despise *me*—felt like hostility toward motherhood itself. The mercurial nature of a woman who shunned fashion and beauty, who barely owned a hairbrush and refused to buy me *Seventeen* magazine, but who I heard critique her own body and the bodies of the women around her, left me tangled up inside about how I should approach the physicality of being a woman. In retrospect, she was undoubtedly working this out for herself, not realizing how it might confuse me. But for some reason, it all made me not only perplexed but also furious.

Yet every night, my father would stroll through the door unscathed by my teenage rancor, which lurched and spun magnetically toward my mother's every little twitch. Was this just mothers and daughters? I wondered. Forever sparring, with the dads eternally exempt? Or was it just Indiana, where dads went to work and moms tended the hearth? The flat fields rolling on and ever on toward the softly undulating far horizon. Later, I would come to question this: not Indiana and its ways but my blithe acceptance of these roles and their meaning. The way I adored my father and oh-so-casually wore my animosity toward my mother like my abbreviated cheerleading uniform. I knew I would one day regret my nasty tone—and I really was a bitch—as I stood, weeping, over the gaping maw of my mother's open grave.

On paper, when you think about how much older Tom is than I am, I guess I could be misunderstood as having *daddy issues*, whatever those actually are. Like my whole attachment style and relationship with men can be chalked up to the ways in which my dad was or wasn't present, was or wasn't good. The ways I do and don't feel about him. But the reality is my dad has always been solid and kind; I knew just what to expect of him. My mom, on the other hand, did not do things *wrong* per se, but she could not be depended on. When I look back on the idyll of my childhood, I know that while I was living it, I couldn't recognize how I revered the man whose benevolent presence held court at the head of the dinner table. Is it any wonder how I was able, years later, to allow my husband to get away with being less than I needed during my pregnancy or to allow myself to deprioritize my baby? I was Goldilocks, figuring out how much care was the right amount to give and receive, and that seemed de rigueur–I had watched it all my life.

On one level, my mother's refusal to feel guilty or apologetic for her disinterest in consistent mothering left me with a gnawing, persistent voice in my brain, and all it seemed to say to me, on repeat, was that my needs were annoying, and I was burdensome. I didn't have the words to tell her how sometimes I thought I despised her almost uncontrollably, or why, and I also did not know how to adequately express the depth of my overwhelming love for her. I couldn't have found words to describe the way I felt when her cells were around me: complete, like a puzzle that had its final piece clicked into place. How could I describe my calm when she put a cool palm on my cheek and called me *sweetheart*? Or how I sobbed in the shower, thinking that no matter where I ended up in the world, I wanted to be buried with my mom? She made me so mad sometimes that I could feel myself smoldering when I looked at her. Then, at night, when the house was dark and I was alone in my bedroom, I cried to myself about how much I loved her–a primal, desperate yearning based on a profound connection that severed every time she "wronged" me. I'd think about something bad happening to her, like a car accident or plane crash, and know that if our last interaction was tarnished by my anger toward her, I would die of guilt and sorrow. I didn't know how to say that.

Instead, I turned outward: I looked for companionship outside the home, devoting myself to my girlfriends with a religious fervor. I spent hours talking to them every night, watching TV shows with plastic house phones pressed against our ears, murmuring about Pacey and Dawson and their love triangles. We wrote one another letters, and we kept group journals and wore friendship necklaces, passed notes at our lockers and stood in tight circles on the playground. My cravings for endless girl talk were earnest and pure, and I kept no secrets from my friends.

IN THE DARK PIT OF MY HEART, I knew I was ungrateful for feeling resentment toward the distance between my mother and the mother I, on some level, wanted her to be. I had a home, and two parents, and I was fed. I wasn't Lizzy Domino, who always wore dirty underwear, whose mom was bipolar and came to school screaming, throwing groceries at Lizzy in front of everyone. I wasn't at the fringes of society, nor in a shelter for people without homes, nor fleeing the Nazis, like some of my relatives. I was not beaten or starved or orphaned or touched by male family members at night. Still, when I went to bed, I closed my eyes and dreamed of one of those mothers I saw on TV; someone who felt fully devoted to mothering, whose sole purpose in life was to float down the stairs and deliver kind wisdom at all hours, to work without working and love without exception.

THERE'S THAT FAMOUS TOM PETTY SONG—I don't know the name, the one everyone sings along to in bars: *Indiana boys on them Indiana nights*, that one. When I croon it in my head, I hear a chorus of white frat boys, with drunk half-smiles on their faces, eyes pinched halfway closed. One of them has sunglasses on even though it's midnight.

It was on the radio that June night, the eve of my sixteenth birthday. I was pressed against the blue door of a 1990s Land Rover, a car passed down from sibling to sibling, finally landing with the baby brother of three kids, Mark, the one I wanted to love me as much as I thought I loved him. I looked up at a round, warm summer moon, letting the sticky air emanate from crop soil and flood over me like a bath as he lifted my tank top above my head, thinking that I was well on my way to becoming the kind of girl that song was written about.

Maybe I was just singing along to it in my head, trying to distract myself, calm myself down a little bit, retain some sense of control over the pounding thump I felt in my crotch, the hormones swelling up so thick it felt like my sex drive was going to explode out of my low-rise jeans. I could feel it, some little square inch of my body, pulsing a tortured, lovesick heartbeat to the tune of that song as this boy put his hands on my tiny hips, their bones about a foot apart, perched on top of a roughly shaved groin, which I kept bare and powdered in case he touched me down there.

I was so grateful whenever he touched me. In fourth grade all the boys had called me a *wet dog*, a moniker from a family vacation to the Caribbean during which I begged to get three cornrows with little shells on the ends braided into my hair by a lady on the beach. When I took them out a week later, I loved the crimp they left behind–I felt like the mermaid in the movie *Splash*–and my mom took me to her hairdresser, who said she could perm my whole head to be like that. It turned out horrible, frizzy and huge, so I'd shower right before school every morning, hoping that if I came in soaked, my wild hair wouldn't dry fully until the end of the day, and no one would know how much uglier I'd made myself. A few years later, on the phone with Phillip Main and his friend, I heard them looking me up in the yearbook while they thought the phone was on mute. *She's kinda hot, I guess. But she has sort of a schnoz.*

So, when Mark laid me down in the back seat of that blue Land Rover and pulled off my pants, I knew I owed him my eternal gratitude. But when he rammed his dick inside my small, girlish body, I groaned primally, like a woman in labor, unable to perform the sexiness I owed him for finding parts of me tolerable enough to want to kiss me.

This is impossible, Mark said bitterly. *You're not even fuckable.* I started to cry, which set him off, and he grabbed a plastic Evian bottle tucked into the pocket of the back seat, lobbing it at my head. *Grow up*, he muttered. When it hit me, the lid spun off, and my hair was suddenly drenched with stale, lukewarm car water, faintly plastic scented. He looked annoyed as drops slid down my face. *I'm taking you home.* Had I been hotter, a better prize, more docile, I wondered if he would have been nicer or tried harder to hide his frustration.

Later, when I walked in the front door, opening it slowly so that it wouldn't squeak, I felt a rush above me, like the air right at the top of my head had been sucked up into an unseen vortex. As my eyes adjusted to the dark, I saw that an owl had flown in the door with me and was circling the living room, shitting as he went. I ran toward my parents' bedroom, which looked out at the peony bushes in our front yard. It was at the opposite end of the house from the kids' rooms, which were upstairs, and my mom almost never came up there; she said it made her nervous. The hallway leading to my parents' room was pitch black, but I could see the outline of their antique four-poster bed and hear their soft snores.

Mom, I whispered. *There's an owl in the living room, and I don't know how to get it out.*

Goddamn it, Sarah, she said sternly, shooting up out of bed, throwing off the antique quilts my great-grandmother had made that covered all of us at night. *Are you on acid?*

I'm not even drunk! I whisper-shouted. *If you don't believe me, go look for yourself.* She thumped out of bed furiously and pounded into the living room, where the owl was sitting on a silk lampshade. He spun his head around in a circle at us and hooted. Otherwise, he didn't move.

We sat on the floor and watched him for a minute.

Wow, she said. *I thought for sure you were on acid.* We started laughing, and soon we were gasping for breath.

I swear, she wheezed, *I was going to be so pissed if you woke me up because you were high and had imagined an owl. When I walked in here, and there really was an owl . . .* We started laughing all over again.

We ended up calling a man we found in the Yellow Pages named Critter Bob. He was listed under "Animal Control," and said he'd be there in an hour because he was on a raccoon emergency call down south. That set us on another round of laughter so hard that we had tears running down our cheeks, trying to keep it in so he wouldn't think we were completely crazy.

He advised us to take a heavy blanket and walk toward the owl slowly. When the owl made a break for it, he'd likely fly into the blanket, and then we could gently cover him with it. He'd calm down in the dark. My mom didn't want to sacrifice any blankets, so we used an old outdoor tablecloth, each holding one side. After the owl was safely sleeping in the dark in his little tablecloth bed, we waited up for Critter Bob together, eating ice cream out of the tub.

Why did you have three kids? I asked her. *It seems kind of miserable. Us waking you up when we let owls into the house and all.* We both laughed as she watched me dip my spoon into the vanilla. I could feel Mark and the car floating away—my life with my school friends, the things I did with boys in the back seats of cars, the drinks I had in basements—all parts of another, secret life I wanted to share with her but was never sure if I was supposed to.

I'll never forget it, the first time I heard you laugh, she said. She was smiling, and everything about her got softer. *I was shaking a bag of cereal, to get some of it out into a bowl, and you must have* been, I don't know, four months old. You burst out laughing, and it was like music to my ears. I imagined myself as a four-month-old as I took another bite of ice cream. I'd seen pictures of myself from that age, and I looked like a squished little monster. The minute I heard your laugh, I wanted as many kids as I could have. I could see in her eyes that she was thinking about a memory, because she was looking right at me but was somewhere else.

But it doesn't even seem fun. Like, usually I feel like I'm just an annoyance, I said.

Oh, you are, she said, and laughed. Something about it made me laugh too, the shock of the honesty. Kids are so much work. But who else would I share this life with? You know how sick I'd get of your father if we didn't have you kids? What would all of it be for, if not for you?

Suddenly she put down her spoon. All right, you should go to sleep, she said. I have work I want to do. I hugged her good night, taking in her smell. I could have stayed up for hours more chatting, but the fact that she didn't want to do that, the fact that she had some other parallel life, confirmed a theory I sensed: maybe all moms didn't owe you their entirety, no matter how much you craved it. Is that why I never told her how I felt about boys, how confused sex made me? Is that why I didn't ask if it was the same for her and every other woman? Or was I afraid it would have made her upset, that brutal severing of my own girlhood?

I'm still not sure. But I know that I dream of a night where we'll stay up waiting for Critter Bob, no clock ticking or distraction from our time together. And I know that, most likely, I will be sprinting, breathless, oxygen deprived and burning, chasing that type of love for the rest of my life, trying to soothe my sore, exhausted heart with the promise of that connection.

• • •

WHEN I LOOK BACK AND THINK about my own reaction to impending motherhood, I can't help but see that my extreme distress was informed by anxiety that I wouldn't be able to be a mother and be happy at the same time. Though my mother had three children, something about dealing with them consistently had been anathema to her core identity, as if she were allergic to it. Like giving in to all the demands of the maternal would make her itchy and swollen, or provoke multiple organ failure. I saw her fear, and I think I feared the same anaphylaxis. I would get married and have a baby, and I would be lost, lost, lost, buried under the goo-goo-gah-gah of it all, the carpooling and the poopy diapers and the deranged spatchcocking. If I became a mother, it meant my mother would die, a generational patchwork of anguish like a quilt my grandmother's mother had made in some Indiana backwater town. But more than that, I knew that the pressure to be some specific kind of polite and perfect mommy would ruin me from the inside out.

6

Birth Story

New York
October 2–3, 2017

YOU'RE IN LABOR. You need to go directly to the hospital, my doctor said, looking straight at me.

I can't, I told her, wiping the sonogram gel off my big, round belly. *I have an appointment at Bergdorf's to get highlights, and it's impossible to reschedule with Jennifer. She's there only two days a week because she has young kids, and look at me, I'm desperate. If you get close, you can see premature GRAYS.* I leaned my head toward her, presenting my hairline, where I'd found suspiciously pale hairs before. It would be fine: everything on the Upper East Side is practically a twelve-minute walk from everything else, and Bergdorf's was just a few blocks down Fifth Avenue. I could go get my hair done and then go have my baby.

My doctor looked at me. *I don't think you understand,* she said. *You thought you peed in your pants last night at four a.m. By the time you finish with your hair, it will be eight p.m., and you will have been open to the world with a torn amniotic sac for all those hours,* she continued, writing something down in her chart while the nurse nodded behind her.

My roots won't take that long, I explained. I started preparing for my stroll, climbing off the exam table and putting on my shoes, flats I'd had to buy a full size up because of how swollen I'd become in the third trimester. *It usually takes me about an hour and a half or two hours, depending on if I get a trim. I can just meet you then.*

I felt completely nonchalant. It was a beautiful early-October day, still warm and sunny, and I was in a minidress I'd bought in a size much larger than normal and tailored to be as short as possible. I felt like Rosemary Woodhouse from *Rosemary's Baby*. A walk in the deep fall sun, down the side of Central Park, with my giant belly and still-tanned summer legs and long pregnancy hair sounded gorgeous.

The doctor snapped me out of it: *Sarah, no. You're not listening. Think about it. It's dangerous for your baby; you need antibiotics*, she said with finality. *You've been open to the world for far too long. You'll be hooked up to an IV within the next hour and a half.*

We argued back and forth. I couldn't imagine pushing out this little alien with my hair dirty. I'd done my morning dance cardio and hadn't shampooed afterward. It would all be a much happier experience for me if I could at least get a blowout. We settled on a compromise: I'd go to the blow-dry bar near NewYork-Presbyterian, the hospital where my doctor worked, while Tom went to fetch my overnight bag, and then I'd be on a gurney, laboring under her watch.

I waddled down Seventy-Seventh Street to get my blow-dry from a random walk-in hair salon, dripping something into my undies the entire time. I could see the hospital from the hairdresser's chair, its old ivy-covered brick walls, perched right over the FDR Drive. It looked like an asylum from a bygone era, built to house hysterical Victorian women in floor-length white nightgowns. It looked like the kind of place women went to get tied into straitjackets and hooked down into beds, injected with sedatives against their will. It looked like the kind of place women walked into and were never heard from again, leaving young children and best girlfriends behind to wonder whatever became of them.

I sat on a rock wall at the edge of the hospital entrance, hunching over my belly, and inspected a small rose garden while I called Augusta and cried.

I don't want to go in, Auggie. I'm so scared. I stared at the scraggly plants, left over from the summer, holding on to their last, tenuously lived moments in the sun. I could relate. I thought about my friend in med school, herself already a mother, who'd said, *It's the most dangerous day of your life and your baby's life when you give birth.* And my sister, she'd already been through one birth, and she didn't even get a living baby at the end of it, just a beautiful little boy with full blue lips and a cold body. I could feel mine kicking around inside me, alive, jamming my upper hip bone area on repeat—a reminder that my problems seemed stupid in comparison to hers, just a little bit of pain compared to a lifetime of grief.

What are you scared of? Augusta asked me, seemingly surprised that I wasn't more excited. *I never took the birthing class,* I sniffled. *I–I don't know any relaxation techniques.* I should have told her I was scared of needles. Scared of the epidural. Scared of pushing. Scared of tearing. Scared of dying. Scared of my baby dying. Scared of my baby living. Scared of not being pregnant anymore, something I was just getting the hang of. Scared of becoming a mom. Scared of never being myself again. Scared of all the ways Tom would disappoint me. Scared of all the ways I would disappoint Tom. Scared I'd love my child so much that it wouldn't be worth it—wouldn't be worth the potential immeasurable devastation of something bad happening to him.

Who takes the birthing class?! she answered. I could tell she was making her kids a snack, the clatter of a cabinet closing in the background, and I felt bad for bothering her. *No one has time for the birthing class and birthing books and all of that. That's why you have a fabulous doctor who delivers babies at the best hospital in New York. Success is correlated with experience, and she has tons of experience. Plus . . .* Her voice dropped low, like she'd turned away so that the kids couldn't hear her. *You have no choice. He's coming out one way or another. And I promise you an epidural hurts way less than a contraction.* She laughed at me, but sometimes she laughs when she's scared or uncomfortable. I couldn't tell which kind of laugh this one was. *Just trust me: it's the best day of your life. You get to meet your best friend.* She was silent for a few seconds while I gulped in a sob.

Where is your husband? Augusta asked. I felt embarrassed that he wasn't here already, with me for every step, and she'd noticed.

He's calling me now, actually, so I'll try you back later. I picked up the call beeping in, but it wasn't Tom.

It was the doctor, and she sounded mad. *You need to get inside this hospital right now. Time is up.*

Tom isn't here yet, I told her. *He went to get my hospital bag, and I don't know why he's taking so long, but he's not here, and I'm scared.* It was obvious I was crying, but that didn't make her any nicer.

Do not make me come find you, she said. *It has been two hours. Get inside this hospital.* I stood up, sniffling, and called Tom.

Sorry, baby, he said after the fifth ring. It was so windy behind him that I could barely hear. *I had to do some final meetings and calls, but I'm in a cab, and I'm almost there.*

He must be cruising up the FDR, I thought, *and can't be too far.* I wondered who he'd been meeting with; probably the unnaturally pretty friend of some friend who wanted a "tour" or who came by to "drop something off," again. I sat back down on the rock wall, watching exhausted-looking women get rolled out in wheelchairs, clasping little bundles in their arms, waiting for their cars to pull up at the grand cul-de-sac in front of us. They called this place the *lying-in hospital*, which had seemed like a chic euphemism indicating it would be comfortable and relaxing, but these women looked pale and almost vacant behind their eyes.

My hands had been trembling the last thirty minutes or so, but as I sat, I realized they'd stopped, and I felt sort of bizarre, as if someone had put me on a conveyor belt I couldn't get off of, and everything was moving forward but not because I was willing it to be that way. Some part of me gave up at that moment, like I realized my fear was futile: Tom was on his way, and I'd be going into that hospital no matter what. I replaced my foreboding with a sort of floating complacency. I could almost see myself sitting there, as if I were reading a book about a scared girl sitting on a rock wall and imagining it instead of being the scared girl sitting on the rock wall and living it.

When Tom pulled up, I was staring at the ground, listening to the birds, and feeling the sun start to go down, the temperature dropping the way it does in the fall once the sun is behind you.

Before we go in, let's take some pictures, he said. *I want us to remember these final moments when it was just us two.* He was trying to be sweet, I knew, but I smarted at the word *final* and explained to him that the doctor had already called to yell at me and now wasn't the time for photos. Though I didn't want to pass into the grand old hospital lobby, his lack of urgency felt antagonistic, a repudiation of all I was feeling. I wanted him to meet my fear or at least acknowledge it, because I knew I was right to be afraid. I remembered something a friend of mine who is a Latin teacher said about life expectancy in ancient Rome: that it was thirty-three years, not because people didn't live to be seventy, but because the average age factored in the high infant mortality rate and also women who died in childbirth. Wasn't this still true in the United States? Didn't we have the highest rate of maternal mortality in the developed world? Why wasn't Tom more scared?

I let him lead me inside, without apology, to the check-in desk. They sent him across the hall to make sure we'd have a room in the maternity ward once the baby came, and he returned quickly, reporting that it cost as much as a very nice hotel room in a major city, but he'd secured me a private room starting tomorrow. I shot off the text I'd promised my mom weeks before: *I'm at the hospital, call Tom for details. Get on a plane.*

An overly cheerful nurse strolled me into a labor and delivery room that had a gurney on wheels in the middle–I knew that was in case they had to take you into an operating room quickly; my doctor had once told me she could perform an emergency C-section in under two minutes if she had to.

Next to it was a small couch. *That folds into a bed*, she explained, *so your husband can sleep there.* The nurse started fiddling with screens and monitors while I dropped my bag in a corner, next to a shelf and faux leather chair, and started slowly unpacking, not really knowing what else to do. I pulled out a comforter for Tom, my phone charger, some Gatorade. *No snacks from now on, okay?* She said it in sort of a singsong voice, part of a script she'd repeated too many times to realize how hard it is for me to go more than three hours without food. *It's in case you want an epidural later. Here's a hospital gown, and then come sit in this bed, and I'll get your drip started.*

She pulled out a needle so thick that I could see it from across the room where I was unpacking–more like a small rod than anything else. I must have looked sick, because she said, *I know, it's the biggest needle in the hospital, this one that we give to women in labor. It will be fast, though!* She sounded so confident as she led me to the bed, and before I knew it, she'd slid the needle into my skin at my wrist. I could feel it tear through my flesh, and while it didn't hurt as much as I thought it might, I couldn't believe she'd done it to me. *Now what?* I asked her. *What comes next, and what's the worst part?* She was not making eye contact with me, busy putting a bag of something on the IV stand and typing into a computer, wrapping a monitor around my belly, and fastening the Velcro strap. Tom was furiously texting someone on his phone. I briefly wondered who–and if it was a woman–but I couldn't take the added stress of worrying about that, and I forced it to the bottom of my mind. I turned my head toward the nurse.

The worst part is when you're pushing, she answered. *Some women call it the ring of fire.* Just then I heard someone scream from down the hall, and the nurse laughed a little bit. *Speak of the devil!*

At that moment, my doctor walked in, smiling at me, like I'd been a good girl by coming inside.

You haven't had a single contraction, she said, looking at the monitor. *I think it's because your water isn't fully broken, so we may need to break it for you.* She sounded so casual. I had no idea this was something that could be done to a woman, this breaking of the water. I wish I'd googled it or had an expert tell me I could say no to this. I wish I'd known better.

Because sometimes, if your water doesn't fully break, the doctor will use what looks like a long knitting needle with a hook on the end to go through your cervix and rip a hole in the amniotic sac. That's what happened to me, and it left me breathless and gasping for air, shocked by the violence of the plastic tube plowing through my cervical opening and snatching a corner of my membrane. It made my legs and hands shake so badly I had to get up and go into the bathroom attached to my room, shut the door, and stare at myself in the mirror, just to confirm I was still there, still real. I had blood all over my legs when I sat to pee, and more of it on the scratchy hospital toilet paper when I wiped. By the time I got out of the bathroom, someone had changed the sheets on my bed, but I could still remember the feeling of warm water exploding out of my body and wetting everything, a feeling so jarring and out of my control; pain so deep inside my body that I didn't even know it could hurt there.

As soon as I climbed back into bed, some other doctor, a tall, brown-haired man with a silent gaggle of nurses around him like a coterie of admirers, burst in, offering to give me an epidural.

He started mansplaining anesthesia, barely looking at me as he repeated what a nurse had already told me when I signed the paperwork that absolved the hospital of any legal action in case my last-chance Texaco for pain relief also happened to leave me paralyzed. *Thank you, doctor*, I heard myself saying, even though I wanted to burn him alive and listen to him scream. I turned toward the window at his cold instruction, peering out at a dark view that overlooked a far East Side cross street and swung my legs over the side of the bed, rounding my back and clutching the nurse, whose face I'll never forget. I heard the doctor's voice again as he said, *Oh, do you have scoliosis?* right before he jammed a long-ass needle into my spine, not even giving me time to respond.

Look right at me, the nurse said strongly and kindly. *Just hold me and look into my eyes. I got you.* I was grateful for her consideration, but I kept slipping back to the first doctor breaking my water. The cold, hard shock of that pain was scrambling my thoughts, flicking through my mind like a demonic Möbius strip. I found myself transported out of the room to various moments of my past, with seemingly unconnected memories popping into my brain like a cinematic storyboard of trauma visited upon my vagina. I thought about the first appointment I'd ever had with a gynecologist, before I went off to college, when my mom thought it was a good idea for me to talk to one, *just in case.* I thought about an ex-boyfriend whose name hadn't come up in years and also about this asshole dude I met in Paris. The anesthesiologist's leaving the room without so much as an "All done, good luck!" slammed me back to the present, and part of me wanted to be alone with Tom, to grab him and immediately compare notes. Perhaps he was as terrified as I was? As lost as I felt? We were both so ill prepared. Neither of us knew to stand up to the doctors or ask them to slow down and explain the repercussions of things. Neither of us knew what any of it meant, what our options really were. We were mistakenly dependent on the idea that the medical system would take care of us—we didn't know we needed protection. And while I blamed us both for not making time for a birthing class or a hospital visit, would it really have mattered? Weren't those things taught by the very people who were surrounding me now?

Maybe it was imagined, due to stress—or maybe my needs were impossibly large, unable to be met by any mortal. However, to me, Tom's mind seemed elsewhere. He took phone meetings and sent texts, not even asking me if I was okay. Or maybe he did, and I couldn't remember it? I'm not sure, but I know I felt a disconnect, like I didn't have his full support and attention, and without it, it seemed like there was no one trustworthy to remember and share the details with me later. I wasn't sure if he saw me staring at my shaking hands or gasping for air, too desperate for oxygen and shocked by pain to even sob. No one but him knew what my eyes looked like when I was happy or could tell when something was wrong, and I don't think he was even watching me. There was no one else who would have noticed I was going into shock, that the world was moving slowly around me as I turned my head from side to side, taking it all in, but at a snail's pace, or that I'd gone dead inside and the shades had come down.

THE EPIDURAL MADE THE PAIN GO AWAY, but it also made me high as hell and detached and out of it and lonely. I was awake all night, not allowed to eat, gushing amniotic fluid all over my legs and bedding with every contraction. Listening to Tom snoring next to me, I spent half the night staring into the darkness, aglow with the light of the medical monitor, wondering how this experience could be so lonely. Wondering how to breathe through that awful feeling of something unwanted entering my body, and why it had disturbed me not just physically but also in my emotional core. Why was I suddenly thinking about Mark and the lukewarm car water? The

English teacher in high school who asked us to write about our orgasms. My friend's dad who used to put his hand on my teenage stomach when I wore baby tees, stroking me lightly and saying *Mmm, soft.* The father figure who called me to his fancy office in Midtown, offering to help me find a job, and instead touched my knee under his desk. The musician everyone loved who put his fingers in my underwear at the bar on Twelfth Street. That horrible night in Paris, that horrible night in New York, that other horrible night in New York.

The last time I was in a hospital, I remember being so small that my dad could carry me. I must have been three years old at best; I have this memory of him taking me to a window, probably the nurses' station, and giving me a sippy cup of warm milk. I remember feeling soothed and safe in his grasp. I remember how calm his energy was, how the noise of his gentle, deep voice vibrated in his chest while I rested my head against him.

It wouldn't be until later that I was told about the procedure I had as a kid, when a strange blood disorder left me mottled with bruises, and the doctors tested me for leukemia. They refused to give me an anesthetic, then drilled into my hip to extract bone marrow, claiming it wouldn't hurt, that kids didn't experience pain, that this was the only way to find out what was wrong. My mom could hear me scream from the waiting room where they'd made her sit. She lost her shit on the doctors and nurses, shrieking until they let her back to see me. But I don't remember any of that, only how safe I felt in my dad's arms, how his comfort made the pain melt away.

AROUND SEVEN IN THE MORNING, when Tom woke up, he yawned and stretched and stood up on legs that worked, barely looking at me, then went to stare out the window at the street below.

I'm hungry, he announced, and then he left to get a hot dog from the Nathan's hot dog truck, which he spotted from the very same window I'd spent part of my lonely night thinking about using to launch myself to my death. I buzzed for the nurse, alone and suddenly experiencing intense, dull pain in my lower back.

I think the epidural is wearing off, I told her. *I think I need more drugs, another epidural, to be sedated, put out, killed—who cares? Just make the pain stop.* The doctor came in for a final check. She looked too exhausted to sugarcoat anything, her mask hanging off, her hair rumpled.

I think the baby is lying on your spine, and no matter what we do, you'll have this pain until he moves. I think it's time to push. So, let's find Tom. As if it were normal that a husband left the delivery room to get a hot dog without taking his cell phone. Or maybe it *was* normal—he had to eat, after all—and what did "normal" even mean in this dystopian hell? *Also, the nurses told me your mom just arrived, so I'm gonna send her in until Tom gets back, okay?* I nodded and rested my head back down on the pillow.

Soon enough, my mother breezed in, carrying a box of Balthazar donuts.

There's my baby girl! she announced, putting the baked goods on the windowsill. The pale yellow and brown logo brought me a moment of comfort until I remembered I wasn't allowed to eat. She came forward to kiss my cheek, and I could smell her powdery skin and freshly blown-out hair. *I brought food for the nurses,* she added. And then, more quietly, *Pro tip, sweetheart: you want them to like you.* She pursed her lips. *You couldn't get your roots done before you got here, honey?*

Mom, no, I fucking could not, I said, reverting immediately to a teenage version of myself. My hands went up to my hair and pushed it off my face. *There wasn't time.*

In the fifteen years I'd been out of the house, my mom had unlocked the next level of feminine self-care. In my adult life, she was always perfectly coiffed, always in a Chanel jacket, still with her signature tropical lip color. She'd gone from repudiating fashion and makeup and pampering to a much more high-maintenance version of femme in the years since I'd moved out. She didn't need a man's signature on a loan document anymore, and she'd jumped headfirst into the land of Botox, facials, and blowouts. It was curious–she'd never taught me a thing about how to take care of myself; she'd never organized a pretty dress for me to wear at the lower school holiday pageants, or bought me a tube of concealer or a blow-dryer as a teenager, but she felt just fine lecturing me about how I didn't meet her newly delineated standards at one of the least opportune moments of my life.

Just as I was considering which juvenile insult to hurl at my mother, which verbal slamming of my childhood bedroom door, Tom returned, smelling like French fries, and I did not know my heart was capable of such derision and hate.

You went and got hot dogs? my mom said, laughing. *What did the fries taste like?* She play-whispered, as if it was a funny joke for me to hear their exchange. Tom giggled, swallowing as if he still had a bite in his mouth.

They were crinkle cut, and there was a deep fryer in the cart. I've never seen a mobile deep fryer, Tom said, as if that were the most miraculous thing about today. *The fries were so hot I burned my mouth*, he complained as he dug in the bag I'd packed, looking for floss. Only he could somehow make today about *his* physical pain.

Get the fuck out! I screamed at them both, and then immediately, as they started to shuffle out of the room, I cried for them to come back. *No, wait, Tom, I need you*, I begged. The nurse pretended not to hear any of this as she checked the monitors. I hated Tom, but I recognized that someone was better than no one. Also, my Beyoncé playlist was on his phone.

AFTER THE TERRORIST ATTACKS OF SEPTEMBER 11, Dr. Bessel van der Kolk studied first responders and their trauma. After a person suffers a traumatic incident, the brain pumps hormones such as oxytocin through the body, which elevates mood and alleviates fight-or-flight responses once they're no longer advantageous. A side effect of oxytocin is that it dulls the memory. What Dr. van der Kolk found was that when first responders came off the field and immediately described what they had seen to other professionals—the gold standard protocol for the Red Cross at the time—it prohibited the flood of memory-dulling chemicals and kept the first responders in an adrenalized state, inscribing their trauma in the amygdala, the primal part of the brain from where the fight-or-flight response originates, rather than moving it to the prefrontal cortex, where it can be stored as a gentle recollection.

The entirety of the nineteen hours I spent pinned to a hospital bed, I texted each of my five best friends real-time updates, describing how everything felt in meticulous detail so that not only did I ensure they would never forget but also that I would never forget. I essentially did what Dr. van der Kolk warned against. Instead of letting the oxytocin flood me, dulling the memories, I made sure that every thought would be etched forever in my brain. It seemed normal, in the twenty-first century, when iPhones are more ubiquitous than babies, to live text my labor.

Tom's back! my doctor exclaimed, barreling in, ready for her moment. She looked refreshed and enthusiastic, smiling and very awake, her eyes darting around excitedly. *Time to PUSH! Let's meet this baby!*

The nurses explained that they'd look at the monitor and see when I was contracting, and cheer me on to bear down, one leg held up by each shoulder, like I was squatting but on my back. I burst into tears—full sobs I had been too embarrassed to let out earlier. I was exhausted and had no energy to hide my fear. All at once the nurses and the doctor said, almost in unison, *Oh no, what's wrrrooonnnggg?* As if I were a little kid who'd stubbed my toe.

I don't want the ring of fire! I wailed and wailed. The room went silent for a minute.

You have an epidural, said the doctor. *The ring of fire is only for women who don't get the drugs. You're not going to feel a thing.* I wasn't sure I quite believed her, but it calmed me down enough that I managed to stop crying. *This is it*, I thought. *This is where I die—or worse.* I had no choice but to move forward. I put my hair into a ponytail and turned on my music.

Tom clutched my left leg, and a nurse held my right and they all started screaming, *Go! Go! Go! Push!* I smiled because it seemed like they were all having fun. The actual birth didn't hurt. I didn't feel anything. The baby was out in just a few minutes, almost like an afterthought. And what should have felt like a triumph, shooting a healthy baby out of my vagina using muscles I couldn't feel, numbed from the waist down so completely that when Tom put my leg down it flopped to the side uselessly, felt instead like just one more assault in a long list of assaults, so mild in terms of the other tortures inflicted upon me that it was hardly memorable.

When they put a baby on my body, I looked down at him, and my heart sank. I felt nothing. No overwhelming love or happiness, no excitement, not even curiosity about him. I didn't count his fingers or his toes. I just looked at him, grossed out by the white stuff from my body that he was covered in. Someone had told me to scoop it off his body to put on my face—that it was like nature's Crème de La Mer—and I complied, but still looked like shit when I glanced in a mirror a few hours later, only a bit more ghostly.

You didn't tear, the doctor said, as I saw her hands moving between my legs at the end of the bed.

I guess that's good, I replied meekly. It was as if the place in my body where I'd normally feel love or sadness was floating away. I don't think I could have gotten angry if someone had come up and slapped me. I don't think I could have gotten excited if someone had said I'd won the lottery.

I felt a tugging against what I guessed were my labia; no pain, thank God, just a sort of pressure.

It's good, she replied. *But I just gave you a stitch, mostly for him.* She nodded at Tom, who looked at me a little bewildered, furrowing his brow but not saying anything. I tried to think of something to say, but she'd already continued. *And now I'm taking your placenta and cutting it into pieces to store in the fridge here, for testing in case we have any issues.* I couldn't see what she was doing now, but I noticed a bucket get carried away by a nurse, and then I heard blood slop to the floor, and Tom's eyes widened. She pushed down on my stomach, and I felt some sort of clumps fall out of me. I didn't have the nerve to ask what they were or what was going on. I just wanted to go somewhere alone and sob.

Tom, what time is the sushi coming? I asked, but he'd forgotten that I wanted sushi and champagne as my post-birth meal. I'd had fantasies of cheersing with him in paper cups, my infant asleep next to me as I tasted my first spicy tuna roll in ten months. But he'd forgotten and ordered mediocre street pizza instead, with the hospital food abysmal and nothing else nearby.

Oh, you're going to New York Hospital?! everyone said beforehand. New York Hospital is what people who *knew* called it. *You know, you get a Chanel gift bag of toiletries when you leave because they sponsor the lying-in wing. It's the best hospital in the city—you're so lucky to be there.* And I know that, on some level, they were right, but it was the scariest place I've ever been. I remember waking up in my hospital bed that first night, shaking uncontrollably from the anesthesia leaving my body, trembling so wildly that it woke up Tom, all the way on the couch across the room. I remember the nurse coming in, flipping on the bright lights, and telling me it would be over soon, to go back to sleep.

Around seven the next morning, they wheeled my baby in from the overnight nursery.

Can't you keep him in there? I asked. The nurses explained it was better for him to be in here with me, bonding, which, while sensible, sounded like the absolute last thing I wanted to do. I pondered lying, telling a nurse I was in pain and needed a couple of Vicodin so that I could spend the day in bed, passed out on painkillers and forgetting my circumstances. But when Tom announced he was going out to get breakfast and for a quick walk, that my mom should be here any minute, I decided it would be too risky. I spent an agonizing twenty minutes alone with my baby, terrified he would start to cry, and I wouldn't know what to do. Thankfully, he stayed asleep until the lactation consultant found me. I hoped maybe she'd know what to do if he woke up. She came breezing into my room in her blazer and pencil skirt, nothing but smiles.

So how is breastfeeding going, Mamma? she asked me like we were old friends.

I can't breastfeed, I told her. I knew that much. Though I wanted to say, *Read between the lines, bitch. I've never felt so violated. I cannot give any more of my body than I've already given or I'll die.*

Instead, I smiled and just said, *I thought about it a lot, and no thank you, not for me.* As I sat propped up in my hospital bed, on a pile of ice packs, I looked over at my baby, asleep in his plastic bin, and shuddered at the thought of him sucking on my body.

The lactation consultant came toward me, as if she was going to give me a hug, then grabbed my right breast and squeezed it.

But there's milk in there, she said. *See, I just got it to come out. Breast is best. Plus, it will help you lose weight.*

I have never cared less what is "best," I wish I'd said. *I have zero feelings on breast milk versus formula. You could tell me breast milk would give me the body of Elle Macpherson in 1989, the bank account of Steve Jobs, and would turn this baby into an immortal superhero, and I wouldn't do it, because the very thought makes me want to find the nearest scalpel, take a deep breath, and slam it between my ribs, right into my heart.* But I just stared at her and said, *Okay, thank you, I'll think about it.*

She put some pamphlets down next to me and waved a cheer-ful goodbye. I stared down at my oozing breast and felt like noth-ing about me would be mine ever again.

This was how Tom found me when he came back from his walk, sobbing in my bed, the baby still asleep in his bin.

The lactation consultant violated me, and my right boob is to-tally fucked up now, I choked out, looking down to see a floppy breast resting against my stomach. The pores of my areola were stretched and open, milky liquid dripping down my belly.

Can I taste it? Tom asked. I glared at him, though I knew he was trying to be funny. The thought of attaching a baby to my body made me feel like I was suffocating. But the thought of my husband sucking my breast made me feel like a self-aware zoo animal–filled with rage and trapped.

Being pregnant had put such stress on my abdominal mus-cles that they'd split apart, and my organs sort of hung out and I couldn't suck them in; it would take eighteen weeks of physical therapy to "fix" it. But worse than pregnancy and labor and its aftermath, as well as the strange rage toward my husband that lingered in the interstices of my mind like a low-grade fever, was feeling pressured to fall in love with this stranger-baby, who I thought came out looking like a malnourished frog. All I saw in him were my flaws, the things I'd hated most about myself since childhood. And I'd felt the pain of my homely face so many times in my life; I knew the way it correlated to my value as a person. So when I looked at him–when I looked at this creature I had some-how birthed from my own loins, this being that supposedly was my whole raison d'être–I saw my hideous nose, my weak chin, all the insults from boys on playgrounds written all over him, and I felt like I'd lost my entire life and identity to this ugly baby in one day. Only unlike the baby doll in the Safe Sitter class, this real human was never going back on the shelf.

In the hospital, my parents came in and out, and my in-laws

stopped by. I refused to get out of bed, letting them hold the baby and wondering if they saw him as ugly and alien as I did, but afraid to say it out loud. Did other moms feel this way? I wanted to pull my mother aside and ask her, *When do the maternal instincts kick in?*

Only I was afraid she would say, *They should have already.* That would not be something I could have handled hearing, so I sat on my little throne of ice packs and thought about how badly I wanted to turn back the clock.

7
Coming Home

New York
October 2017

WHEN I GOT HOME FROM THE HOSPITAL with the baby, everything looked the same, but nothing was the same. It was like walking into the movie set version of my apartment, frozen in time from a whole other reality: coconut water in the fridge from the dehydration headaches I'd get while pregnant, a to-do list on my desk, my closet filled with heels I couldn't imagine wearing ever again.

The whole ride downtown, I'd kept my eyes on the baby's tiny car seat, staring catatonically at him as he slept. In his face I saw nothing to love, but I stared anyway, as if a sudden burst of maternal obsession might wash over me. I hoped that this staring contest might tuck us both neatly into a private little microcosm of adoration and care, but I felt like a scraped-out shell. I remember my mother telling me how television stations used to sign off the air at midnight, that they would play the national anthem and then go static. That's how my brain felt, like static nothingness, a void punctuated by terrifying flashes of memory I had to pinch myself to make go away.

Tom and I said nothing to each other as he drove, and I wondered if he felt like I did or if he was just tired. I didn't have the energy to ask. If he looked back at me in the rearview mirror and met my eyes and said something as startling as *That was terrify-*

ing. I don't know who this creature is, and I don't know how to feel,
I think I would have collapsed. The little support columns holding
my brain's architecture together would have crumbled, leaving me
in ruins. But he didn't. Instead, he said nothing, perhaps himself
trying to understand a reality neither of us had processed.

I preferred, in a way, to consider that most of what I'd experienced in the hospital was standard and normal and weathered by
thousands of women every day. I preferred to tell myself that I had
been weak and unprepared but that I could be tougher, and things
were going to be okay from here on out. I fingered the baby's gray
cashmere onesie, the "going home" outfit I'd been told I absolutely
had to buy him—a tiny, newborn size he'd never fit in again—and
tried not to be sad that I'd left with zero sense of euphoria or excitement, just this parasitic alien baby and a husband who had
cared more about French fries than the process of expelling our
child from my womb.

After the chaos of the hospital, nurses I didn't know coming
in and out of the room and babies crying and having to shower
with flip-flops on and terrible cafeteria mashed potatoes for dinner, I was longing for the luxury of my own house: the quiet of the
classical music we always played in the kitchen, the loose-leaf tea
I loved waiting for me in a beautiful pot, the fully stocked snack
drawer, and my big, fluffy bed.

When we pulled up to our small apartment building in SoHo,
the street was full of people, just like it always was, but past the
fire escape our windows were dark, curtains drawn. The crowds
terrified me. I put on sunglasses, scared I'd see someone I knew
and have to say hi, or worse, have to show them my brand-new
baby, standing there smiling as I pretended the birth had gone
well, and I was in some sort of blissful motherhood dream state.

As quickly as I could, I wheeled the stroller from the street into
the elevator, almost bumping into the exposed brick walls where
the hallway turned, terrified to wake the baby. I still looked preg-

nant, much to my dismay, but without the heaviness in me, I was unmoored. When the elevator opened into our apartment, late-afternoon autumn sun warming the wide-planked wood floors, I knew my parents were somewhere inside, waiting to help us. My dad had arrived yesterday, and after a short visit, they'd left for dinner, promising they'd fill our fridge before we got home.

Well, hiiiiiiii, you two! my mom cried out in her most cheerful southern accent. *Or should I say, you three? We can't forget our new little man, Guy.* Her welcome felt mocking, domesticity by force. We'd named Guy after my paternal great-grandfather, J. Guy Hoover; my paternal grandfather, J. Guy Jr., an army surgeon who'd won a bronze star for bravery at the Battle of the Bulge; and Little Guy III, my father's beloved oldest brother. I'd fought Tom bitterly to get my way, conceding his middle name in our negotiations.

Bring me that baby! my mother said, much too excited. She was somewhere in the living room, sitting comfortably on my deep-green couch, probably holding a martini. Even without seeing her, I could tell she was faking a radiant positivity, trying to make sure I would fake it, too, something I knew from a lifetime of training as her protégé. It pissed me off. How dare anyone expect anything of me right now?

She came into the kitchen, her smile plastered to her face, highlighted by the tropical lipstick she'd made her signature as she'd aged. Her voice was three times louder than necessary, and she nodded at me, urging me to partake.

How was the drive down? she asked, seemingly fascinated, as if it hadn't just been your standard thirty minutes in New York City traffic. Before I could even answer, she complimented Tom. *Aren't you just the best daddy, bringing my Guy home safely! I refuse to call him my grandson. I'm simply too young to be a grandmother, even to a baby this gorgeous!*

I wondered if she believed that if she playacted happiness, it

might rub off on me, but she was overdoing it. A flicker of annoyance traveled through my body, reminding me of when she'd
introduce me to her friends as a kid, nudging me forward and
demanding I talk about what I was studying in school. I felt myself
revert to teenage irritability but didn't have the energy to shush
her, not even to roll my eyes. Instead, I stared down at Napoleon,
who was sniffing around the infant stroller, some folding contraption I'd been told I had to have for my life to be at all tenable in
the city. It cost as much as a designer handbag, and I had no idea
how to operate it or where it was going to live in my home, since
it was the size of a small car and had disgusting wheels that rolled
all over the SoHo streets, through dog shit and piss and garbage.
I remembered my dad once telling me that the most exciting days
of his life were when he brought his babies home from the hospital
and wondered if this reminded my parents of those moments and
why the same experience had me focusing on sidewalk gunk and
toxins entering my home.

Tom dropped our bags on the floor. I don't know who he imagined would be relocating and unpacking them, but it wasn't going
to be me. I watched my dad unbuckle Guy.

If you guys are going to be here awhile–Tom looked at his cell
phone–*is it cool if I run to the studio? I just want to check in on this
resin job I started before I left for the hospital. It's probably almost
dry by now, and I had this idea in the car about it that I want to
implement, but I have to do it before the resin is totally set.* He'd
been working on some new furniture prototypes using epoxy, and
I knew there'd been some complications with the drying time, but
the thought of him leaving made my stomach drop a little, even
though I wasn't sure what I needed him for. I was so disoriented
that I didn't even know what I was supposed to be doing: What
would I do if the baby started crying or threw up or was awake for
more than the time it took to drink a premade bottle of formula?
What if SIDS happened? My eyes darted around the room, as if I'd

find some secret code behind my lacquered kitchen cabinets or painted into the muraled sepia walls.

Yet again, I wished that I'd asked any friends what they did the first hours they got home with their baby, what the first move was, and then the second and third, fourth and fifth. I wished I'd asked Augusta when her husband had gone back to work—but I hadn't even thought to. Besides, most of my friends were married to men who worked in corporate offices and got paid time off and had long commutes, so it wasn't the same as Tom and his constant need to be at his studio, a few blocks south. I looked at my parents, as if they might provide some direction, but they were making funny faces at Guy. I wondered if they remembered babies don't smile back for six weeks.

Yah, I think I'm good here. I smiled weakly, hoping Tom would change his mind and carry me gallantly to our bedroom and talk to me for hours about every detail of what had happened in the last horrible days. I was desperate to compare notes, to process them with someone and dissect every second.

I'll take Napoleon with me so he gets a walk in, he said, grabbing the leash from the console table by the door. He leaned down and kissed Guy very lightly on his cheek, which already had little baby acne bumps on it, incongruous imperfections that not only grossed me out but also made me feel embarrassed, like I already wasn't keeping him clean enough or had passed on my bad-skin genes. Tom gave me a little wave, tugged the dog's leash, and they were gone before I knew it.

Give me that little nugget! If I hadn't been so despondent, my mom's cheerfulness might have seemed hilarious—I don't think I'd ever seen her hold a baby with such unbridled gusto before. I wasn't even sure I'd ever seen her hold an actual baby, apart from my siblings. She gently lifted him from my dad's arms and sat down with him on a kitchen chair. He stayed asleep against her, and she bent to smell his head. *Should we give him a bath?*

I don't think we are supposed to until his umbilical cord stump falls off, I said flatly. I could feel something dripping into the giant mesh underwear the hospital had given me, which I'd stuffed with the boat-sized pads they also passed along, a nurse telling me to fill my duffel bag with whatever supplies I wanted. What a shitty consolation prize: free hospital crap.

Well, hasn't that happened yet? my mom asked. I noticed her lipstick smudged on the baby's head. *Is it normal for that not to have happened yet? Should you tell your pediatrician he still has his umbilical cord?* I sighed. My uterus had started cramping. And my breasts were so tender that the denim of my maternity shirt felt like it was skinning them.

Mom, I have no clue what's normal. You've done this three times. You tell me. But please don't give me something else to worry about.

Oh, honey, she said, as if I were exasperating. *Just go shower or something. Write your baby gift thank-you notes. And call some-one to come do your roots. People are going to think I'm the baby's mother and you're the grandma.* She giggled at her own joke.

Martha, my dad warned, then walked over and cupped my face. *Why don't you go rest, and your mother and I will watch Guy. Just text me if you need anything, and don't worry. At least one of us actually enjoyed raising three children and remembers how.* My mom rolled her eyes and laughed at him.

At least my dad loves babies, I thought. He cried when I told him I was pregnant, over red wine at his favorite steakhouse. My mom always said he was the baby whisperer of the family when we were kids, the kind of man who waves to them in restaurants until they smile and had already sung all his best grandpa songs to Guy when he saw us in the hospital, staring into his vacant eyes—dark as if there were no soul behind them yet—with emotion that I doubted I would ever muster.

At the time, I honestly wasn't worried to leave Guy with them.

In fact, I figured he was better off in their care. I had no clue what to do with him. I preferred the idea of alone time rather than trying to figure out feeding and diaper changing, something I'd been happy to let the nurses handle in the hospital. No part of me thought either of those activities sounded fun or remotely interesting; I guess no one thinks those activities are fun, but it seemed oppressive to me, that I was supposed to find them somehow fulfilling. And while I'd anticipated them as part of being a mom, I thought it would all be so different right away. That I'd do anything to be close to him. Even wipe up his shit and feed him using my engorged, tormented, violated body parts.

I did not feel a desire to touch him at all, the same way I had zero desire to touch a stranger's baby. It was as if my own baby, this clump of cells my own body had grown for all these months, my offspring, was a nobody to me. More than that, it was as if this baby were the offspring of some nemesis who had dropped him at my doorstep, and now I had to raise him as my own.

I felt nothing for him. I was blank inside, hoping no one would enforce any mandatory snuggle time–*skin on skin*, they called it. I could look at him only as if he were some sort of scientific sample, a case study I was meant to analyze. I thought about those paintings from the Middle Ages, *Madonna Lactans*: devotional images of Mary feeding Christ at her breast, in which the virgin usually resembled an old, haunted woman and her tiny infant looked more like an entitled, middle-aged man than a darling baby. I looked at Guy and saw a medieval Christ in his stern little face and shuddered inadvertently. This lonely, miserable creature was now my life's responsibility and sole purpose. The thought made my chest tighten and my brain feel too big for my skull. It was like all seven pounds, eleven ounces of him was my evil captor, and I'd be subject to his tyranny for the rest of my living days.

This feeling was contrary to what so many friends had described as the best moment of their lives. *Your heart literally ex-*

plodes, said Augusta, *and you can, like, feel the love hormones surge through your body, and you just know that this is your best friend for life, almost like a new limb on your body that you could never be apart from. And breastfeeding is so tender. It's so beautiful to have that quiet alone time.* She'd said this in the dressing room at the lingerie boutique on University Place where I'd worked in college, her hands filled with fancy nursing bras she wanted me to try on. *It's as if you and your child are meditating together,* she'd sighed wistfully.

I'd been looking forward to that moment of connection, holding out hope through nineteen hours of labor that meeting my son would be a fireworks display of exquisite emotion, just like Augusta had described. I didn't think that had happened for my own mother, based on many of my memories of her, but I wanted her to be so anomalous that I had a chance at a better experience. I hoped that I'd look at his tiny mouth, that he'd have my husband's beautiful lips, which I loved so much, and I'd place Guy immediately to my breast, compelled by adoration to feed him the best milk a creature can provide for a newborn, the free and nutrient-dense ambrosia that I'd secrete proudly. Staring into his dark, searching eyes, which would look so much like mine, I would relax profoundly when they landed on my face, knowing I was the ultimate nurturer.

I remembered being five or six, watching my mom feed my little brother, while *Murphy Brown* played in the background on the TV. She'd told me as an adult that it was her favorite part of early motherhood. *It was the only thing I knew for sure I could do*, she'd explained. But now, the thought of doing so made me panic, the expectation of having to share my body. I bristled at the idea that the whole world would consider me good only if I complied with a feeding system that seemed both invasive and time-consuming. I just wanted to beg everyone: *Please. Please. Leave me alone.*

I got naked in my bathroom and stared at myself in the mirror, the same mirror that a week ago had seen a woman adjusting to her pregnant body, in her fortieth week. Now I was grotesquely distorted, but no longer a fetus-making machine. My stomach was huge and loose, I had brown nipples the size of saucers at the end of massive, heavy breasts. I hadn't realized my stomach wouldn't shrink immediately and that every part of my body that had changed in the last ten months would look so much worse without the baby inside. The hot water didn't feel as good as I wanted in the shower, and then none of my pajamas fit comfortably, and when I climbed into my bed, the light in my all-white bedroom hurt my eyes. I looked at my cell phone. I had a plethora of unanswered texts from friends welcoming me home, asking me about labor, wondering when they could come meet Guy.

How's your pussy? asked Petunia. *Can you drink now? I'll come over day or night.*

When can I come meet the little man and give you a quick hug? I'll bring muffins! wrote Augusta. I ignored them and everyone else. I didn't want to answer their questions or watch their faces as they registered my body or wonder if they, too, thought my baby was weird-looking.

WHEN THE DOORBELL RANG a few hours later, I was relieved to find the baby nurse, Sharon, whom I'd hired months before, waiting outside.

I'd have been here sooner, she said, *but your husband didn't call me when you went into the hospital like he was supposed to.* Sharon pulled me in for a hug, and she smelled like jasmine tea and vanilla. Then she stood back to look at me, unwrapping a heavy purple coat to reveal leopard print leggings underneath, all while moving big brown eyes up and down my body. *Okay, Mamma, you're cute*, she said. I remembered from our phone call that she was originally from Trinidad, which explained the touch of an accent that I could just make out. She had a shaved head and not a wrinkle across her face; not a single visible pore. I'd soon learn she'd never had a zit, owed her youthfulness to staying extremely hydrated, and shaved her head in solidarity with her best friend who had suffered from breast cancer.

I'll be having a talk with him about that later, she continued. *I don't tolerate nonsense with the husbands, you'll see.* She shook her head, laughing, and her attitude put me immediately at ease. I needed honesty, and I needed an ally. *Show me where I sleep.* She handed me a small overnight bag, and I walked her to the nursery.

Feel free to verbally bitch-slap Tom as often as you feel is needed, I said. The baby was asleep in his crib, swaddled up like a dumpling, the way the nurses had told us to wrap him in the hospital. Against the opposite wall was a daybed for Sharon. There was also an upholstered rocking chair, which was the only thing she'd requested I get for her when I hired her.

Lovely room, Mamma, she said, admiring the wallpaper, a pale-toned zoo animal pattern I'd chosen with my mom. *You did a great job. And that fucker left you home alone with a newborn?* I laughed at her casualness. It was like I'd invited over Petunia, and we'd already had a bottle of wine. *Add it to my list of things to talk to him about. He brought you flowers yet, or do I have to add that, too?*

I have a really good baby, I said, not wanting to admit how bad everything seemed to me. *He kind of just sleeps and doesn't even cry.* I opened the dresser drawers so she would know that I'd left some of them empty for her things.

They all start like that. Soon he'll wake up and realize he's on planet Earth, and you won't be able to shut him up. She started putting her T-shirts and underwear in a drawer. *He doesn't look like much, poor fella. Sometimes they don't.*

Right? I exclaimed. *I almost thought something was wrong with him when he came out. I mean, he looks like a fucking demon, his eyes don't focus, and I think he's possessed or maybe something isn't quite right . . . I don't want to say it out loud, but do you think he's okay? I am so glad you get it.*

She squinted at me. Her vanilla smell, which I would later come to associate with tranquility, wafted.

Oh my God, you're such a hater! She laughed so loudly I thought she'd wake the baby, but he didn't twitch. *He's a little unfortunate, but you would be too if you'd just come out of a vagina. The eyes will settle. Takes about six months.*

She bent down next to me to grab her phone out of her purse and, on the way, looked at my breasts, which were swollen beyond belief. I could feel them grow minute by minute.

When was the last time he fed, by the way?

I looked down at the floor, and then, before I could chicken out, I blurted: *I don't want to breastfeed!* It came out like a whine, like I was embarrassed. I'd already told her I thought the kid was ugly, now I was admitting I didn't want to feed him.

No worries, Sharon reassured me. I felt a relief at her nonchalance, the opposite of the nurses in the hospital. *You got formula? Easier for me if we just plump him up that way.* I showed her where I kept the boxes of powder the hospital had given me on the way out. *Gonna need much more of this*, Sharon said. *I'll make you a list. But go do you! Let me get him all fixed up for a little bit, and you rest. Take the hottest shower you can and press on your stomach, so the clots come out.*

I already showered today, I told her, peering over the crib at Guy, trying to conjure a semblance of a desire to hold him, but my arms dangled, leaden at my sides. He looked content in there, anyway; I don't know what he needed me for.

Okay, then take a Sudafed and put some cabbage in your bra. We need to dry out those breasts. Get your kisses in before you go, she said, picking Guy up and handing him to me, supporting his head in the crook of her arm.

I held him very gently, sort of balanced on my big stomach, and bent down to kiss him.

I can't believe I have a baby. I said it in actual disbelief, which, considering everything I had gone through–the pregnancy, the long and terrible labor–sounded insane.

A lot of new moms feel that way, Sharon told me. *You'll get used to it, and then you'll want five more.* But I didn't want to have to get used to anything. I wanted to love it because it was lovable and amazing, not because I resigned myself to the fact that I was trapped in a hell of my own making, where I couldn't turn back the clock. I tried kissing him again, still not feeling a spark when I smelled him or grazed his head with my lips. Briefly, I experienced a flash of pushing his head out of my vagina, Tom holding my leg. The giant knitting needle pushing into my body to break my water, me twisting in pain to get away from the doctor as she forced it in.

It's good to kiss him on the mouth, Sharon told me. *It gives him your good bacteria.* I did it, but only because she was watching. It seemed silly to kiss him on the mouth when he didn't know how to kiss back, if that makes sense. He couldn't pucker or make a kiss noise, and he didn't seem to even know I was doing it, keeping his face peaceful and unresponsive no matter how close to him I got.

Now what do I do? Do I read him a book? I don't really remember any bedtime stories. She waved me out of the room.

He's four days old, you crazy girl, she said, laughing, then reached out for Guy. *Pass the spliff,* she joked. As I held him out to her, held out his tiny, light body, like a small misshapen loaf of bread, he slipped out of my grasp and fell headfirst on the floor, his tiny skull smashing open, and his brains, devoid of a single memory except the still waters of my womb and the slime of my vaginal canal, popping open like ripe fruit.

I gasped, glancing up at Sharon panic-stricken, horrified, waiting for his cries, and then she said, *Are you gonna give me the baby or what?* And when I looked down again, I was still holding him.

I shook my head. *I think I need a nap or something. I felt for a second like I dropped him.* She eyed me strangely as she started to undo Guy's swaddle and readjust it.

Yes, just go ask your parents to get you some cabbage leaves, and then go to bed. It's almost bedtime anyway. I backed out of the room and felt nothing but relief to be away from the baby.

As soon as I closed the door to the nursery, I heard my parents chatting, their low voices seeping out of the living room.

Would one of you mind running to the Whole Foods on Houston? I asked as I walked in. It was just my mom on her cell phone, facing the window.

Oh, honey, Daddy went to our hotel to pack and leave for the airport; I told him you'd want him out of your way so you could spend real time with the baby. This information rocked me. I felt my eyes widen, but my mom wasn't looking at me. The room felt off-balance, like the floor was suddenly crooked.

Why would you do that to me? Isn't it a little soon for people to be abandoning me with that infant? I tried to make it sound like a joke by ending with a weird little laugh.

I've got to run to the airport now, too. I stayed a few hours extra because I could take some meetings from the hotel, but your father needs me at home. I felt like my stomach was going to drop out of my body, pulling my giant, battered uterus with it.

What could Daddy possibly need from you, Mom? I just gave birth. She seemed to not hear me.

I'll text Tom and make sure he brings whatever you want on the way home, okay, sweetheart? She touched my head like I was a little kid who needed comforting. I felt that first chest compression like when you're about to start to cry, and it was so deep and long that I thought I might not breathe again, but finally I surfaced, broke through the water, and drew in a shaky breath.

Sometimes when I was sick, my mother would let me sleep in her bed, and she'd come in and place her cool, soft hand on my cheek to check on my fever. Other times she'd be exasperated that I was unwell and throwing a wrench in whatever plans she'd had for the day. Watching her now, I felt myself slip down beneath the surface of the water again. I wanted to take it all back: kicking her out of the delivery room and being annoyed with her for asking me stupid questions about Guy's bath. There are women who don't have mothers, who don't have doctors, who don't have clean places to give birth and homes to return to. I had been so stupid, so selfish, so spoiled; no wonder she was leaving me. I hadn't appreciated her mothering, and now I didn't deserve it at all. I didn't deserve any of it.

Oh, sweetie, she said. *Why are you crying?* She caressed my hair. Her features were soft. It made me think of the coldest winter days when she'd let us sleep in from school and wake me up with hot chocolate and whipped cream for breakfast, bringing it into my room and gently nudging me out of bed by tickling my arm.

I don't think I can do this, and I'm so–

I saw your new stationery, by the way, and it's adorable. How'd you get it so fast? Don't forget to write your thank-you notes. My friends will be expecting.

I'm so upset, I said, sobbing. *I don't know how to do a single bit of this. I don't know when I'll start feeling magic for him and–*

I'll be back in a month, honey! No time at all. She was talking to me like a little kid, almost patronizing. *By the time I'm back, you'll have it all down pat.* She was already looking at her phone again.

But when will I fall in love with him? No one told me he'd be such a stranger, Mom. Mom! She jerked her head up from her phone.

Look, Sarah. She sounded annoyed now, a little bit stern. *You have full-time help–more than your father and I ever had with you three. You have Tom. I'll be back, and we'll talk twenty times a day in between. This time next year, that baby will be your best little friend.* I wanted to cry even harder at that line, which I'd been fed so many times and still couldn't see as being true.

I couldn't explain how devastated I felt at the idea of my mother not being physically with me, right next to me, holding my hand for this. I couldn't explain how long a year seemed. But I knew she was right, too. I was in a really lucky position, and I did not, on paper, have a thing to complain about. So even though I hoped secretly that Sharon would kidnap the baby, and a fairy godmother would come and restore my body to its factory settings, I smiled.

You're right, I said, feigning confidence. *It's going to be fine.* I wondered if my mom would come back sooner if I made this seem a little more fun. Plus, I knew she was right: I wasn't technically alone. Sure, I had a husband who wasn't always available, a mother who was almost never available, and friends who seemed to like motherhood way more than I did. But I had more help and good fortune than millions and millions of parents out there. I was resolutely not alone. So why did I feel so lonesome?

My car's downstairs, but I'll text you when I'm settled at the airport. And make sure you get your roots done, so we can go out for a fabulous dinner when I'm back.

And then suddenly my mom was gone, and it was as if she had never been there at all.

I SPENT THE REST OF MY NIGHT IN BED and then well into the next day, too. I kept getting woken up by Guy crying, but when I'd open my eyes, there would be total silence in the house. I'd sniff the wilting cabbage, originally cold when I shoved it into my bra, then warm with a ripe smell a few hours later. It mixed with the faint scent of curdled milk, which seeped from the clammy skin between my boobs, where the milk had run while I'd slept. I felt disgusting, like I'd never be clean again.

When I'd fall back to sleep, I'd hear Guy wailing in my dreams, like he was mad at me; almost as if he was doing the baby version of yelling at me. It was like he was trying to tell me something, trying to tell me someone had hurt him. I woke up maybe four times, once gasping for breath like I'd been sobbing myself. My sheets were so wet that I thought for a minute I'd peed the bed. I rolled my tortured self to the dry side of the bed–Tom must have left for work without wanting to wake me–and remained there, curled into the fetal position.

By midafternoon the next day, I hadn't moved except to turn over or use the bathroom. I had no appetite and nowhere to be. I was glad to just lay quietly, staring at my white walls, at the curtain of ivy on the tenement buildings across the street, the deep fall sun warming the room, the pigeons and soot-colored doves swooping past my view. When it was quiet and calm, I could pretend nothing had changed. I could pretend there was no baby in the room next door. I wondered if I should make a hair appointment like my mom had suggested or schedule a mani-pedi. Would that make me feel better, a little pampering? I wasn't sure–I was grasping at straws, attempting to use the language of a previous life, not realizing that language was deader than dead, the ancient Greek of emotional contentment. I considered writing some thank-you notes for shower gifts, but the idea of getting up was too awful, the shift of my empty, flabby stomach falling to one side as I climbed out of bed too demoralizing. I tried to make a to-do list on a scrap of paper I found lodged in a book on my bedside table.

One, place Amazon order for Sharon. Two, write thank-you notes. I couldn't think of a three or a four, and when I tried to log in to Amazon on my phone, I couldn't remember my email address. Damn it, I was tired. This baby must have sucked out half my brain when he was pulled from my body.

I thought about journaling, which I'd done every morning for years. Every ten or so days of babbling seemed to produce one good idea I wouldn't have had otherwise. I flipped the scrap of paper over, dated it, and decided to start a little entry, but my pen hovered, words clogging in my brain like a traffic jam. I forced myself to put the tip of my pen onto the paper, to start a sentence. *Today I have a newborn baby.* Ugh, I didn't want to write about that; it was too miserable to dwell on.

I grabbed my phone and opened my gallery email. Maybe a better use of my time would be making sure my colleagues knew I was still alive. Maybe knowing I still had the ability to do my job would make my new normal seem less permanent. But I had to scan the first email I opened three times just to get the gist. It was as if it had been written in another language on a subject I knew nothing about. My brain felt useless and empty.

When I finally got up to shower, pulling my adult diaper off gingerly, I let the room steam up like Sharon had told me and sat down on the cold tile floor. I pushed on my stretched-out stomach and watched as dark chunks streamed out of my body into the shower drain, some so thick they couldn't pass. It smelled like iron and mud, rank and meaty, like the innermost, dense part of me; like a serial killer had dumped the fresh remains of his victims in a blender and heated up the puree. I couldn't believe how much blood was pouring out. It couldn't be right. I stood to finish washing myself and felt dizzy but wasn't sure if it was from all the blood loss or just general disgust. I got a trash bag and cleaned up the mess like I was covering up a crime scene.

I brushed my hair and put on some serums and thought about how much I needed Botox as I looked in the mirror, something I hadn't noticed when I was staring at myself in the hospital bathroom just a few days before, puffy beyond recognition from the IV. What if I was an anomaly, and I just wasn't cut out to be a mother? Worse yet, what if I was like my own mother, who so often in my memory seemed aggrieved by the very act of mothering? What if the rest of my life would be spent battling against my instincts, hating this new job I'd thought I would love and could never quit?

My phone pinged, and it was Tom texting me: *Want to bring leftovers over to the studio, and we can do dinner here just us?* I was surprised to find his offer appealing; we had barely been talking, neither of us knowing what to say. I imagined that he was feeling a bit stunned like I was. But our fridge was stocked, and the weather was nice out. I could use a walk. I could use a check-in with him, too. Maybe we could commiserate.

Sure, I typed, then put some chicken and vegetables in Tupperware for my husband, whose life had seemingly continued along its usual course—which I tried not to dwell on, though my mind kept coming back to it.

I wrapped my stomach up in the belly band I'd ordered on Amazon to hold my floppy, stretched uterus in place, and put on one of Tom's button-up shirts over my shorts. It was a five-block walk, so I figured I'd put in headphones and call my mom. But before I even got out the door, as I was packing the Tupperware into a grocery bag, I felt a clot slip into my shorts. I felt it slime its way out of my body, hot and thick, then drip onto my leg. I'd forgotten to put on an adult diaper, so I went back into the bathroom to do that, and it was all over my thighs. I had to rinse off, peeling my shorts down so that I wouldn't drip anything onto my pristine white bath mat as I climbed back into the shower. As I ran them under the spray, watching yet another trail of red circle into the drain, I heard Guy wailing, which was strange because Sharon never let him cry.

They cry if they're hungry, lonely, cold, wet, or scared, and we don't let them be any of those things, she'd explained to me. I wondered if Sharon had fallen or hurt herself and couldn't get to him. What if she'd died in her sleep, and he was in there, all alone? Or maybe someone had just broken into the house and had murdered her and was kidnapping him.

I slammed the faucet to the closed position and was met with a silence so complete it was startling. Had I imagined the wailing? The colicky cries had been so convincing that my breasts started throbbing.

I tore into the nursery like a berserk Hansel and Gretel, not even processing that I might be leaving a trail behind me, not of breadcrumbs but of footprints stamped in blood and shower water. Sharon looked up, surprised I was back, and I clocked her doing a double-take as I lunged toward the crib. Guy was in there, all right, swaddled like a skinny, misshapen dumpling, pink cheeks and barely parted lips. He stirred slightly, and I felt the carpet sink under my wet feet. *It's your house and all, but could you not come in here like a bat outta hell?* she groaned as she stood up and shuffled to her bathroom. She came out with a towel and handed it to me as soapy water rolled down my forehead and into one eye. *I . . . I just wanted a good night kiss*, I lied, wincing. She sat in her glider chair and opened the slot machine game on her phone.

I wanted to make sure the baby was breathing, ya know?

She gave me a quizzical look but said nothing.

You must think I'm a horrible mother for not doing more of this mom stuff, I said, sort of egging her on. I was curious to know how harshly she judged me.

You're not my business. You pay me to take care of the baby, and that's what I do. She did not look up from her phone as she explained this, like it was an obvious rule that I should understand. Or maybe she just didn't want to make eye contact now that she'd seen my bare, soaped-up tits.

I know in an employer-employee sense you don't judge me, but I mean as a mother. You did this four times yourself, and let's not kid: I've known you, like, two days, and I can tell you're a judgmental bitch. We both smiled. *Give it to me straight.*

Oh, hell no, I am not falling for that. You act tough, but the last thing I need is you pouting. I'm not saying shit. She sighed and put down her phone. *Okay, I'll say one thing, mamma to mamma, but then you have to leave me be.* I nodded, as if to agree to her terms that I'd go away. I was sort of expecting her to say I was worthless and crossed my arms to brace myself.

I always had my sister and friends that helped when I did this. Plus, I have never met a baby I didn't love. It's my thing. I started my own family young because I have always loved babies, but I've worked with hundreds of other families, and it's not always the mom's thing. So no, I don't care, particularly, that you don't seem so into it. Easier for me if you're out of my way, actually. What you did was hire me to ensure your baby would be cared for, the same way I hired a driver to take me here the other day in a car, because driving isn't my thing, but I wanted to make sure I got here without anyone dying on the road. You are fine by me, just like that driver thinks I'm fine. Can you go now?

I didn't quite know what to make of that, but I appreciated her bluntness. She picked up her phone again and resumed her game.

Okay, thank you, I guess, I started. *On that note, I was thinking of running to Tom's studio to take a little picnic over there.*

We'll be here. Lay lay. That was her standard sign-off. She seemed unbothered and content as I slipped out of the nursery.

I was relieved by what Sharon said, but also embarrassed. She'd noticed that motherhood "wasn't my thing," as she'd put it, which I guess in a way gave me permission to be myself but hadn't really alleviated my shame about who I was. As I rinsed off the suds, finishing what was technically my second shower, and slipped on another adult diaper, Velcroing my belly binder tightly, I wondered how I could be so pathetic, unable to care about my own kid as much as she cared about another woman's, whom she barely knew. I'm sure had I been locked in a dungeon with Guy, I could have figured shit out. But the thought of feeding, burping, and changing sounded like launching myself into a black hole. When would I rise to the occasion and be able to do all of these maternal tasks that everyone seemed able to perform with little or no afterthought? Would I ever feel like motherhood was anything but a vacuum of joy and hope?

Back I went to the kitchen to grab the picnic. I lifted the bag, took the few steps to the elevator, and rode it down to the street.

Outside, it was warm and bustling, a perfect fall city night. Evening light had triggered the streetlamps to turn on, and groups of young people stood under them, glowing with laughter, puffing on joints whose peaty smell I drifted in and out of as I marched by. Cars drove past with snippets of music blasting, giving my walk a soundtrack. I'd missed it out here, and even though it had only been a few days since I'd arrived home from the hospital, the before times felt like eons ago. It was reassuring to feel free. I *could* just leave and go for a walk if I wanted to. I could leave and keep going. I could walk all the way uptown or down to the Financial District. I could go to a bar by myself, bring a book and read it with a martini. I could sit at my corner restaurant and eavesdrop while having a spritz. I could walk to a hotel, check in, and order a club sandwich and fries from room service. I could walk and walk, and never come back.

I hadn't made it far, maybe the end of the block, and the plastic of my diaper was stuck to my skin uncomfortably. I had little rivers of sweat running down my legs, which I feared were blood, so I kept looking down to check, trying to be surreptitious. I sat down to rest and took a deep breath, tossed my hair into a ponytail. I shouldn't have worn long sleeves. At the end of the block, turning the corner, I thought I saw a horrible man I once knew, a guy from a really bad night, but I blinked, and it was no one, just someone with the same beard. My heart started racing, and I fanned my face. I lifted the bag back up, heard it rip before I felt the weight in my hand shift to nothing, vegetables spewing onto the sidewalk. As I bent down to pick up the stuff, I heard a female voice.

Let me help you with that. Pregnant women should not be on their knees on the street picking up groceries.

I looked up at the face of a curly-haired young woman in a jumpsuit and clogs. She smiled at me kindly, then extended her hand as though to help me up. I felt my cheeks get hot.

Oh, I'm, I'm not pregnant, I said. *I just had a baby.* She blinked at me. *Like, literally, my hospital bracelet is still on.* I held up my hand to her. *You look pregnant even after you have the baby, don't you know that? What is wrong with you?* I choked.

Jesus, sorry, I was just trying to help, she said. *Have a great night, bitch.*

She walked away, and I was alone on the filthy New York City sidewalk, crying over my pile of busted Tupperware and roasted vegetable detritus. My hands flew up to my head, and I felt my frizzed-out tresses, remembering what my mom had said about my roots. I must have looked completely crazed.

Screw this, I thought. *Screw Tom for thinking this was a good idea. Screw him for even suggesting I walk to him, let alone bring him dinner.* The whole thing reminded me of the time he invited me to meet him in Paris, and a few hours before I left, he'd had someone from his studio bring me an extra suitcase of art supplies to take to him, then was mad when I left it behind, even though he'd thrust it on me last minute, the bag was overweight, and I was scared the power tools would get me kicked off the plane.

I shot off a text while I sniffled, telling him I was too tired to come over.

What happened, my love? Are you okay? I was looking forward to our little date, he replied right away. His sweetness only annoyed me, and I sent back an eye-roll emoji. If he really cared, he'd be rushing to me, rushing to re-create our date in our apartment, where a newly postpartum woman should stay. There he was, safely ensconced in the shrine he'd built to himself, while I was covered in leftovers and bleeding from holes in my body. I wanted to text back that I saw how he and the whole world were against me and it made me hate him and maybe all men. Was I being irrational? I wasn't sure. But my anger felt explosive.

I returned home and stormed back upstairs. I passed by the nursery with barely a glance at the door, slightly open, the warm glow of Sharon's cell phone illuminating the cozy room as she watched over my son. I was shaking with anger at the audacity of Tom's request, the sting of humiliation at a stranger calling me pregnant. I took my third shower of the day and got right back into bed.

If this was motherhood, I fucking hated it.

8

First Signs

New York
Late October–Early November 2017

I THINK IT'S TIME FOR ME TO GO BACK TO WORK, I told my sister exactly three weeks after Guy was born. Sharon and Guy were on a walk, and I was sitting on the carpeted nursery floor, sprawled in front of Sharon's cushioned gray rocking chair. I had on workout pants and a maternity bra, which was all I had felt like wearing for the last three weeks of October weather. My butt cheeks touched each other differently, and my rib cage felt wider, straining against my bra straps; my thighs rubbed in new places, and the one time I'd been stupid enough to try on jeans, I'd been horrified that I couldn't get them over my knees. Normally, I didn't pay attention to a little weight fluctuation, but the inability to fit into any of my clothes for going on the eleventh month was starting to wear me down.

Okayyyy, my sister said a little skeptically. I didn't say anything else, instead examining the dark line on my belly that hadn't gone away yet. Her tone was familiar and annoying, and I wanted to say something snippy but held my tongue, reminding myself of all she'd been through. It embarrassed me that I'd witnessed so much of her pain and still couldn't get my shit together to be an acceptable mother. Also, my brain felt dead. Over the past couple of weeks, I would try to make grocery lists and start to cry.

I'd shake my head, as if that would set things right in there, but I remained discombobulated as if I'd had a tiny stroke. When I tried to journal, I'd wince and focus, write a half sentence, forget my train of thought, and end up paralyzed, unable to finish even a simple paragraph.

I wasn't sure my aphasia had been noticeable to anyone else, but my sister's hesitant response made me wonder if everyone could tell I felt lobotomized. And while I resented Tom for leaving me to go back to work that first week, abandoning me to the abject monotony of Babyland, I was also jealous. I would have loved to run away like that, run back to my old schedule and my old life. But my old life was unreachable, and Tom's work was right there where he left it at his studio. No one had told me how lonely this new existence would be or how angry I would be that such disparity was still happening in the twenty-first century, when women supposedly–*supposedly*–had a semblance of parity with men. Why did his life return to normal, while mine couldn't? I thought of the character Jane in Penelope Mortimer's 1958 novel *Daddy's Gone A-Hunting*: "*What happened to her during the six hours of labour nobody ever knew. Something snapped or something fell into place or her brain, under pressure, tossed about like the coloured pieces in a kaleidoscope, settling in an entirely different pattern.*" Was I Jane? When the knitting needle hook pulled out my insides, had my brain dripped out with the remnants?

The group of mid-nineteenth-century British artists, mostly men, who comprise the Pre-Raphaelites painted feminine hysteria almost as a prerequisite for female beauty. One woman, Lizzie Siddall, modeled for all of them, and I have always loved her look, even though that style of painting gave her a square jaw and odd nose that wasn't particularly pretty. What I admired was her long, wild red hair, which seemed to be a creature of its own. Everyone knows her from the famous nineteenth-century painting of *Ophelia* by John Everett Millais, her hair billowing around her in the water like a capsized life raft studded with peonies and roses. She was the perfect picture of female suffering: in Shakespeare's *Hamlet*, Ophelia drowns, caught between her murdered father and the demands of her eponymous boyfriend. In real life, Lizzie Siddall was marginalized as an artist in her own time, cheated on by her husband, the painter and poet Dante Gabriel Rossetti, and found solace in an addiction to laudanum. After suffering a stillbirth in 1861, she committed suicide by overdose, unable to overcome the grief of wanting a baby more than anything.

No one had me chained to the radiator, I guess, or forced me to stay with my newborn. No one told me babies were my only hope at happiness in the world. No one held me in my nineteenth-century home against my will, forbidding me from having a career while some mad woman clanked around my attic. And yet I felt gaslit and broken, as if some phantom presence were controlling the manse.

Between the hopefulness I had that spending time with my child might spark some sort of love for him, and the fear I had of being judged for being a bad mom—whatever the fuck that actually meant—I hadn't felt it was acceptable for me to try to dip into normal life and routines. I tossed the idea out there, wondering how Deechie would react before I let myself get too excited about the prospect of trying to become myself again.

It's not like you do that much at home, she said with a slight tone, adding, *No offense.*

Actually, I'm trying really hard. I'm doing bath every night, and we go on walks. It's just not as natural as I thought.

Whatever. Maybe work would be good for you to kick-start your brain a little bit and put your new hair and nails to good use. I glanced down at my manicured hands, the shiny polish making it look like I had a little candy on the edge of each finger, and I smiled faintly. Despite the sibling attitude, my sister's approval made me feel immediately lighter. I fiddled with the waistband of the leggings, trying to see if I could cover up my bulging midsection enough to look chubby but not newly postpartum.

I couldn't tell her the rest: that I couldn't bond with Guy, that the minute I even saw him I'd start to feel short of breath. The other day when I'd gone into his room for my requisite afternoon visit, my stomach had fallen because he was awake. I would have to interact. I couldn't just pretend I'd done something by coming in while he was sleeping and standing there staring at him in the crib. I thought of the pictures I saw on Instagram of new mommies gazing lovingly at their cradled babies, and my mom friends who described their newborns using words I found appropriate only for ice cream desserts or nachos, like *delicious* and *yummy!*

I couldn't imagine feeling that way about my little sack of human organs. And then there was that trope that was all over social media, the whole *Thank you for choosing me to be your mamma* bullshit. Who gave women the idea to say that crap? That somehow a fetus's soul *chose* its growth receptacle. From what religion did that heinous sentiment even hail? Was I to believe that Guy willingly chose me—a woman who found babies and baby activities so god-awful and boring, I could barely keep my eyes open the second I started reading *Goodnight Moon*? Shaking rattles and singing along to nursery songs made me feel like I wanted to unzip my skin and crawl away from it, leaving the outline of myself there to pretend to care.

The other problem was when mothers I knew told me about their postpartum journeys, they didn't resemble anything like what I was going through. If they had "depression," it looked like graceful bouts of weeping sadness on their beds, which didn't remotely mirror my pockets of rage or what I would later come to recognize as something akin to cyclical psychosis wherein I aurally and visually hallucinated nightmarish traumatic events that I thought would come true if I spoke them aloud. My friend Barbara had told me that after her third baby, she was so overwhelmed with love and fear for him that she'd hide in the bathroom, sobbing and clutching him to her. She didn't even trust her nanny. She thought everyone was trying to steal her child. Meanwhile, I wanted to give mine away to someone who could parent him better than me; part of me wanted to send my baby down the river in a basket like Moses and pretend none of this had ever happened.

Over the previous three weeks, when friends and family wanted to visit, I made every excuse to keep the baby hidden away. I ignored phone calls and texts, claiming sleepless nights and a chaotic schedule, terrified they'd know his ugliness, and mine by extension. When Sharon suggested I start taking him on a daily walk, my biggest fear was that I'd bump into someone I knew. How would I cross the street quickly with an ungainly stroller? I'd time my walks around his nap schedule, hoping that at least if I was caught by an acquaintance, I could give them a quick peek with an excuse to keep it moving. So, I chose to isolate rather than come clean. Looking back, I would realize that his unattractiveness–a common side effect of having just been flung unwillingly from the safety of a womb out into the world–was actually comical, and had I approached the situation with a sense of humor, I could have embraced it. But at the time, nothing was funny to me.

Nobody judges you for going back to work, my sister interrupted. *Plenty of people don't have that choice. They either have to go back to work or don't even have jobs. I judge you for thinking you're the only person who wants to have their own life and have a baby.*

Okay. I don't think I'm the only person who has ever wanted the best of both worlds, Deech, I said, horrified by the adolescent lilt of my voice. *All I'm saying is, why does my baby look like an alien frog?*

I could hear my sister take a drink of something. *Oh my God, Sarah, I can't believe you're even saying this to me. Do you know how lucky you are? Jesus fucking Christ.*

Of course, on some level, intellectually, I did. I knew it was deranged to say anything to my sister whose baby had died. Yet something kept me from adding that I was having nightmares about a car jumping the curb and wiping out my stroller. Last night, I'd dreamed that a man in an SUV had pulled up into a bike lane, edging a delivery man onto the sidewalk, where he slammed into my baby carriage. It had toppled, and I'd seen Guy's little body get thrown into oncoming traffic. I'd woken up in a pool of sweat, my sheets stuck to my body. And while I'd been relieved that it was all in my head, the visuals had left me feeling jagged and uneasy all day. The border between memory and dream blurred to the point of nonexistence, which, at the time, seemed normal–an indication of maternal concern that I hoped would morph into love.

LATER THAT NIGHT, Tom's reaction to my return to work was positive, which part of me knew it would be. He loved when I got excited about my work; I think it reminded him of how much he lived for his own. *The reward for good work is more work*, he always said. He'd listen to my symphonic late-night rants about different art shows or performances I'd seen and laugh at my critiques. *People would pay to hear the shit you tell me after you've had a martini, you know*, he said all the time, which made me blush as if my parents were bragging about me to one of their friends. I pretended it annoyed me, but I also felt secretly flattered that he believed in me so much.

That's so great, babe, he said, emphasizing the *great*, as we ate delivery sushi in the kitchen. I'd set out plates and napkins on the table–even remembered to put a bottle of sparkling water in the fridge to get cold for him–but he was dipping his little rolls into soy sauce and bending over the sink to eat them, droplets of brown splashing on the counter. He seemed not to notice his mess as he took a chug from the Gatorade I had been drinking to flush out some of the residual bloat I blamed on my epidural, even though it had been three weeks before.

I fully support you in whatever it takes for you to feel like yourself again, he said between mouthfuls and gulps. It was a sweet sentiment, but the sushi rice backwash I saw floating in my drink made me twitch. *Your hair looks great, and your nails too! I think if you get one of those massages you like, or maybe a facial, you'll feel really ready to face the world.* He dropped a piece of ginger off his chopsticks as he finished. I glared at him until he noticed the soy sauce stains on the counter. He muttered an apology, then took a sponge from the side of the sink and started wiping down everything. I thought about what he'd just said and felt annoyance rising in my throat.

You think I need a facial? What is that supposed to mean—I'm ugly? Is that what you're saying? My voice sounded wobbly as I threw open a cabinet, grabbing the Clorox from it. I began spraying aggressively.

Sarah, Tom said. His voice was measured. *Baby. I hate seeing you like this.* He said it so gently that I wasn't sure if he was being condescending or not. The idea that he was speaking to me in some sort of *Mister Rogers' Neighborhood* voice like I was a toddler when he was the one making messes everywhere ignited something in me.

Well, I hate feeling like this, Tom, I sputtered. *Why can't you clean up after yourself! It's some sort of learned helplessness. Women have been doing that for you your entire life. Well,* no more. *I'm going for a walk.*

I grabbed my keys and stormed into the elevator, leaving Tom with his soy sauce. Outside on the street, I called Petunia as I paced around the block, pulling my sweater over my hands. It was one of those cold late-October evenings that would disappear around Halloween, giving us one last burst of sixty degrees before turning into true New York winter. Petunia picked up on the first ring.

Tom is the reason I can't love Guy, I blurted. *It's all his fault, and it's all because he's a subconscious misogynist who thinks my sole purpose is to clean up his soy sauce dribble.* I took a deep breath and looked at my ghostly reflection in the window of the Prada store across the street.

Whoa, whoa, whoa. Slow the eff down, you psychopath. Did you, like, find an old bottle of Adderall and take all of them at once? Inject cocaine into your–

P, I'm serious. I took a deep breath and started speed walking back in the general direction of my house. *Men subconsciously know that if they are lazy, women will just pick up the slack for them. We are badass and strong and trained to be polite and say yes to everything plus keep adding tasks to our plate. Maybe if I didn't have to manage that man-baby, I would be able to feel something for Guy.* Another deep breath. *I'm coming back to work tomorrow. We can discuss at lunch?*

I guess? Petunia gave a small laugh that I would now clock as being confused. I put my key in the door of my building as she continued, her voice softening. *Why are you freaking out about soy sauce? Tom is on your team, babe. He knows how to wipe counters, and when he doesn't do it, I don't think it's on purpose. It's like how you sometimes leave ponytail holders all over the place. Everyone is a little bit messy in their own home.* But I was barely listening, and before I could turn the lock, I told her we'd catch up in the office, and I pivoted to march right back down the street to the café on the corner. I was out, and I had freshly highlighted hair and a manicure. I was going to get drunk by myself and people-watch, and then I was going to use that new massage app I'd downloaded to have someone come rub me down, make sure I was feeling my best before work the next day. It had been Tom's idea, I thought, as I plopped down in a bistro chair and ordered a vodka on the rocks from the model-slash-waitress. I knocked it back, tried to read a novel on my phone, and when the words stopped making sense, planned my outfit for the next morning on my walk home.

• • •

I HAD SEX EDUCATION in gym class once a year for my entire school career, and I took AP bio my sophomore year of high school. I even got a five out of five on the exam. Plus, I followed a bunch of mommy accounts on social media, and I had mom friends. You'd think I would, at some point, have learned that mothers bleed for weeks after they give birth. But my only warning had been a side-note from my doctor, who once mentioned: *You should have some pretty heavy pads waiting for you at home when you leave the hospital . . . maybe even adult diapers.*

That I was still gushing old-looking blood twenty-one days after birth was unexpected, to say the least. I hadn't imagined going back to the office with the damp cling of Lisa Rinna-approved plastic underpants distracting me, but that's what I was dealing with when I took my first client meeting at the gallery the next day.

I have five minutes, and I don't want to hear any of your art history stuff, my client Jim announced as he waltzed into the gallery from his idling Range Rover. When I'd called to tell him I was back in the office and had a painting to show him that he was going to love, I could practically hear the drool from his slobbery mouth dripping onto the phone, like a pitiful, hungry dog who was also desperate for the social status that owning expensive art might get him. Jim had made his fortune by turning his parents' independent publishing house into one of the country's largest Bible distributors, though the minute they'd died, he'd sold the whole company and never looked back. He'd gone on to work at a friend's hedge fund, and they were early investors in YouPorn. He thought this made him young and cool. That his wife was twenty-six, beautiful, and affluent only seemed to exacerbate Jim's misguided self-perception.

The gray morning light from the open front door flooded the

gallery as he entered, which, combined with my slight vertigo, gave the spare space in which we were standing an almost other-worldly ambience. Yet again, I felt as if I were in a dystopian sci-fi film of my own devising, one in which we would possibly have to kill each other to survive.

Jim! So nice to see you. Can we get you anything to drink? I welcomed him at the front desk and started leading him into the exhibition. *I think you are going to be really impressed by the integrity of this show. The artist's practice has really developed, and I think the paintings are extremely potent at this scale.* Jim ignored the walls around us, covered in gorgeous paintings, and walked toward the door of a private viewing room. Transom windows about twenty feet up let in cold, natural light, and it made every brushstroke on the canvases visible. I tried to imagine the meditative quality of applying that paint. I felt my diaper squeak a little bit as I walked.

Jim took one look at the painting we were in front of before going back to his phone.

I'll take it. Can you invoice to Southampton? And can I get a Diet Coke? He started walking toward the back conference room and plopped himself onto a beautiful Jean Royère couch, a 1940s rounded shape covered in soft, nubby beige bouclé cashmere and draped with a Hermès blanket. I opened a cabinet and poured him a Diet Coke into a crystal lowball glass, plus one for myself, then sat down next to him.

What else are you shopping for? Anything I should keep an eye on? I asked him, hoping to get his attention back from his phone and onto some business transactions. He downed his drink and stood up to leave.

I'll text you later. I gotta get back to the office. I bought this company yesterday, and I have to tell a bunch of C-Suite losers that they're fired.

Trying not to react, I stood up to say goodbye, and before I could even look down, I knew I'd leaked onto the couch. Praying that Jim hadn't noticed, I yanked the Hermès blanket down to cover my red stain and led him to the door, then walked to the bathroom with my back against the hallway wall, hoping I wouldn't see anyone. I ducked into the all-Carrara marble bathroom.

Santo Pietro, the mountain from which this marble derives, has been depleted for its use in toothpaste, of all things–the demand for it being higher among the titans of industry than among rich people looking to redo their bathrooms. It's very hard to get large chunks of Carrara, unless you're Johnson & Johnson. But this bathroom was an exception. There was even an all-white marble trash can, and as I inched my diaper down my thighs, blood-soaked and wet, I could smell its warmed-up plastic. Slowly, carefully, I dropped it in the trash, but even though I tried to be meticulous, it left a smear of blood down the marble. I wet some toilet paper and tried to wash off the streak, then cover it the best I could, half laughing, half crying, readjusting my Spanx and the corset I wore over them to fit into the loosest office-appropriate skirt I owned.

I went back into the conference room to try to wash the stain off the sofa and thought about how my mom had gone back to work at the prosecutor's office after she had me. What must that have been like? Did they even have disposable diapers then, let alone adult diapers? Did she wear them in court? And why didn't she tell me to expect this? And then suddenly, as if an alien charged into my brain and sat on the rational part and squished it so that the synapses couldn't fire, I started thinking about what it would feel like to be alive on this earth without my mom, and I started to cry. I tried to stay as silent as possible, but my whole body shook with deep, slow sobs. The tears just fell down my face, and I felt an intense heat in the center of my forehead down to my nose, which meant it had probably turned bright red.

Even during my epic monthly PMS shower-crying sessions, I'd always been able to stop the tears when I needed to. But now all I could think of was how humiliating it was to bleed all over expensive midcentury furniture and try to do my job with these huge tits in the way. I wished I could ask my mother why she hadn't warned me. I knew if I asked her, or any mother, they'd all make the same joke: *If I told you how hard it was, you'd never have done it.* Or something like that–some excuse for why they were perpetuating this cycle.

Just then Petunia walked in. *Um, what is going on?* she asked me, her face awash with concern. *Why is it* Girl, Interrupted *in here?* I stood up and pointed at the sofa stain and showed her the matching red splotch across my ass.

Oh shit, she said. She started laughing. *It's not* Girl, Interrupted, *it's* Carrie.

It's not funny, P. I miss my mom so fucking much, and she's going to die, and then I will die. What if she's already dead? Then I will have to die, Petunia. How will I ever live on this earth without my mother? I looked up at the ceiling and closed my eyes as more tears leaked out. P was silent.

You know, I read that you leave cells inside your mom's body when you're a fetus, and they stay in there forever. And you have her cells in your body forever, too. I swear I feel that, P. Even when I hate her and I'm so angry at her that I feel like I'm going to burn down into a pile of ashes, even then I can feel that we are part of each other. Even then I feel like I need her just to exist if I'm going to keep existing. P let me wail on. I wiped my nose with the side of my hand. *Like, why don't I love Guy like that? Why don't I feel him in my body? It's like I'm already dead.*

P touched my arm, and a shadow fell over her face. Her eyes looked wet. *Babe. You're so sad, it's making me sad. This is not normal. Your mom is, like, fifty, and she's in great shape. I think I should call Tom and get you home. Let's start this over tomorrow.* She guided me out of the conference room with her arm around me. *I'm getting you an Uber, and we can go out the back, so you don't see anyone, because, frankly, you look next-level insane. Your mascara not being waterproof is very much a problem.*

I had to laugh at that. She peered around the corner of the hallway leading to the service entrance. *No one's back here, the registrars are probably still at lunch. I'm gonna tell the car to come around to the service door.*

I nodded, looking around the storage area where we were huddled, remembering my first days at this job, coming back here and being so excited to see giant wooden transport crates with labels on them saying the names of the greats: Rauschenberg, Stella, Mitchell . . . It had seemed so incredibly rare and glamorous to be in this position, but now I forgot what I was looking at sometimes.

Do you have sunglasses in your purse? Or, like, one of those hats that covers your entire face? Anything that could double as a disguise? She smiled as she pulled me through the service entrance and loaded me into the car like I was a child. *I'm worried about you, babe. This isn't like you.*

I rolled down the window before the car pulled away. *Don't call Tom, okay? I know I was being a little dramatic back there, but I already feel better. You know me: I just appreciate a dose of hyperbole.* We smiled at each other. I could tell from her face that Petunia felt genuinely concerned for me, but she didn't need to be, I didn't think. She just couldn't understand what I was going through because she didn't have kids. Plus, it's not like I was actually depressed, I reasoned. In my mind, a depressed person wasn't capable of going out and having drinks, of making jokes and having fun with friends. It's not like I just laid in bed all day with dirty hair, crying, and avoiding everyone. I'd had a vodka in a café last night while I people-watched, for God's sake. I considered myself on the up, not realizing that just because I wasn't a textbook definition of something didn't preclude me from having a version of it. I didn't understand that the collision of my previous anxieties and a new level of depression was taking me on a wild roller-coaster ride.

Back in my apartment, cleaned up and showered, I went into the TV room. In the last month or so, I had ordered every book I could find about the "fourth trimester" and postpartum depression. I started skimming, searching for any description I could relate to–some story that would warrant my state. But all I found were tales like *Poor Ingrid, she suffered so after giving birth, alone in Nova Scotia in the dead of winter, no anesthesia, only dental floss and a whale bone with which to sew her wounds. She spent her days reading books about feminism by candlelight and holding her baby for warmth, while eating only potatoes and the water they were boiled in for sustenance.*

I felt bad for Ingrid, but at the time, I didn't see myself represented in what I was reading. And so, after an hour or so of flipping through the texts, I deduced that what I was experiencing was just motherhood. Rich, nanny-assisted motherhood, for which I had zero justifiable complaint. My feelings could not have been postpartum depression, because the postpartum depression I read about was not comparable to the strange rage and discomfort and confusion I was feeling. There were women out there who were overcome with paranoia: they murdered their children, believing them to be satanic or ghostly apparitions, or they killed themselves. I told myself I was simply having nightmares, triggered by extreme disappointment and some misdirected stress over a life that was not comparatively difficult. Looking back, the worse things got, the easier it was to believe I was just a bad fit for motherhood, yet I was a mother–so my reactions, my mental shifts, were because of that and nothing more. My experience of the job seemed both rational and irrational at the same time, and I was caught between Scylla and Charybdis.

Two hours later, I was still sitting on the couch, surrounded by my books, when Augusta FaceTimed to check in on me. I could see she was at her weekend house in Connecticut.

Are you all right? I heard about Sunday Bloody Sunday from Petunia.

Auggie, what's wrong with me? She cocked her head to the side, her usually perfectly coiffed blonde hair in a messy topknot. Behind her, through a picture window, I could see the last of the fall leaves in an expanse of meadow. *I make myself go into Guy's room to hold him every hour or so, and I do the evening feed. I'm trying, but it's just–* I choked on my own words, moving my hands in small circles, as if to show her there were no words I could pull from the air in front of me.

You know, she said slowly, *this usually applies to the father, but my grandmamma says they start to realize what the kid means to them the first time it gets sick. Knock wood that Guy doesn't get sick anytime soon, but when he does, you'll see how you feel. You'll get it then.* She was so gentle and understanding. Most people would think I needed electroshock therapy. *It's like any other relationship, honey. Love at first sight is rare.*

IN MID-NOVEMBER, IT GOT COLD. Tom was out of town for a few nights on some work trip, and Sharon and I were home with Guy, snuggled into our respective beds. The forecast said we had a big snow coming, which was early for New York. Usually it didn't snow until right before Christmas, and it was still before Thanksgiving. I hated winter, ever since my first lonely winter in New York as a teenager. I was terrified, expecting this year's dark months to be a bleak, frigid slog.

A knock on my bedroom door woke me up in the middle of the night. I shot out of bed, and Napoleon gave a half-assed growl, too sleepy to attempt actual guard dog duties.

Who is it? I grabbed for my cell phone so I could call the police or at least take a photo of the murderer before he raped and killed me.

It's me, S. I tried to text you and call for you. I shook the sleep out of my head and opened my phone screen. Sharon had been trying me for fifteen minutes, I saw.

Guy has a fever, and I wanted to tell you before I gave him meds. I think you should call the doctor. It's high. It's a hundred and four. I reached for the curtains and opened them, seeing snow falling in the green city light. *I think we should take him to the ER, because what if we get stuck in a blizzard and can't get out and he needs something?*

I opened the door and looked at her in her robe.

Okay. I'll get an Uber, I said. *I just have to grab shoes and my coat.* I looked around, still a little disoriented, wondering where I had put my keys. Should I bring a book with me?

Maybe also put on a bra, Sharon said as she went back to the nursery to get Guy, who I could hear crying in his crib. He sounded irritable. I went in to pick him up myself, grabbing extra blankets to carry him to our waiting car. He was burning up, and I remembered being a kid with a fever—the worst feeling. Everything in his entire tiny body probably hurt. I felt so sorry for him.

I handed him to Sharon as we headed to the stairs out of the building.

I can't take him on the stairs, I told her. *It's against my rules.* I'd had enough nightmares of him slipping out of my hands, bouncing down to the landing. No way was I going to test that luck during an emergency.

You're insane, Mamma. But I get it. You know, I never, ever mess around with a fever, Sharon said as she loaded Guy into a car seat, kissing his sweaty forehead. There was no one else on the street, not even the sound of traffic. Just the colors cast from slowly changing traffic lights reflecting on quiet snowflakes. The first snow was always like this, hushed and tranquil. *When my youngest daughter had a fever, about Guy's age, it spiked and went to a hundred and seven. It gave her a heart murmur, and she had to have surgery. She has a pig valve in her heart. That's why she has a scar on her chest.* Sometimes her daughters would come over to say hi, but I'd never noticed this scar. *She keeps it pretty hidden under her clothes, actually,* Sharon explained. *They had to crack her rib cage, and after ten years, she had to have it replaced. So, we don't mess around when it comes to fevers. And I guess for your crazy ass, you don't mess around with stairs.*

I felt suddenly very awake and on a mission to get to the doctor quickly. I called Tom as the Uber pulled away from the apartment. He picked up, groggy and annoyed.

Babe, I'm still sleeping. It's, like, three a.m. here.

I'm not calling for fun. I'm taking Guy to the emergency room. I put my hand against his chest and felt him take a shallow breath, reminding myself to breathe, too. *He has a high fever, and it's dangerous because it could give him a heart murmur, and I'm not sure if I should be nervous or not?*

Poor little dude, Tom said. I watched small flurries glide past the car window as we drove, clouds of them seeming to hover around the traffic lights. *Glad you're going to get him checked out. Call me as soon as you know more. Love you guys.* Before I could say anything more, he hung up, which I almost couldn't believe. I stared at the phone, wondering what to do next, and decided that I was absolutely enraged by the conversation I'd just had. Why wasn't he making a bigger deal out of our tiny son's vulnerability? I turned to Sharon.

Did you hear that? I asked, adding, with a small, angry laugh, *Tom didn't even sound that worried. That's weird, isn't it?* I looked at her for validation.

It's not part of my job description to judge the parents, she said, *so I'm just gonna say this: Tom is not here, and this one's up to us. We got this, us three. We don't even need Tom.*

I'm so sick of men always getting a pass. Actually, shorten that: I'm just so sick of men. I shook my head, checking my phone again to see if Tom had sent a follow-up text. He hadn't, which also pissed me off. I felt tears coming on, a hot lump brewing in my throat. The car pulled up to the emergency room entrance, and even under the portico, I could tell the snow was coming down faster and faster.

Focus, Mamma, Sharon said. *This isn't about Tom.* We ran inside to the bright lobby and found the admittance desk.

In triage, Sharon got to work as soon as we'd checked in, making friends with everyone. She called all the nurses *lover* and got coffees from a vending machine for the two that worked in our little area. We were the only people there, so they saw us quickly and calmly. They told us the best course of action would be a Tylenol suppository. I laughed at the little dumpling. He had no idea what he was in for.

We were home within two hours, Guy back in his bed, snow still falling outside. I called Tom, but he didn't pick up. I felt energized, like I'd crunched through a bag of espresso beans. I decided to call Augusta while she got ready for work and told her how happy I was to feel so worried about Guy after our hospital excursion.

What? she said, sounding confused.

You told me that's when I'd probably love him, the first time he got sick. And I think I do maybe love him? He didn't even cry when they put Tylenol up his ass. More than I can say for you.

Petunia and I had an inside joke about butt chugging, some terrible fraternity practice we'd heard about where you give yourself a wine enema to get drunk quickly. We tried to bring it up as often as possible. It drove Augusta nuts; she'd shake her head and say *I'll pray for both of you* every time we managed to work it into a story just to torture her. I sat on my bed and quickly stood up again. I wanted to be moving.

Bitch, it is, like, six a.m. I thought something was wrong. She didn't even laugh at my butt chugging reference or remind me that she found the joke disgusting.

I was worried *about him, Augusta, actually worried. That's what moms do, you know? Worry! I'm still shaking. I'm so excited. I'm not going to work today. I'm going to organize my memory box about Guy and make some scrapbooks. Maybe journal about this.* I walked across the room to my closet to see if I had an empty journal stuck on a shelf somewhere.

Here's an idea, she said. *Instead of making a scrapbook about your child, why don't you go hang out with your child? Or don't. I don't care. But I'm going back to sleep. You should too.*

She hung up, and I thought about what she said. Was I being crazy? I walked to the kitchen to look in our junk drawer for a glue stick so I could start a scrapbook for Guy. I'd include one of his sonogram pictures and a corner of the blanket they sent home with us from the hospital. Oh, and the footprints they made of his newborn feet. But then it struck me that if I wrote down a bunch of stuff about Guy, it might tempt the universe. It seemed too dangerous to affirm his life so clearly. I shuddered and felt the energy that had been bouncing around my body start to drain out, leaving me cold. The thought of unwittingly willing something bad to happen to him with my brazen scrapbooking efforts was too horrible to dwell on. I needed a distraction.

Suddenly overcome with exhaustion from a night spent adrenalized, I went into my bathroom and swung open Tom's medicine cabinet, rifling through various orange pill bottles and jars of pomade he never used. When I found the expired Vicodin, I popped one in my mouth and chewed it, the bitterness familiar to me. I deserved some stress relief, I rationalized, and Sharon was right next to Guy, keeping vigilant watch. I deserved a little self-prescribed medicine once in a while.

In the novel *Valley of the Dolls*, Jacqueline Susann writes that *giving a party was not as simple as going to one. You could always leave someone else's party. You were stuck with your own.* I did not realize, as I chewed my second and then third powdery pill, letting them rock my body into a sparkly sleep, too deep for nightmares or dreams, how lonely and miserable being trapped at the party could be. What I saw as my escape, as my reward, as a short-cut to feeling good and slowing down the ever-present worries ricocheting around my electrified brain, would not end up being the salvation from my own mind that I so needed and craved.

9

Off the Deep End We Go

New York
December 2017

WHEN AUGUSTA SUGGESTED I TAKE GUY to music class at our neighborhood public library as an attempt to do something actively maternal and fun, I already had a list of potential emergencies in my head.

What if he starts crying? What if he poops? I asked her, half joking, half serious as she stood in my tiny apartment foyer, strapping him into his stroller. She'd shown up that morning with hot croissants and a vanilla cappuccino for Sharon, then marched into my room with a robe in her outstretched hands. *Wrap yourself before I have to see you naked for the thousandth time*, she'd said.

What if a lone gunman comes into the library and finds the music room? I wanted to ask her. I didn't, though: I didn't like sharing my deranged private thoughts and nightmares, in case it made them come true, like some version of manifesting gone wrong. One of my main occupations was avoiding catastrophe by trusting my arbitrary instincts that, at the time, I believed were foolproof and rational.

First of all, you already made it through an ER visit with him, she said, *and this has got to be easier than that.* Augusta reached into the coat closet to pull out my puffy winter jacket. *Put your coat on—you're going. This will be good for you.* She pulled a cashmere blanket off a shelf at the top of our coat closet and cloaked Guy in it.

Now, this is his fancy travel blanket. He needs to look nice at music class–the best-dressed kid in the room, always, she said, pressing the button for the elevator and turning around the stroller so that it was aimed to go inside. I felt a ripple of nervousness shimmer through my body but decided to ignore it. Maybe this would be the bonding moment of mother-son intimacy I'd been hoping would awaken my love. The hospital visit, which felt like such a victory for stirring up a kind of concern that was new, had left me even more deflated when the high wore off.

And listen, he's not going to cry. He's a happy baby. If he poops, come home right away to change him. Sharon told me that she's seen people use that library bathroom to shoot up, so don't change him in there. You don't want him grabbing a needle. The elevator arrived with a *ding*, and Augusta looked at me. I must have appeared a little panicked. *Sarah, this isn't that hard*, she said. *It's two blocks away. I have a meeting at the kids' school; I just came to get you out of the house.* I closed my mouth and zipped up my coat.

The frigid December air sliced right through all my layers, and I burrowed my hands into the giant stroller gloves as I navigated around ice patches and small hills of gray snow. Guy did not seem perturbed by the weather. When we got to the library, we hit the wheelchair accessibility button to be able to maneuver the stroller inside, and I looked around for the music room.

If you're here for music, it's downstairs two floors, said a librarian who didn't glance up. She was flipping through books from her desk chair and putting them on a cart. *Don't leave anything in your stroller that you want to be there when you come out of class; don't let your kid use the bathroom alone because people use it to shoot up, and sometimes there are needles in there.*

I liked that the library let anybody use its bathrooms. It was a safe place, for everyone, and it was where I was about to have a gorgeous bonding experience with my kid.

I peeled Guy out of the layers of blanket and his warmest coat and took everything out of the stroller and inside the music room with me. There were about twenty other mothers and nannies with kids around my son's age, mostly sitting on their caregivers' laps. The grown-ups talked to one another, arranged in little cliques. There were some young moms in one corner, their Cartier Trinity bracelets blinking in the bright overhead lights, and I saw one man–I guessed a stay-at-home dad, because he seemed extremely confident and prepared–who was talking to no one. He was wearing his baby in one of those hippie scarf-wraps around his body and had on a fanny pack, which I saw him reach for when he needed a baby wipe.

I took the only available seat, and one of the moms leaned toward me.

Hi, I said cheerfully, *this is baby Guy! He's almost three months.* I lifted Guy's arm and had him wave to the baby sitting on the woman's lap. *And I'm Sarah. This is my first music class at this library. I tried going back to work last month, but I think it was a little premature, so here I am! Momming! Gonna try this for a while!*

The woman smiled. *That seat is where Aubrey's mom's assistant usually sits*, she said, nodding to a little girl with a tiny puff of hair and three bows in it.

Oh, no problem. I'll just scoot one over, I said, blushing a little. I thought the woman had wanted to meet me, not chastise me, and I wasn't sure why Aubrey's mom's assistant couldn't sit one over herself. I knew none of these moms would like me. I knew I wasn't like them; that I wouldn't fit in. I knew they would take one look at me and know I wasn't cut out to be a mom.

The woman smiled again, and this time she rolled her eyes. *Sorry, I wasn't trying to be a bitch. People get very territorial at this class. I'm Caroline. This is Casey. Where are you applying to twos programs?* she asked. She bounced her baby Casey on her knees and leaned back into her plastic folding chair.

Oh shit, I said. *Am I supposed to already know that?* About four heads turned when I said *shit*. Guy squirmed in my lap, oblivious.

Oh, he's just so delicious! Caroline exclaimed. *Do you just nibble all over him? I would chew his thighs and suck on his tiny baby toes and kiss his rolls.* She made her voice sound like she was a little kid, high-pitched and silly. Her behavior was as odd to me as my saying *shit* in a room full of babies probably seemed to her. I'd never considered chewing on Guy's thighs before, nor sucking on his toes. All I'd done to his rolls was powder them, at Sharon's insistence, since I knew they could get chafed and rashy. Caroline's appetite for the body of her infant was anathema to me. I rarely even thought of my baby as cute, which I knew was alien-level behavior on my part, not to be openly shared. This class was yet another instance of my outsider status, unless, of course, I could find one other mom who was like me, somehow. An ally; someone who could admit they'd also never wanted to chew on their baby.

You should come for coffee with us after this, she said, gesturing to a mom crew in the corner. I smiled back and nodded an enthusiastic RSVP, my eyebrows lifted in excitement. This could be the opportunity I needed. Maybe one of these women felt a little bit like me and was willing to chat about it, willing to break down the wall that kept most mothers conscripted to the good girl rhetoric. *There's a group of us mammas that go every week,* Caroline continued. *It's nice.*

Then an older man walked into the room and rang a bell at the front. *It's starting*, Caroline whispered, nodding at him. He began to blow bubbles from a pink plastic jar, and suddenly all the bigger babies were watching him, enraptured. It was like they were all on the same dose of shrooms. Guy seemed indifferent, his dark infant eyes staring at the action but not revealing any response.

Maybe it would be good to make some neighborhood mom friends, I thought, even though I didn't think of myself as a "mamma." Maybe it would endear me to motherhood or force some shift in attitude if I had comrades. Maybe, once I got a few of them in a room alone, they would drop the act, and we could get real about motherhood. After what could be described only as an endless, percussive, cutesy singalong of the goddamn bubble song, class ended. I filed out after Caroline, and she introduced me to three other women. I immediately forgot their names because I was trying to load Guy into his coat and then into the stroller, under his blanket, which I was not going to let myself forget. Even though I listened to her and repeated their names as she said them, I couldn't retain a single fact these days.

We steered our drooling human cargo down Prince Street to the La Colombe Coffee on Lafayette, placing our orders separately and finding a table where four strollers could also park. We all began the process of lifting our babies out from under their blankets and seat belts, then unwrapping their winter coats and scarves, wiping away the snot under their noses with paper napkins, meanwhile starting to sweat a little bit in our own winter coats and scarves.

You'd think with how much work it is to move a baby around in the winter, I'd have lost more baby weight by now, said Caroline. Woman #1, with her visible, dark circles, agreed: *As if I needed another reason to be tired. It takes me about thirty minutes to get all these winter layers on him.* She nodded at her little boy, asleep in his stroller, oblivious to the noise around him.

Caroline blew on her chai and yawned as the espresso machine whirred behind her. *So, so tired. But it's so worth it. Look at our babies. It's so fun to be out and about with them and other moms. Isn't it just the best?* All the women nodded and smiled and sipped their drinks, and I wondered if I'd been initiated into a cult where all women were always happy and wanted to eat their offspring, or if, underneath the surface, someone was just waiting for an invitation to talk shit.

Yah, it's so nice to connect, I heard myself saying, a smile plastered on my face. *I don't know that many moms, to be honest. The ones I'm friends with . . . I guess you could say they're more uptown types. You know, organized. Preparing their three-month-olds to get into the right eating club at Princeton and all of that.* I studied their faces to see if anyone betrayed a glimmer of commiseration, but they all just nodded and smiled at me.

The truth was, I did appreciate the invite. It was a kindness to be included. Yet it was hard to know how much of myself to reveal. I didn't like being outside with my baby: I was scared of all the things that could go wrong, and I found the activities we did together about as fulfilling as sitting in traffic. No one had told me that it would be simultaneously terrifying and boring to be around my own child, and these women didn't seem to think so. Or, if they did, they weren't saying it yet. I worried that something anti-baby was going to tumble out of my mouth and alienate them, while desperate to know if a more honest approach might endear them to me. I was too lonely to be making enemies while drinking a cappuccino at La Colombe. I had to tread carefully.

Caroline, how are you feeling? asked Woman #2, her arm full of rose gold Cartier bracelets. *Different . . . ?* Caroline turned to me to explain as she slowly rocked her stroller back and forth with her foot, soothing Casey, who was starting to fidget.

I started antidepressants last month. I was just hating my life. I mean, obsessed with my baby, like totally in love with the baby— but everything else made me miserable. Thank God for my baby, though, or I'd have really lost it. The other women murmured their agreements like a Greek chorus.

I felt my chest tighten, as if my heart were squeezing at the wrong times. Something about this stranger opening up about her need for antidepressants hit me. It seemed almost impolite, her vulnerability. Where I came from, no one talked about their psych meds, of course, but even in my adult life in New York, I hadn't often encountered women willing to do more than hint at their problems. Here she was being real, or at least her version of real, and it both scared and intrigued me. Maybe I could do the same, and it would all turn out okay?

Sometimes I think maybe I need meds, too, I began. No one seemed offended, so I kept going. The warm coffee cup in my hands felt cozy. *Like, I know this is a weird example, but when you look at my baby, do you think he's a little off-looking?* I said. *He's abnormally ugly, right? Sometimes I find that his ugliness makes him hard to love, you know?* Seven pairs of eyes stared at me, blinking.

Absolutely not. Your baby is precious! Caroline exclaimed, then laughed, as if she thought I'd been joking, so I laughed too. I looked at the other women, hoping one of them would be honest with me, but they had each turned to gaze at their own children, appreciating them in a way I wished I could with my own. I looked at Guy. The kid was objectively a tiny worm; even worse, a worm with my nose.

Honestly, it's hard to say anything bad about my baby be-cause I did three rounds of IVF to get her. Caroline cocked her head, like she was thinking hard about what I had to say. I felt my heart fall because I knew that I'd misjudged; laid my vanity and insensitive idiocy bare. *And a lot of babies are funny-looking at first. But they are all miracles, and almost all of them turn out perfect–eventually.* She smiled at me like she understood but felt sorry for me, or maybe like I was stupid.

My friend Diane's baby had blood in her diaper, Woman #2 said. *She's been to all these specialists, and they are running test after test.* I got lost in her sad eyes, which were so beautiful. She must have been a former model. Everyone sucked in their breath, me included. *We are just so damn lucky to not have those prob-*

lems, she added. That part I understood. The fragility of life was simply astounding.

That's when you really *need psychopharmaceuticals,* Caroline said with a little laugh. *My God, it makes me sick to think about.* She shook her head.

I had the sudden urge to leave these perfectly nice women, and I wasn't quite sure why. Something about Caroline's admitting to being on antidepressants made me want to leap from my little stool and run out into the cold without my coat on. If she was so depressed that she'd accepted a dose of medical help, yet she managed to love her baby and find her beautiful, then meds weren't going to help me. They were being prescribed to people who seemed so functional; how could they cure whatever ailment I had? I didn't know that refusing medication is a sign of depression. I decided I wasn't depressed. I was just an aggravated, spoiled little shit who didn't like responsibility and thought my baby was ugly. In other words, I was a monster. And while part of me wanted one of these women to turn to me and say, *Do you ever dream that your baby drowned? Do you ever think about holding him and feel your chest squeeze and your stomach drop? Do you hate your husband? Do you hate yourself? Do you ever wish you could be anywhere else but your own life?* I knew they never would. I knew I was alone in my monstrousness. The all-too-familiar feeling of being the odd one out made me vertiginous and dizzy. How on earth would antidepressants change the facts?

I was embarrassed as I stared at this crew of women. They seemed so together, so maternal, so lit from within. They also seemed so interested in whatever domestic responsibilities occupied their lives. I wish I would have asked them how they managed to find themselves again next to these squishy sacks of flesh to which we were each beholden, apparently until our own deaths. I wish I could have just come out and asked them, *Do you think I need antidepressants too? I am so sad and out of sorts. Is this normal? Do you all see the bad parts about motherhood that I see?* But in my desire to seem strong, and capable, and good at being a mother, I could not have admitted my shameful truth. So instead, I decided to lie through my teeth. And also, agreeing with what they were saying would have made my own version of it too real. I preferred to hold out hope that I might wake up one morning magically adjusted.

Caroline brought the conversation back to her new meds. *I'd just been crying so much. I had no choice. It was either cry, cry, cry all day and night or take this little pill.* She said it matter-of-factly, and while I was so glad that she had found a fix for her sorrow, I wondered if whatever was wrong underneath was still there. That was my fear for myself: that I'd medically lobotomize myself to the point of some dreamy contentedness, but the real problems of my life would still bubble beneath the surface.

Oh gosh, that sounds so hard, I said, sipping my coffee. *But good for you for doing what you need to do for yourself. Was your husband helpful with Casey while you were crying and stuff?* I hoped I seemed empathetic, but like I had my shit together. I wanted to make up for the gaffe of admitting to my preoccupation with Guy's face. They all laughed at my question.

No, God love him, he's barely changed a diaper, replied Caroline. *But he would just do it wrong anyway!* This was not something I could even pretend to laugh at; thinking about weaponized incompetence and ineptitude made me so mad. It was like all the husbands I heard about were on some giant, cis-hetero male group text about how to suck. I wondered if I'd find sympathy among this crew if I explained how every one of Tom's coffee stains on the kitchen table or crumpled paper towels *next to* the trash can made me feel like it was chipping away at my brain power and my will to continue in this life. I wondered if they also scrolled through their husband's cell phones late at night, suppressing their tiny wounds in favor of keeping the peace?

Speaking of husbands, I gotta run home, Woman #3, with her thick, gorgeous ponytail, said. *Mine gets back from a work trip this afternoon, and I can't wait. See you girls next week?* We all said yes and started the complicated process of getting the babies dressed, wheeling our giant strollers out onto the sidewalk. I wondered what it was like in Woman #3's house and if I'd ever feel excited to see Tom again. If I'd ever feel comforted by him coming home, if I'd ever feel like our house was our joint refuge.

Let's talk about baby-led weaning next time, one of them called. The thought of that conversation made me want to burn down the library with me in it so I wouldn't have to ever use those words, but I said bye cheerfully and started the two-block walk home. Guy began nodding off as I looked down at him. Lucky him, being able to sleep whenever he wanted.

I felt so jumbled up inside that I couldn't go home just yet. If Sharon asked me what I'd done after the library and I had to tell her about the mom cult I'd accidentally joined, where I'd brought shame to our family by admitting to four normal women that I found my kid to be physically heinous, I thought I'd feel even worse. It was somehow more isolating to be around a bunch of women who didn't seem to feel any of the things I was feeling about my baby, even though I also hated meeting people whose flaws mirrored mine.

It was curious. I'd faked being happy to fit in at one moment, faked loving my baby to get them to like me. But I'd also been scared to admit that I was depressed like Caroline had copped to. And I wasn't totally sure why I'd done either. Maybe this was why my mom never really had mom friends. Maybe she just felt totally different from the other women around her. Maybe she didn't want anyone to know her, so lost herself in a lonely vortex she could never escape. Thinking about my mom feeling alone in her motherhood journey made me so sad. I'd judged all of her faults so harshly for so long, and it still cut me to my core that she wasn't always the mom I craved. But when I thought about her suffering, and thought about how my hostility toward her just added to it, I almost couldn't handle it. A wave of tears hit me so hard it took my breath away, and I could feel sadness spread through my whole body, weighing me down and stopping me in my tracks. I turned toward the brick wall of an apartment building so no one could see me, one hand on my stroller, and silently ugly sobbed for a second, my whole body contracting, wincing so hard that the pressure in my ears changed. I sucked in air and started on the next wave of hot tears, the old-tenement bricks blurring in my vision. I shook the carriage back and forth a little, to make sure Guy was okay in there.

I was just such a bad person, and a bad mother. I missed my old self and my old life. I felt like I was grieving: yearning for who I'd been before, yearning for connection to my mom, yearning for a time in my relationship with Tom where we'd been more in tune. The next full-body, aching, wrenching sob passed, and I wiped my cheeks, trying to reel in my little spiral, shaking my head and patting my eyes to get the wet off my heavy eyelashes.

The day was gray and cold, but SoHo was bustling, people walking by me energetically, hustling to run their errands and get to wherever they were going. I wished for that busy energy, the sense of normalcy that came with quotidian tasks. I decided to window-shop a little and get another manicure, so I texted Petunia and Augusta to see if either of them could sneak out of the office and meet me at the nail shop near my apartment.

You have to keep up with yourself, older mothers I knew had told me. *Keep the spark alive in your marriage by losing the pregnancy weight and putting on lipstick and making time to leave the baby. Get your nails and your hair done! You have to let your husband take you on dates!*

Friends instructed me to be sure that I took Guy on walks outside at least once a day, even though I couldn't understand how a little baby who was mostly asleep would know the difference. *When Tom comes home from work, make sure you've taken the baby out for a stroll and washed your hair! Answer the door naked with a rose in your mouth!*

I wasn't sure if I wanted to keep the spark alive, if I wanted to leave the house, or go on any dates—and I certainly didn't think a rose in my mouth, with my oozing, sagging breasts and my loose stomach skin from diastasis recti, was going to do the trick. But I would have gone to any length to feel like myself. I would have done whatever it took. I heard their suggestions and followed them blindly, willing to spend all I had if it meant that I could tele-port back to the days of being young and baby-less.

And while I savored all the indulgent self-care experiences that were recommended to me—an advantage I couldn't ignore—I hadn't yet had any luck emerging as either my former self or as an independent, happy, new person. Plus, the minute I left the spa, finished the hair appointment, or walked out of yet another yoga class set to rap music, there I was all over again. And worse yet, there *he* was. The baby. But I kept trying.

I walked into the salon, a cheap neighborhood mani-pedi mill that turned out beauty services faster than a Wendy's drive-through. It was a long, tiled room with massage chairs and nail stations all down one side, little UV dryers down the other. There was only one guy inside, talking quietly on his cell phone while getting a foot massage. His feet were huge, like paddleboards at the end of his long legs. They were immaculately pedicured and had French tips painted in black.

Hi, Christine, I whispered when I walked in. Christine met me with a big smile and came over to give me a quiet hug. *I'll get the spa pedi, and Petunia will be here in twenty. Can we get seats next to each other?*

I hadn't had to ask P very forcefully. She'd practically jumped in a taxi when I told her we could have a glass of wine afterward.

Augusta had to pick up her two boys from school but was going to try to meet us later for the wine.

How were all those bitchy moms at the library? Petunia wanted to know, rushing in twenty minutes later. Guy stayed asleep in his stroller next to me, and P barely clocked him as she chose a bright blue color for herself from the shelves of nail polish.

They were so nice, actually. Not sure I need to hang out with them again, but you don't need to be judgmental, okay? Not all of us can just go to work every day without gushing blood on things. Some of us make other choices. I winced as I thought back to my attempt at returning to the gallery in person and thanked my stars for Wi-Fi and cell phones so that I could work from home.

Did you work out today? Petunia asked as she reached her arms across the little table toward her manicurist. *You're in a better mood when you work out. Less fragile.*

I'm not being fragile. Remember when you took pottery lessons? Was it fun to be that bad at something? Manicures are fun. Going out with my friends for wine in the middle of the day is fun. Going to the bathroom to do coke, even though I hate coke but love doing illegal shit in bathrooms, is fun. I don't even think Guy could have looked into that crowd of mothers and known I was his. I probably could have kidnapped someone else's baby, and Guy would never know the difference. I picked a nude polish and shook it. What I didn't say was that I'd always imagined the tedious tasks of mothering would transform magically into some sort of delightful honor once it was *my* baby whose ass needed wiping and brain craved playtime, but that my lack of connection to Guy made it all not just grueling but also a reminder of my own maternal failure.

Petunia squinted at me and said, *You're kind of unhinged.* I rolled my eyes at her.

I work out every day. I got a pedicure already this week, I got my eyebrows waxed. I went to acupuncture. I haven't missed a hair color appointment since this baby came, and my mom told me she looked more like the baby's mother and I looked more like the grandma. I've had so much Botox since Guy was born that my dermatologist invited me out to dinner last week–her treat. And I still don't feel so great or pretty, for the record. And I still hate Tom.

You know if you need to kill him, I'll help you bury the body. She laughed and closed her eyes as her manicurist started on the hand massage. *Did you tell your new besties that you're plotting a husbandicide?*

Of course not. I want them to like me. I have an annoying condition where I want everyone's approval, I said. *You know this. I can tell you and Auggie my truth but not them,* I continued. *They were perfect mommy robots. They wouldn't understand me.* I stared at my nails.

Why do you care what they think of you? Petunia asked. *You don't need them. They were probably lying, anyway. Either to you or to themselves.* She shrugged.

I don't know; I think some people are simply more suited to this than I am. I'm just bad at it. I'm jealous of anyone who finds mom shit easy and natural and fun. I watched Christine whip out her shiny cuticle tools and wished I could use one to snip off the part of my frontal lobe that made me so uncontrollably averse to parenting.

Well, even if they are naturally brilliant moms, don't you want to be friends with people who can complain about the whole motherhood thing with you? I mean, complaining endlessly is kind of your entire personality.

She wasn't wrong. I'd long looked at New York City as a mecca for those who wanted to be different; who wanted to interrogate everything that seemed conventional. When I left behind my cushy suburban life, it hadn't been to do coffee dates with women who didn't seem to want to question our societally defined parental roles, who I couldn't be honest with about my experiences–least of all my experience as a mom. I'd always relied on my career and extracurriculars to help me feel like it was worth it to have strayed far from home, and somehow I'd ended up knee-deep in the perspectives on parenthood that I thought a life in New York would insulate me from. It's not that I thought enjoying motherhood was bad: I *wished* I enjoyed it. But I didn't think that in New York, of all places, I'd have to pretend.

Plus, the calendar of my work and social lives–another advantage I'd always associated with life here–suddenly made me terribly anxious. I thought about the upcoming fashion parties, gallery openings, museum fundraisers, client dinners, travel to Europe for art fairs and fashion week, a show of Tom's new ceramics in his Tokyo gallery, the contemporary art auctions, squeezing in time with Guy when I used to squeeze in time with my friends, and I felt a foreboding settle over me like a thick, heavy fog.

The other day, I'd popped into Tom's studio to give him a kiss and see the work before it was shipped off to Japan to be installed, and he'd been out buying plywood. Everyone was racing around, their heads down, finishing up last-minute tasks before the shipment left, and it seemed like no one had time or even wanted to chat. I felt like they were all avoiding me, as if I were some interloper; then I realized I didn't even know which objects were going to be exhibited, and what they were about. Usually Tom and I talked about all of his ideas, and we fleshed them out together. And then I'd get sent a draft of the press release, and I'd add my two cents, and he'd ask me to come over and look at the work and make final edits. I'd tell him which paintings I thought should stay behind, those that didn't feel fully finished; I'd suggest a sculpture for the back rooms, to be offered only to VIPs. But everyone seemed so busy without me now, like I didn't even count.

What if I just went away? I thought to myself as they finished up our polish. *What would it look like if I just vaporized?* It seemed like I'd probably be better off if I just didn't exist at all. This thought process, a fax of a fax of suicidal ideation, didn't freak me out. I mostly just felt numb. I was reminded of Millais's *Ophelia*, floating in her beautiful, still lagoon, her hair radiating out from her dead figure.

Back at home, as I kicked off my shoes at the kitchen door, I thought about pouring a glass of wine. It was barely midafternoon, but I needed to relax a little. I could go grab another expired Vicodin, but thinking about it made me nervous. I'd made my way through several drug categories in my twenties, and I didn't want to push my luck. There'd been a cocaine moment, which ended when I did too many lines and drank too much one night and puked my brains out in my bathroom. I decided to shower to wash off the bile, and then showering seemed too hard, so I drew a bath. The next thing I knew, it was ten in the morning, and the sun was glaring through my tiny bathroom window overlooking Houston Street. I'd been asleep in a freezing-cold bath for hours, my nostrils barely a millimeter above the waterline. I got scared after that and hadn't messed with non-pharmaceuticals for years after.

Plus, Adderall worked better as a party drug. I'd keep one next to my bed and take it when my alarm went off, then let the medicine kick in to wake me up for the day. I got so much done, never had to break for food, and I could drink and drink and drink all night. By the time I decided to kick that habit–really less by choice and more because I ran out and couldn't find a crooked doctor or a good dealer in time–I hadn't felt hunger or fullness in probably a year, just eating at mealtimes out of habit, my appetite completely suppressed. For weeks after I quit, I felt like I was under water. Noises seemed slow and every movement felt delayed, like my life was some distorted freeze-frame at the end of a movie.

My phone buzzed as a text from Tom came in. *Don't forget we have the Guggenheim Gala tonight. I can swing by and pick you up at six?* I put the phone into my lap and took a deep breath. I didn't fit into any of my clothes, and I didn't want to see people.

There's no way I'm going to that, I responded, hauling myself up the stairs and into my bedroom. I took off all my clothes and got into bed under my white comforter. My phone buzzed again.

You have to. We are guests of the Baldwins—they just bought a huge sculpture from me—and you're sitting next to Tracy Emin. My head throbbed behind my eyebrows, and I closed my eyes, pressing my fingers on top of them.

Tracy Emin was a British artist who'd risen to explosive fame in the nineties with her work *Everyone I Have Ever Slept With 1963-1995*, a tent appliqued with the names of all her sexual partners, family members such as her grandmother and twin brother, and her aborted children. A few years later, she exhibited a confessional work called *My Bed*, which was her actual bed after a four-day depressive episode during which she hadn't left it. The sheets were stained and rumpled, cluttered with empty vodka bottles and a pregnancy test, and dotted with cigarette butts, period blood-stains, and lube splotches. A night with her sounded like it might be a sort of relief.

I rifled through my medicine cabinet, knowing exactly what would make this gala tenable. Inside a little dopp kit I kept on my highest shelf was my stash of mushroom chocolates. I pulled out a square, dusty and old, closer to gray than brown. I chewed it before I could second-guess myself, then swiped on a big, exaggerated cat eye of liquid liner. I could always rely on Cleopatra-inspired makeup to make me feel more glamorous, so I added an extra coat of thick mascara, blinking against the heaviness of the waxy makeup on my lashes. Maybe I could distract from my puffy stomach with excessive makeup.

In my closet, I reached with one hand into my underwear drawer, searching for the most comfortable pair I could find, and pulled out a pair of cotton briefs that read *fuck me* on the butt—a joke gift from Petunia. I yanked them on and then pulled down the one long dress I had that fit, zipping it tightly over my swollen tits. It was black Gucci, a PR sample my pregnant friends had passed back and forth. The material, having been home to several en-gorged bodies, sagged a little in the wrong places, but it was my only option, and the buttons were ornate cloisonné and beautiful, so I couldn't complain. I didn't even look in the mirror as I shoved lipstick and a credit card into a black clutch. I put one of the Vico-din I'd been avoiding in my mouth for good measure, then chewed it to a powder before swallowing.

BY SEVEN THIRTY, I was standing at the base of Frank Lloyd Wright's Guggenheim Museum rotunda, staring up and pretend-ing I was inside the eye of a tornado. I was thinking about the first exhibition I'd ever seen there–the Matthew Barney one where he covered the banister of the central staircase in Vaseline–when Tom came up next to me and put his arm around my waist. He led me gently to our table, steering me between the banquet chairs.

You okay, babe? he asked as he let his hand rest on the small of my back. The warmth of his palm made my stomach flip-flop, and I remembered the first time we'd ever walked into a room with his hand in that same spot; how I'd beamed at his touch.

I'm fucking great, I whispered back. *I'm on so many drugs that I feel like a tiny baby.* He turned and looked at me.

All right . . . he said. *That is a weird choice.* I shrugged at him as we sat, and felt my dress loosen a little in the back as my butt hit the chair. My giant boobs must have stretched a seam, but I was too high to care. The servers were pouring wine, and Tracy Emin was there, and I knew so many people in the room–people I hadn't seen in months. I felt like I was being rocked back and forth in the sturdy arms of my former life.

As soon as dessert hit the table, I stood to make my rounds, smiling and waving at friends and colleagues I would have prob-ably hid from had I been sober. I saw Tom by the bar, talking to a very pretty woman I didn't recognize. I saw her touch his arm at the elbow, and I knew that he was looking at her with a sparkle in his eye. I looked down at my bulging middle for a second. Part of me wanted to go over and put my arms around him, stake my claim. Instead, I just sighed and tried to relax into my high. I felt like I was floating among the tables, my black silk Gucci train gliding behind me. As long as I didn't think about Tom, over there in the corner, I couldn't stop smiling, tossing my long hair and laughing at people's mediocre jokes.

When a hand came to touch the small of my back again, I was surprised to feel skin on mine.

Babe, Tom whispered. *Your dress is unzipped in the back. I think the zipper's broken.* I laughed a little.

Ugh, my boobs ruin everything, I said. I wanted to add, *I bet that woman you were just talking to has perfectly perky ones, if you want to go home with her instead*, but I didn't. I bit my tongue and just said, *Can you force it closed?*

I could feel his fingers clawing the fabric together.

I think we need to go, he said. *People are looking. Tracy Emin is looking. Your butt's out, and did you realize it says "fuck me" across the back? I can't fix it.* I started laughing as he scrambled to keep the two sections of cloth as closed as possible. *What the actual fuck are you on?* he asked, sounding a little annoyed at me. In retrospect, that was the moment my spiral really got going. It felt so good to not care. Drugs were a miracle, I thought. I can feel like this any time I want, like nothing matters and everything is funny and silly. I can feel stupid, and okay with being stupid. I can feel euphoric. As I sat in the taxi with Tom, watching him silently scroll through his phone, I thought about which crooked doctor from my twenties I could call to get more pills.

THE NEXT WEEK, I had an appointment at my gyno, a three-month check-in at which I planned to get an IUD inserted. When I got to the old-fashioned office with its floral wallpaper in the waiting room, I showed the nurse, Vani, a couple of baby pictures. She'd asked, pretending to care about a baby she'd never even meet, and I indulged her. I showed her the ones I'd saved with his eyes closed, so she wouldn't see all the evidence of his weirdness.

So-ooo cute, she said, and I knew she was lying. *Look at all that hair!* As if hair was something to applaud on a newborn. I could sense she was faking it, or she would have complimented something else besides his hair, which was so *easy*. Had she found things to admire in his face, she would have named those instead. And while I didn't hold it against her–I understood she was compelled to be polite–I was annoyed at the constant conspiracy of lies regarding babies. *They're cute, they're magic, they bring happiness and enrich your life.* That shit made my eyes want to roll out of my head.

Here's a cup to pee in for your pregnancy test, which we have to give you before we put the IUD in. It's just protocol. I'll come get you when the doctor is ready. I headed to the bathroom to pee in the cup, laughing to myself because I couldn't imagine being pregnant so soon after a baby. I'd had sex with Tom only twice since I gave birth, and both times I'd been pleasantly surprised to find out I was so numb from the traumatic horror show otherwise known as labor and delivery that it was like my nerves were totally shot. I could barely feel anything at all, and it came as a relief that I could just lie there with no discomfort, even though it inversely meant there was no real pleasure, either. I was just sort of detached from my body, like it barely even existed, or maybe like its existence didn't matter.

A few minutes later, Vani came to get me in the waiting room.

Sarah, if you want to step into exam room one, I can discuss the results of that test, she said, a little too seriously. I felt my adrenaline surge at her tone. I wondered what there was to discuss. She led me through an open door into a small, cold room with a bed and ultrasound machine and handed me my hospital gown. Every second felt like it was moving through syrup.

Vani, what did the test say, if you don't mind? I asked in a small voice, taking off my clothes and stepping onto the scale for her. I had a lump in my throat, for some reason. The thought of her saying, happily, *Guess what, you're pregnant!* filled me with a terrible chill. I took a deep breath.

The pregnancy test? Oh, you're not pregnant, if that's what you're wondering! But your sample looked a little dark—make sure you're drinking enough water. She wrote down my weight. *The doctor will be in shortly. Stick your head out if you need anything.* I let all the air out of my lungs.

Thanks, Vani! I said with my best Indiana-cheerleader sweetness. Blood rushed to my limbs, the relief of her update washing over me. I sat on the bed and put my feet into the stirrups, covering my lap with a flimsy blanket. *Dodged that bullet*, I thought. The doctor rapped on the door and stuck her head in.

How's that baby? And how's Mamma? she asked as she entered the little room, Vani behind her. *We're putting in an IUD today, right?*

I nodded. *It doesn't hurt, does it?* I asked, suddenly nervous at the sight of her putting on surgical gloves.

For a postpartum woman, it is usually so simple. You won't even know I've done it, she said. *I'm gonna do a quick Pap first, which should also be completely tolerable. You've probably noticed if you've had sex that your nerves have been impacted by the cervix's expansion in labor.*

Vani handed her something that I couldn't see, and she pulled a little roller stool down to the foot of my bed, then disappeared from my view. *How's the little one?* she asked as she started with that same lubricating gel they always use to medically fist me, followed by the cold metal speculum. I winced as it slid in, cranking me open, and then sucked in my breath as it clasped my cervix and yanked it toward the doctor. I thought about how a doctor had invented this barbaric tool in the 1840s by experimenting on enslaved women who could not, by definition, consent to his exams, nor his surgeries, during which he did not administer any anesthetics or palliative care. The tool felt heavy inside me.

He's very sweet. How are your kids? I felt almost frozen, suddenly having someone reaching around inside my body again. Next came that pipe cleaner thingy. I swear I could feel it gag me, daring me to protest. The doctor twisted it around a few times while I picked at my cuticles and felt my brain empty. Though I couldn't see what she was doing, exactly, I noticed that one end of it went in clean and came out bloody, and it made me feel lightheaded to witness that evidence of a private place wounded and suffering.

My kids are wild, she said. *We just took them to Disney. Just wait until you get into your Disney days!*

She handed the pipe cleaner swab off to Vani, who put it into a plastic vial and walked the sample out of the room while checking her text messages.

Now I'm going to do the IUD, the doctor said. *How's Tom, by the way? He's too funny. The girls miss him around here.*

As she spoke, I felt like I was holding my breath again, my chest too tight to move. I felt like I'd fractured into two people. There was the one who was watching the doctor's every move, frozen in terror, sick to her stomach. And then there was the good girl, following her training, unable to say stop, or ask for help, rambling on with casual conversation at almost double speed.

Tom's great! He's just the best! He's such a good new daddy! I felt like my synapses were going haywire, firing at random, and it was all I could do to try focusing on the words the doctor was saying so that I could reply adequately. *Guy has peed on him, like, six times, and we had one major diaper blowout experience, but he's taking it all in stride. My mom is coming back this month, I think, which is wonderful because maybe she will babysit, and I'm back at work, and everything is going great!*

She withdrew her hands and started peeling off her gloves. *All done! You can get dressed and check out.*

I pulled on my clothes the second the door shut, ignoring the lubricant smear that transferred to the inside of my leather pants. My hands and thighs were trembling so much that my signature looked different when I signed the credit card slip at the front desk. I thanked the receptionist, all smiles, holding back tears, but the minute I got into my Uber, I burst into rough sobs. I called my mom, my mind spinning, the small of my back sweating against the leather of the seat.

How will I ever get through a second pregnancy if I can't even get a pelvic exam? I cried to her on the phone, ashamed that I'd been so scared on the exam table with no clear catalyst, and even more ashamed that I'd been unable to tell the doctor to stop, to admit to her that I wasn't well. *What if I have an only child because I'm too scared of doctors and needles to have a second, and Guy turns out to be a Republican because he never had a sibling to teach him to share?* I blubbered, remembering how formative it was when my baby brother told me he'd put my photo on HOTor-NOT.com and I was getting a four, or when my little sister told me everyone could tell I had a crush on Adam Mohlman, and that they all knew I got so drunk at homecoming that I peed on him when we were making out. Tough sibling love had made me more resilient and realistic and self-aware.

It's so scary, my mom said. *I remember feeling the same way.* This made me cry harder. *I wish I could take it away,* she continued. *I really do.* She was quiet for a minute, letting me sniffle. *Sweetheart, I'm getting a call on the other line, and it's from the restaurants.*

It's okay, I muttered. *I'm almost home. I'll talk to you later.*

I wasn't worried about what my Uber driver was thinking or even if he was listening. My main concern was getting home, getting in my bed with a hot tea, and crying my eyes out to anyone else who might be willing to listen to the details of my newest and latest disappointing vagina-related crisis.

I called Petunia when I was finally under my covers, and, strangely, she was crying too. She'd just had a fight with her boyfriend.

You're so lucky you're a mom, Petunia told me. *I cried to mine all morning. There's nothing like crying to your mom.* I'd never thought of that before, since crying to mine never really worked, and I liked the idea that my newish role was one that could bring a very specific comfort to the world. Because every other aspect of this new parenthood life seemed to completely suck.

P, when I saw the doctor's head bobbing around down there between my legs, it was like I was right back in the delivery room. I took a sip of tea and put it on my bedside table, pulling my white comforter around me like a cloud. *Remember that time that hot, older Brazilian guy put his hand up my dress in that bar? Maybe thirty seconds after we met him? I froze like how I froze then.*

Yes! Petunia agreed. *That dude was aggressive. I know what you mean, though. All the times I've ever been in bed with a guy making out, and suddenly he's just sticking his dick in without asking? So fucked up.* I could hear her chewing on something. She liked to stress-eat Japanese gummy candies that her sister sent her from Tokyo. I thought about all the times that had happened to me and realized that I'd always just perceived it as sort of normal. I remembered that joke from the movie *Wedding Crashers*–*just the tip*–and something clicked in me; some little floodgate holding back a lot of anger sprang open.

We all have the same damn stories! Is any woman ever exempt? It's so pervasive to the point that it's not even something I think about. It's just a fact of life. You're gonna get groped in bars or flashed on the subway. You're gonna get surprise-dicked at the end of dates. I was getting worked up, memories flickering through my brain. *It may not be violent in the traditional sense—like, there may not be a firearm or a Taser involved—but you're definitely gonna get knifed by a dick at some point. Ugh, it's like a whole generation of men just silently raped us all, using their horrible dick-knives as weapons, and now we are all married or coupled up with them or their brothers. How do any of these dudes dare to think we want to have sex with them for the rest of our lives?* When I thought about it, maybe I needed a whole truckload of gummy candies from P's sister in Tokyo.

Dudes don't know what they want, Petunia replied. *They only know what porn has taught them. They're never taught how to convey emotion, and they are never held responsible for any actions. You think mommy cults are bad? Imagine being so brain-dead that you're trapped in a rape-culture, toxic-cesspool porn cult of dick worshipping.* She had a point. I was getting mad, and it was making me hot, so I threw off the comforter and sat up in bed. I thought about how fucked up it was that the same way an entitled, horrible man might make me feel at the end of a third date was the same way a doctor could make me feel when I was naked, my legs spread in front of her face.

P, I simply cannot feel terror for this body anymore. I need to feel good, in my bedroom and at the doctor's office and everywhere else. How do I do that? How? I was crying again. I took a shaky, deep breath. *How do I just feel safe for fucking once in my spoiled life? I have everything, and I still can't feel safe. What the fuck do I do? And WHERE THE FUCK IS MY FUCKING MOM?*

Petunia was quiet on the other end of the line. I heard her take a breath like she was galvanizing herself. *Honestly, Sarah. I'm not sure how to say this, but . . . bitch, you need therapy. Bad. You need a therapist stat, because you're not being normal about any of this, and, yah, having a kid seems like a bummer, and your mom isn't here, and Tom kinda sucks, and, okay, we've all been some version of raped a million times by a million entitled dudes, and your doctor is maybe a medical sadist, but you seem on the edge of a spiral. I could put some pills in an Uber for you and send it on down, but I don't think that's the fix we are looking for. I don't know why no one else is telling you this, and maybe you'll hate me forever, but please: Go. To. Therapy.* I heard her plastic bag of candy crinkling closed. She said nothing, waiting for me to get mad, or maybe start crying, or tell her to mind her business, but I did none of that.

I sat there and thought about what she said. And then, softly, I asked her, *Wait, really? Do you really think something is wrong? Because being a mom is crazy. I think it's irrational if you're a new mom and you're not mad. I feel like I'm saying something that no one else will admit. Maybe I'm the only one who sees it, you know?*

Petunia sighed, as if I was testing her patience. *You're not the only one that sees it, Sarah. But you're letting it drive you off the deep end. I'm, like, scared you're going to pretend to jump into the Hudson River, and I'm going to see a made-for-TV movie in twenty years about how you ended up working in a casino in Vegas under an assumed name. And your hair is not at its best in dry heat.*

I understood what she was telling me: I was in danger of blowing up my life, and in a way that wouldn't get me anywhere closer to where I wanted to be.

Okay, okay, I hear you. I'll call a therapist, I promised, though it was the last thing I wanted to do. The idea of sitting in a chair looking at a stranger and telling them everything filled me with dread. P knew my whole story already, so I could hint at stuff to her, and she could fill in the blanks. But most of this wasn't a narrative I wanted to rehash out loud, in detail, to a stranger. I didn't have the nerve.

When I hung up the phone, I went to the kitchen to make myself another tea, stopping to pet Napoleon snoring away on his dog bed. While I let my tea steep, I sat at my little kitchen table, crumpling into a chair with one leg under me as I stared at the ivy-covered buildings out my window. I didn't want to do this anymore. My life wasn't getting better. I didn't have any right to complain, and I was ashamed that I even wanted to. But I was crying all the time, set off by tiny memories about my mom or thoughts about my baby that led to spirals regarding really horrible shit, like death and shame. I could barely remember my name some days, let alone do anything productive. I couldn't commiserate with mom friends, and when I looked at my baby, I felt dead inside. But when I looked at my husband, I felt *too* alive, burning with rage, even when he was being kind and thoughtful, even when he was trying his hardest for me. When I looked at myself, I didn't recognize what I saw; I knew that all the pain I was feeling was my own fault, and that everything I had done to this point was wrong. I was a wretched mother, a terrible wife, a shitty friend. It was like trying to live life with a constant hangover on a boat rocking back and forth erratically. Everything hurt to the point of distraction–I could hardly think straight. I wished I could just walk off my balcony and end it all, painlessly and peacefully. I wished I could just walk off onto a cloud and float away, without anyone realizing I was gone.

10
Brain Explosion

Indonesia
Late August 2018

I KNEW BEFORE WE LEFT LA that the monkeys in Indonesia were going to be a problem. The night Tom showed up at the Chateau Marmont just in time to drop my baby, we'd slept on separate sides of the big hotel bed, facing separate walls. I think I would have screamed if he'd tried to touch me; I actually think his touch would have physically hurt. Even my skin hated him, and I could picture my individual cells shrinking away whenever he came near me. On an atomic level, my body didn't believe he was safe.

It didn't matter that we were soon going on a fancy trip to Bali; my brain was trapped in a spin cycle of mental tics, thinking about all the dangers that Southeast Asia might pose. Scrolling through the depths of the Internet, I learned that Indonesian primates were too smart to be safe, too feral to be harmless. That they might galvanize into a carefully organized army and come for my baby. It had happened to other people. It could happen again.

Of course, I didn't tell Petunia any of this, nor did I mention anything to Tom, to whom I was barely speaking. I also didn't tell the therapist I'd been "talking" to once a week since Petunia had told me I needed to get my shit together eight months earlier.

I wasn't lying to said therapist per se, I just wasn't telling her everything. I still believed that saying anything I feared out loud would speak it into being. So, when the therapist asked how my day went, I didn't tell her about the painkillers I took when I felt scared by the overwhelming number of disorganized thoughts cycling through my mind at warp speed. I didn't tell her about how I imagined getting hit by cars while walking with Guy, or about his potential kidnappers, or about the sudden deaths or even the long illnesses my loved ones might soon face, ripping the rug out from under me. Instead, I referred obliquely to "my sadness," desperate for her to read between the lines and give me some kind of framework for how to fix it, a list of things I could cross off and feel a sense of completion or accomplishment.

Every time I crept up to the edge of honesty, I pulled myself back. I feared what was on the other side, not realizing how much worse it was to be stuck in my little self-made purgatory. I spent way too many therapy sessions complaining about Tom's failings, and felt camaraderie when my therapist agreed with me that, yes, he could be frustrating. I'd told her, my voice breaking into raw sobs, how mad I was when he had dropped Guy at the pool a few days before, which still made my hands shake when I thought about it.

Here's what I never said: I'd had that nightmare so many times that when it finally happened in real life, when I finally heard the noise of Guy's little body hitting the ground, it was almost a relief. It was proof that my worry had been justified all along, and I felt vindicated. I never *wanted* anything bad to happen to him: my worst fear was that my negligence, or something I did, would cause his harm. But I took his fall as evidence that I was right and that my fears were a harbinger of worse things still to come.

So, when I stumbled upon a news story about a monkey stealing a baby and carrying it over the rooftops of Jakarta until it fell to its death, I couldn't talk about it. I kept it all inside, fermenting with the rest of the chaotic thoughts in my brain, mixing with the anger and frustration and loneliness already in there, seasoned lightly with painkillers, which I chewed every night before my first drink.

If I admitted out loud that I was mad at my mom, then she might die, and it would be my fault for not loving her with zero conditions. If I articulated how much I hated Tom, it would give him the opening to leave me, and though some days that sounded preferable, it also terrified me, the idea of being that alone. If he left me, then I would be alone with the baby. If I didn't keep everything to myself, the universe would punish me for not being polite and *good enough*. So, I didn't tell anyone about the monkeys or anything else I was scared of, like walking downstairs with my child in my arms, or leaving electrical devices plugged in, or kidnappings, and it was a terrible mind frame in which to fly all the way to Indonesia, a thirty-two-hour trip door to door, with my baby not yet a year old.

The week before I'd left for LA, the therapist and I had agreed that some time in a warm, exotic locale might help my mental state—and might even help my relationship with my husband. I hoped it might help me connect with Guy, too, though, of course, I hadn't admitted to her exactly how detached I felt from him.

Real self-care is standing up for yourself and asking for help when you need it, she'd said, putting down her pen and looking over at me. Her office was nondescript but clean, and she always made sure to have fresh flowers in a small crystal vase near the tissues. I often looked at these floral arrangements as I considered telling her what was really going on.

Totally, I responded. *And that's why I've decided to hire a second life coach and a hypnotherapist and maybe someone to organize my closets. I need help, and I'm not afraid to say it.*

She got a funny expression on her face then, as if unpacking all the layers of that idea would send her back to grad school. Was I really aware that I needed help? I was still seething that Tom had sent me off on my own to Los Angeles, and some days I'd FaceTime her and spiral about that, even though I should have predicted that it would occur.

What I didn't know then was that my rage at Tom was a red herring distracting me from the real issue: a deeper, inner grief that I would have done anything to avoid. My anger at him was a symptom of a much bigger problem. If I focused on how often he chose his work over me and the baby, or how he seemed to fuck up everything I asked of him, I could shield myself from my real despair, which seemed to be getting thornier and darker, pulling me down into the bog. It was so much easier to think about all the ways he'd managed to let me down since I'd found out I was pregnant than to think about whatever was at the core of my own sadness.

DRUGS ARE EXTREMELY ILLEGAL IN INDONESIA, so I left my stash at home. But I woke up the first morning in Bali wishing I had some so badly that I thought about risking it all. I'd been in the midst of a nightmare about dying in a plane crash, and the wild turbulence I'd been screaming about in my sleep turned out to be the rumblings of a destructive earthquake two islands over. When I opened my eyes, the room didn't stop shaking, the overhead fan didn't stop swinging back and forth across my vision, and our bed was rocking.

Tom snored away next to me as I spent the next hour refreshing Twitter to look for emergency warnings about a resulting tsunami. Finally, I shook him awake.

Babe, did you feel that earthquake? I pressed the button next to our bed that opened the wide-slatted teak shutters in our thatched-roof hut. The view on one side was of the perfect, rolling waves. The other windows faced lush, green jungle and the little plunge pool that came with every house on the property. There was a main pool near the restaurant as well. The waves looked like they'd been programmed in a simulation, their rhythm as regular as a metronome. The sun had barely risen, and there were already surfers on the break.

Not really, he said, not opening his eyes. *I thought maybe I heard thunder. Was that the earthquake?* He rolled over to face the door leading to our outdoor bathroom. Even the toilet was outside, along with two sinks, a shower, and a bathtub overlooking the ocean. Yesterday a crow had tried to eat my toothpaste, and, before bed, a giant, shiny beetle perched on the sink's edge, so large I was sure it was self-aware.

It was really big on the Richter scale—like a seven, I said. *And it was only two islands away, on Lombok, so I'm thinking we should be prepared to go to higher ground if there's a tsunami, don't you think?* Tom lifted his head off the crisp, white hotel sheets, his eyes taking me in. I imagined what he saw: my messy hair, a face frazzled from the long plane ride the day before, eyes looking rabidly at my phone for any indication of danger.

Baby, he said slowly, like he was trying to be judicious with his words. *They have warnings and alarms that sound for tsunamis, and we are on the first part of a cliff over the sea. It's very high up. Also, the Richter scale isn't used anymore. Can we go back to sleep now?* His nonchalance annoyed me. I was the only person who cared enough to be vigilant about this family, and the pressure of doing that alone felt massive.

I need you to listen to me, I continued. *Guy cannot walk, let alone run. Can we at least get dressed and go to breakfast, so that we can be ready if we need to move quickly?* I was already pushing apart the mosquito net, walking to the outdoor bathroom to brush my teeth. I heard Tom take a deep breath and follow me.

I couldn't believe the humidity when I pushed open the door, and it was barely seven in the morning. The air was thick and heavy, sliced by bright sunshine, already hot enough to sweat in the shade, like getting into a steaming bath. The dazzling sun made me a little disoriented, like my brain was crooked in my skull for a second. After throwing on my bikini and splashing my face with water, I went into the other bedroom to check on Sharon and Guy. They were awake, dressed in swimsuits, and Guy was drinking a bottle, his little ankles crossed like a grown-up. He smiled at me when I walked in.

Good morning, how did you sleep? Sharon asked me. *Did you feel that earthquake? Felt like we were on a ride at Disneyland*, she said. Immediately, I felt a little silly being worried about a tsunami. If Sharon wasn't worried, then maybe I didn't need to be.

Want to go to breakfast? I asked her as she was putting sunblock on Guy, inspecting him as she rubbed it in.

Sorry, she said after a pause. *I just noticed he has some bug bites, or a rash or something. It's all over his back.* I went over to look. He didn't seem bothered by the welts. *You should take a picture and send it to his doctor.*

You think? I asked. *Should I be freaked out?* The fact that Sharon was being cautious made me a little distressed. I watched her pull a sunproof shirt over his tiny body, covering a mottled splotch of red bumps.

Just email the doctor. He can recommend an ointment or something. We can talk to the hotel about a medic visit if we want. We left our hut and went to find the restaurant.

For those first few days, Tom would go off to surf while Sharon and I lazed around at the house. I spent most days swimming in our little pool, the humidity almost too much to bear otherwise. I'd get out of the water, and my hair wouldn't dry completely for hours and hours, sometimes staying wet from when I went to sleep at night until I woke up in the morning. I'd go to breakfast with it still so damp that it looked like I'd put oil in it.

I wonder if this was really all I needed, I thought to myself on day five as I bounced in the shallow end, Guy giggling every time I dunked him to his neck. His legs were wrapped around my body, and he was holding on with his arms for dear life.

When Sharon screamed, I thought she must have been afraid Guy was going to slip, or maybe she'd been stung by a bee. But then I heard a splash and whipped my head around. A monkey's red butt was visible above the waterline. Then his head popped up, and he bared his teeth at me, hissing, showing long fangs on the top of either side of his mouth. He started swimming straight for us.

I scrambled my way out of the pool, clutching Guy to my chest desperately, my scream stuck in my throat. The monkey was paddling toward me with the speed of ten Michael Phelpses. From the corner of my eye, I saw another one scamper across a tree branch and drop down onto our patio. I think it was the first one's girlfriend–he seemed so relaxed to see her in his territory. I half tripped up the steps, then sprinted onto our porch, my arms squeezed hard around my baby.

Sharon and I ran inside, where we watched the monkeys through the teak slats of our windows. One grabbed my watermelon juice, looked right at me, and screeched. He chugged the remains and then threw the glass to the ground. It felt personal. I called the concierge and told him I was afraid for my child's life; monkeys were attacking us and had run us out of the pool. He said he'd send security.

Within a minute, two men showed up with slingshots, slapping the rubber bands against their handles. The minute the monkeys heard that noise, they scuttled off into the jungle brush.

Take these slingshots, they instructed me. *Make little piles of rocks around your house and leave them in strategic places. Keep the slingshot on you at all times. If you need to, hit the monkeys with the rocks. They will run.*

I stared at them, probably ashen white under my tan. I felt like this was how the story of the stolen baby probably started. For the next two weeks, while Tom surfed and sunned, I vowed to stay outside our front door with a slingshot while Guy took his two-hour midday nap, to make sure no monkey opened the door or slipped through the slats of the teak shutters. I visualized their thin monkey arms reaching through, twisting the knob of the door open, letting themselves in.

The next morning, Guy's rash got worse, despite the cortisone cream. I had the bumps, too, and then a few days later, so did Tom. They were itchy and angry, hard and throbbing; not just irritated, swollen skin the way a mosquito bite would be, but so big that the skin around them was pulled taut, strained and shiny. Tom seemed unconcerned, dabbing himself with cortisone every time he got out of the water. Guy's doctor had said not to be worried unless Guy got a fever. But within a few days, the bumps had turned bright red, like from poison ivy.

Come surf with me, Tom urged me. *You're all the way around the world, wasting the best part of every day sitting in front of Guy's door on monkey watch. You're being irrational. You have to come down to the beach with me.* It frustrated me that he didn't take my fear more seriously. The ocean looked chaotic and stormy, big waves coming in at all angles, crashing against one another like Poseidon was having a war underneath.

Why do I have to have fight with you ten times for you to listen to me? I asked Tom. *Besides, it's pouring rain.*

It's totally surfable, he said, ignoring my question. *It's really nice and really warm. Come on, you'll like it. We can spend some time together, out in nature. It's so lush in the water here that when you paddle on the board, you can feel little fish swim between your fingers. It's teeming with life. It's paradise.*

Fine, fine, fine, I said, pulling a rash guard over my head. *The water looks . . . sharky. If I go under and don't come back up, it will be your fault.* I looked out at the gray, churning mess of a sea and started walking toward the door.

Down at the beach, Tom gave me his surfboard: a long, wide one; slow but stable and balanced. I strapped the leash onto my ankle and watched him grab a short board, too fast and scary for me to try. We paddled next to each other, and when we got out past a break, we sat up and watched the sets of waves come in from out at sea.

I'm proud of you for getting out here, Tom said. I thought of my therapist. I could already imagine the fantasy version of this trip I would spin for her: the tropical air and the waves, how much I loved surfing. *I know this trip is a bit complicated*, Tom continued, *traveling with a kid and all, and you have a lot going on. I just want you to know things are going to be okay. I really believe that.* He was looking out at the horizon, watching for a good wave, not making eye contact with me. Fat, warm raindrops made a calming, gentle noise all around us, and caused tiny rainbows to dance on top of the water.

Take this wave, Tom said. *Turn your board! This is a good one!* I worked my legs like an eggbeater and started paddling hard toward the beach. I looked back over my shoulder for a second, and, at just the right moment, I popped myself up onto my feet, my knees angled toward each other, hands out to the sides. I was skimming the water so fast I started laughing—and then I felt a slam. I'd been too far forward, or maybe too far back. Off the board I went, plunging into the frothy water. I tried to paddle up to the top to take a gasp of air, but I got knocked under by another wave.

I tried to let myself be loose, to suspend in the water and give in to my own buoyancy. I tried to just listen to the ocean in my ears, pretend I was a mermaid, comfortable in the sea, unfazed by its power. *Maybe this is how I die,* I thought for a second, surrounded by ocean bubbles, not a fish in sight, all the sharks hiding deep down in the gray water. By the time I surfaced, whatever air left in my lungs lifting me up, I'd swallowed a giant mouthful of salt water and felt the sting of my sand-skinned knees starting to bleed. I towed my board onto the beach and waved at Tom. I was done here. One bad wave felt like enough.

. . .

YOU OKAY? *You look like a drowned rat, but if rats had long hair and really good tans,* Sharon said when I walked back up to our bungalow. She was sitting outside under the eaves of our little front porch with a slingshot next to her and a small pile of rocks.

I think I swallowed about a gallon of salt water. I'm gonna rinse off and lay down for a little. I'm not doing great. Maybe it was anxiety, or maybe it was too much fruit, but my stomach hurt. It was bloated and hard to the touch.

I rinsed off in my outdoor shower, rain sprinkling around me, and climbed into my cool sheets. The weather kept the room dark, and the fan above my bed was whirring, cooling my damp skin. Guy was snoring almost imperceptibly across the room in his crib, and I let the rhythm of it lull me into a doze. When I woke up, the pain in my stomach was disorienting. It was like it had been filled with something on fire. I sat up to get myself out of bed, and my nausea was so bad that it made me dizzy. I started to feel sweat at my temples and in my hairline. I fell back down onto my back, bouncing on the mattress. And that's when it happened.

I turned on my side and threw up all over myself, and the force of my gagging and the ensuing projectile spew of puke released something unholy in me. It was like the power of that vomiting was too strong for me to control, the thrust of it rendering all other bodily functions faulty. I was using so much muscular force to throw up that I couldn't do anything else, couldn't contract other muscles or do anything useful. And before I knew how to stop it, I'd shit the bed.

Shit is not the right word. There was nothing solid about it. Nothing fecal, even. It was just liquid, an endless stream of clearish liquid squirting out of either side of me. The room smelled putrid, and as soon as I could stand, the nausea retreating for a minute, I pulled all the sheets into a ball and put them outside, then immediately went to the shower, where another wave hit me. I had to sit on the floor and puke down the drain, my head feeling like it would burst from the pressure of all the gagging. I'm sure I was leaking out of my ass at the same time, but I couldn't even tell. All I could think about was how I would get to the phone to call a doctor. Was I going to survive my surf session only to die here in my shower?

Babe? You in here? I heard a voice call through the dark room. For a second I thought I'd imagined it. *It smells insane. Do we need to empty the trash?*

Tom came in to find me in the bathroom curled up on the floor. *Oh my God, are you okay?* He seemed genuinely concerned. I must have looked as scared as I felt. *I'm going to call the hotel doctor*, he said. I put my cheek against the cool stones of the shower wall and closed my eyes. Soon Tom was back.

The doctor is coming, but he won't be here for an hour. He's coming from another town. Anything I can do for you? I felt completely helpless and weak.

Not really? I ended my sentence with a question mark because I didn't know what to ask for. Nothing was going to make me feel better, and I was too frail and wrecked to think about it. I either wanted him to know what I needed, or I wanted him to go away. The energy of having to tell him overwhelmed me.

Just go check on Sharon and Guy, I said. *I don't want Guy anywhere they could get to him. They might reach between the slats of the shutters, so he can't be left alone, even if he's sleeping.*

I could tell I was blabbering, spilling out all the fears I'd been trying to keep inside, and I knew that was risky, but it was better than not saying any of it out loud and something going wrong. If I wasn't well enough to be vigilant, I needed someone to know what to look for.

Always have slingshots nearby. If the hotel seems open to it, maybe you should ask for a gun? What are gun laws like here? Tom looked at me like I was delirious. *I'm telling you, they are vicious,*

I insisted. *I saw it in the pool. They tried to come for me and take him.* I tried to make my voice louder so he'd know how bad it had been, but the effort made me dizzy.

Just let the water soothe you, Tom said. His face was hard to read. *I'm going to have housekeeping put new sheets on the bed, and then I think you should sleep until the doctor comes.*

Thank you, I said weakly, unsure precisely what I was thanking him for.

Hours later, when the doctor arrived, Tom was nowhere to be found. I still hadn't left the shower. I hadn't stopped spewing liquids from my body. A nurse came in and helped me up, my legs trembling. He laid me in the newly made bed on top of a towel and covered me with a sheet, like a cadaver.

Have you been drinking unfiltered water or have you had any ice? asked the nurse. The doctor himself did not speak English, but the nurse translated for him.

No, of course not, I said. *Only bottled water.* I even used bottled water to brush my teeth. The doctor nodded.

Have you been swimming and swallowed salt water? I recalled surfing earlier when I'd been pinned down under the waves.

I swallowed some earlier, at the beach here, when I was surfing. I nodded toward the water below the hotel.

When it storms like it has today, he said, *if gutters overflow, a lot of raw sewage can flood into the water at that beach. I imagine you swallowed that.*

The thought made me feel worse; more grossed out for myself. *I can give you an IV of antiemetic medicine we give to cancer patients to control your nausea, and antibiotics. And charcoal pills. But this most likely won't let up for several days. Perhaps a week. Or a month. You should drink electrolyte drinks and rest. It's all you can do.* I wanted to cry as the doctor started setting up a hanging bag for the IV.

I'm really scared of needles, I said. *Do you mind if I just call my husband?* I reached for the phone next to my bed. I sent off a text to Tom and then called him. His phone rang and rang. *I'm so scared of IVs*, I said, my voice pleading. *Is there any other way to do this?* I thought about the giant needle they'd given me at the hospital when I was in labor. *Can the anti-nausea meds be swallowed?*

The nurse and the doctor consulted. *We can give it to you in a shot in your buttock. It won't be as effective, and we should come back tomorrow to do it again, but it's the only other way.* I closed my eyes and grimaced as the shot went in.

All done, said the nurse. *Also, I noticed your bug bites, and on your child as well.* They were all over Guy's face at this point, swelling his left ear in particular. *I don't know the name of the insect in English, so I wrote down the species. But you should keep applying cortisone cream. You may need an oral antihistamine if they don't improve.* I looked at his note. *Cimex lectularius.* I quickly googled it on my phone: bedbugs. We had fucking bedbugs.

Thank you, doctor. Thank you both so much, I said. *I can already feel the nausea receding.* I really could. I don't know if it was a placebo effect or real, but the icky sweatiness had gone away. They said they'd be back tomorrow and left. I truly did not know what to do. I peeled back the bedsheets, and the mattress was clean. Where the hell had we gotten bedbugs?

When Tom finally came back at dinnertime, I was waiting for him in bed, deflated.

Why are there all those empty Pocari Sweat bottles at the front door? he asked, looking clueless and very tan.

Oh, that's *your question?* I started crying. *I shit and puked my brains out today, all day, and as soon as the anti-nausea shot wears off, it's going to start again. My butthole burns, and we have bedbugs. But not from these beds. We have to burn all our clothes. The hotel brought me electrolyte water and left it at the door, and because you weren't here to let them in, the monkeys got to the water. Every single bottle was broken into and drained before I* had a single sip. *Sharon found it there when she got back from lunch. This is all your fault*, I told him, each sob snowballing into the next. *You made me surf. You made me come here. You left me all day.*

I'm sorry, he said. *What can I do to help you?* I wanted to smack him, but I didn't have the energy to raise my arm.

Can you just order dinner for Sharon? She's giving Guy his bath. Just order her some fish? He went to call room service, and I rolled over, letting my tears spill onto the pillow. I felt miserable. Why did I have to tell him to order food for Sharon? Why couldn't he think of these things before I had to think of them?

When Sharon's food arrived, she came into our room to check on me. *Your dumbass husband ordered me a steak, even though he knows I eat only fish. I'll live, but why can't he do shit right?* I couldn't have agreed more.

Tom! I shouted. He came into the room in a towel. *Didn't I tell you to order Sharon fish?* He looked at us and blinked. *Oh, I forgot*, he said. *I just ordered whatever.*

She was caring for our child, and you had one tiny little job to do. Sharon doesn't eat steak. She's lived with us for months now. You know that. Tom looked sheepish, and Sharon was smiling.

Don't you worry, Tom Sachs, I'm gonna leave now so your wife can let off some steam. I hope it ends well for you. But if she murders you, I'll visit her in prison, don't worry. She left to go back to her bedroom. Tom stood there in his towel, fresh from the sea, showered and freckled. *How are you feeling?* he asked softly.

I am feeling . . . edgy. Crispy. Is that even a word that makes sense? It's just . . . exactly how I feel. Like I could flake off into little crumbles if someone touched me. I sat up taller in bed, my voice calm, slightly dizzy.

I'm really sorry I ordered the wrong thing. I know that was dumb. But that is fixable. He walked toward me and sat on the edge of the bed, not touching me.

Nothing is fixable, I said. *What are you talking about?*

I looked at him, amazed at the level of idiocy from a man who was otherwise so brilliant and forward-thinking, an iconoclast who supposedly loved me. The man who took my tampon out with his teeth. The man who told me to be honest with him about my body, who held my leg while I pushed his child out of my vagina, the man I'd spent days with under our white comforter, talking about our futures. I was shocked at how little he seemed to care when I needed him to care the most. *Everything's your fault*, I repeated tearfully.

Sarah. I took a trip I had to do for work and turned it into a luxury Balinese vacation for our family. I called the doctor for you. I don't know how else to support you. I don't know what I'm doing wrong. I don't even know what I'm doing right! He seemed genuinely confused, and that made me so mad because wasn't it obvious? Wasn't it so damn obvious? He couldn't even order fish. The hate I felt for this man, my God.

You know, there were days you didn't even ask me, "Hi, Sarah, how are you doing today? How do you feel today? How is your pussy today, Sarah, since it just squeezed *out my child?" Entire days! I kept a tally. How was I supposed to recover mentally or physically when no one cared about my mental and physical state? Well, you win, because I didn't recover. Nothing is right. From my hips to my belly to my brain to my hair, nothing is right.* I pulled at my hair, roughed it up to show him how frenzied I felt.

Tom took big sigh, let his shoulders fall, and stared at the ground. *I hear you, Sarah. I really do.* He stood up and took off his towel, inching closer to me on the bed. I could hear frogs and insects making their bedtime noises outside, croaking and buzzing in an odd melodic song, almost like they were reading the same sheet music. *I'm sorry that I haven't done enough. And I can tell you are really, really not okay. But I am out of ideas.* Tom hung his head and put it in his hands for a minute. *Do you want me to leave you? I don't mean that in a threatening way. But would it be easier for you if I moved out for a while?* I gasped violently, like someone had just dumped a bucket of water on my head. In my peripheral vision, I could see the red eyes of a thousand monkeys flashing.

You lazy motherfucker. You would *offer that.* My voice was ice cold. My anger felt completely justified. I'd been right. His goal all along had been to get out of our marriage. He had never been committed to me or to Guy. He'd clearly orchestrated this whole trip as a ruse or some sort of exit strategy to get away from me. Maybe there weren't really any monkeys at all. Maybe they were all robot puppets, some marionette art project of Tom's whose sole purpose was to drive me mad. When he'd gone right back to work, and I'd read it as benign negligence from a man who didn't know better, I'd been wrong. It had been a strategy. *You* would *take the easy way out, leave me high and dry with a baby. What is it, you already have a girlfriend, and she hates babies? I'm not pretty enough for you?* My voice was wobbling. It made me sick to think of him with someone else, while I was at home, depressed and trapped with his baby.

No, Sarah, no. That's not what I'm saying. I'm saying this isn't sustainable the way it is. You're miserable. And you have to be happy. For you and for Guy, you have to be happy. You owe it to yourself. He reached out to grasp my hands with his.

Right, sure. You just really want to selflessly fuck other people until I kill myself.

Jesus, Sarah. Kill yourself? I have not fucked a single person aside from you in this relationship, ever. I love you. And I'm deeply *concerned.* He sounded shocked, which enraged me.

Deeply concerned? I laughed loudly, my best Julia Roberts impression. I felt crazed, almost under a spell. *You know what, Tom? Get out.*

What?

Right now. Go sleep on a pool chair for all I care. Just get the fuck out! I screamed and yanked my hands from under his. I didn't care if Guy woke up, or the hotel thought I was being murdered, or if Tom cried or told his friends I was nuts or said I was a bad mom. I didn't care about any of that anymore.

I wanted the anger to shoot out of my body the same way the vomit was spewing from my throat—my body rejecting that which threatened to harm me. I wanted to be free of everything that trapped me. I wanted to escape my own self, to float somewhere else, leave Guy with Sharon, where I knew nothing bad could ever happen to him. She loved him the way I couldn't, and at least I had that. Tom, on the other hand—I wanted to leave Tom for dead outside in the Balinese jungle. I wanted my screams to summon the monkeys and for them to eat Tom in the night, rip off his face while he was still alive.

Go sleep at the pool! I screamed again.

Tom looked at me, and he had this expression on his face that was so sad—sad and sorry for me. He grabbed clothes and left the room. I didn't care where he went.

I was embarrassed. I was messy and ashamed of it; a horrible person, a nasty, ungrateful bitch, a miserable, sad, ugly woman. I was right and I was justified, and I was wrong, and I was disgusting. I was an empty shell in every way, devoid of anything lovable. I was a mother with no inklings of maternal sense and a wife who wanted her husband dead and a human who wanted not to exist. I was everything bad and nothing good, and the only thing that could erase it was me disappearing from this life.

Guy deserved better than me. He deserved to be loved properly by everyone who knew him, and I was so mad at myself for not knowing how to do that. Yah, okay, I'd tried. I'd done everything anyone had recommended. I'd done yoga and acupuncture and cardio, gotten manicures, and I'd meditated and I'd journaled and gone to therapy, but after months and months of all of it, I showed no improvement. There was no progress. I was still so unhappy, in such a dark hole of torment, I could see no way out. Without happiness, I could not love Guy. And without loving Guy, how could I be happy? It wasn't that I wanted to die; it was that I didn't care if I lived or died, because it wasn't right for him that his mother be this way.

I thought about how in first grade, this girl named Janice Thockman would get so angry that she'd throw fits and make herself faint or puke. I remember the smell of her vomit covered in the chemical powder meant to dry it up on the classroom carpet. The teachers had her stand outside on the playground and scream when she felt a fit coming on. I could picture her out there clearly—an image that's kind of funny now that I thought back on it. She was wearing her Brownies uniform: the brown knee socks and the khaki skirt, topped off with her thick, blonde ponytail, like corn silk, badges for sewing and pottery and cooking stitched proudly on her wide sash. She stood outside the classroom door, in the middle of the playground in our school's courtyard, and we all watched her from our desks, pencils hovering over blue-lined penmanship paper. She'd stand out there in the cold and scream. She was like a cartoon with the noise turned off: a little farm girl, thick through the legs, knees together and saddle shoes pointed apart, screaming and screaming into stillness.

This way of being was untenable; this amount of anger eating away at me was unsustainable. I needed a new husband, a new house, a new job. Maybe I'd move home to Indiana. Or to LA. Maybe I'd commit myself to a long-stay mental institution in Austria, the ones where they put you to sleep for two months, and you wake up thin and refreshed, like in *Valley of the Dolls*. Maybe I'd get a second therapist. Or a third one. I honestly didn't know what else to do that I hadn't tried, but something had to give. I had to change my entire life. Because otherwise I was going to die.

11

Brain Switch

New York
September 2018

MY YOUNG, CHIC GENERAL PRACTITIONER looked at me across her big white desk, a Hermès scarf tied around her blown-out hair.

So, she said, *catch me up! I haven't seen you since you had the baby.* A large vase of beautiful pink peonies sat on the desk between us. My dad once told me that peonies smell so sweet that ants are attracted to their secretions. The weight of the ants is just heavy enough on the petals to open up the flowers so that their surface area absorbs more sun. She moved the vase slightly so that she could look right at me.

My baby will be a year old soon, hard to believe. I had a boy. I tried to sound enthusiastic enough so that she wouldn't ask me more questions. *We recently got back from Indonesia, which is why I'm here. I got sick from dirty water, and I'm not shitting the bed anymore, at least, but I'm nauseous pretty much all the time.*

Her hands were poised above her keyboard, ready to type. On her left hand, a fat wedding ring caught the light, reflecting miniature prisms on her impeccable white lab coat. *I've lost almost all my baby weight because of it, which is great, and I never thought I'd say this, but now I just want my appetite back.*

We gotta get you well, she said. *I'm just gonna ask you some general questions, get us up-to-date in your record. How's work?*

I'm so lucky, I said, my voice full of smooth gratitude. *I'm paid on commission, so I just sort of make my own hours, do my own thing. It's totally fine. I don't spend so much time in the office.* She nodded, typing some notes.

And how are things at home? She was still smiling.

I'm honestly just here because my stomach hurts, I said.

Even though she'd asked, talking about Tom sounded too depressing to go there. For the last week in Bali, we'd walked around each other quietly, like we were both too bruised to be anything but careful, the energy between us more sad and silent than angry, even though I had a laundry list of things I was mad about. I knew I'd been an asshole, making him sleep on a pool chair and all, but I also knew I was right to be furious at him. I knew it in my heart, and I wasn't going to let any doctor talk me out of my God-given right to hate that fucker.

I looked around, not wanting to meet her eyes, and noticed a framed photo on a bookshelf with three children in it. They were beautiful, dressed in matching clothes, grinning from ear to ear. It was obvious they were happy.

Your kids are so cute, I said, nodding toward the frame.

It gets easier as they get older. I keep a million plates in the air. My work schedule is so grueling, and my husband will text me and ask me something like what to eat for lunch. I love the man, but it doesn't even occur to him . . . She trailed off, writing something on a piece of paper. *Sorry–I just remembered he has shirts at the dry cleaner. See! I do it to myself, almost.*

I was taken aback by her openness and forced myself to look right at her. No one, no doctor, no professional, no friend, even, had articulated this same frustration so eloquently.

To be honest, my husband drives me insane, I said. *I don't even want to fuck him, or anyone. Maybe this is TMI, but I don't even masturbate.* She looked up from her notes as I tucked my hair behind my ear nervously.

This is a doctor's office. There is no such thing as TMI, she said. *I had a man in here earlier ask me if he could give himself a boner so he could show me that his penis gets crooked sometimes.* She shook her head. *So please, don't worry about anything you tell me.*

I looked at her and thought back to how that wave had pinned me down in Indonesia, forcing dirty seawater down my throat. If I was being honest with myself, I'd considered letting it hold me under. And later, when I was so alone on the shower floor, waiting for a doctor, or when I'd been so scared of the monkeys, I'd wondered if I'd made the wrong decision by fighting up to the surface. I thought back to all the days I sat at my kitchen table, staring out the window, wondering how to slip away from my life. I thought back to all the taxis, bodegas, and museums in which I'd broken down into sobs, unable to stop myself from a sadness that felt like grief. I thought back to the times I had heard Guy crying when he wasn't or saw him falling when he hadn't. I thought about how ferociously I resented Tom, how angry his every move made me—how I couldn't see the good in him or in us. Everything seemed heightened, like an endless pump of cortisol. I wasn't sure if any of this would have been diagnosed as psychosis, or anything close to suicidal ideation, but it did all feel strangely, existentially final. And some little voice, somewhere in my deranged head, told me not to ruin the opportunity to be honest with someone who could help me, who was being frank with me, who seemed to get it.

The week my kid was born, the exposé came out about Harvey Weinstein in the Times, I said, thinking about something I'd been going over in my head for a while but still hadn't discussed with my therapist. *And Donald Trump was in office, and here I was holding this little boy in my arms.* I mimed cradling a baby, remembering the disconnect I'd felt as I looked down at that little lump. *Even the little one, he was just using me for food and, like, a chance at survival. And I was just thinking to myself, everything bad in my life is because of entitled, shitty men. Not that my husband is*

Harvey Weinstein or Donald Trump, but they all exist on the same spectrum, you know? Just by virtue of being men. And I haven't really been able to get rid of that feeling. I resent them all. Not the baby–he deserves better than that. But all the grown ones, all the jerks I dated in my twenties, my husband. I wish I could just ditch them all; ditch the memories of them, too. But they're hooked in my brain like a glioblastoma.

I thought about this guy I'd gone out with in my early twenties before I met Tom, the one I called the Wolf. I thought of him as an animal; it made it easier to examine what happened if I categorized him that way, wild heat emanating from his soft belly, covered in silky fur. I remembered how his sharp eyes dilated when he saw me nude for the first time, as if suddenly entranced by the vulnerability of his prey, and I would never forget the sound of his howlish laugh. The first time I heard it, I hadn't known it was coming from a ferocious beast. I thought it was deep and loud and savage because he found me funny.

I was practically a kid, still in college, studying cultural theory in Paris, and he was an artist who did something with Victorian-era machines. I'd met him in a club in New York when I'd been there on my spring break. I hadn't thought about him again until his text popped up on my phone a few months later, back in my Parisian apartment. It read that he was visiting and remembered I lived there. Then he asked me if I wanted to have dinner.

When we arrived at the restaurant, he asked the hostess for a table in broken French. She told him they didn't have any. I asked again, this time in much better French, and she said she'd double-check. She glanced at her book for a second and ushered us to a small booth, where we sat across from each other on velvet banquettes, and I told myself not to be embarrassed at how sweaty I'd gotten on the walk and to just try to laugh and have fun. I ordered champagne, and he ordered a whiskey. He ordered beef tartare as his dinner; I had the Dover sole.

Whenever I eat raw meat like this, I can feel the blood course through my veins. It almost makes me a different person, he said with a half-smile. *I only do it in Paris.* I sipped my champagne, annoyed that it was in a flute and not a coupe glass. I hated my nose and was ashamed every time it bumped the crystal rim. I wondered if he noticed. He told me he lived in a loft in SoHo, collected photography books, and spoke Spanish.

Do you speak Spanish as well as you speak French? I asked. He laughed.

You're pretty ballsy for someone so young, he replied. *Where'd you get all your strong ideas?*

Honestly, I don't know. I shrugged. *Should we go get ice cream?* I'd had so many glasses of champagne by that point that I could almost see double, and when I was very drunk, I craved ice cream sundaes, which are excellent in Paris, where they caramelize the nuts. He flagged the waiter for the check, and when he plonked down his credit card, I made sure to look at his last name. I'd made it this far into the date without knowing, but I wanted to google him when I got home. *Alex Tolst.*

The minute we got into the taxi, he leaned in to kiss me, and I was scared that the chalky taste in my mouth meant all that champagne had given me bad breath. He didn't seem to mind, continuing to make out with me for the whole drive, drunk and sloppy. The taxi driver even turned around at one stoplight and told us to stop–I think he thought we were fucking or something–and Alex apologized very seriously in his terrible French, which made me giggle. He didn't seem to have any idea how awful he sounded to these people. He took me to the George V Hotel, into the bar off the lobby, all chandeliers and Aubusson carpets, small tables with lamps on each. As we walked in, he waved his hand.

Monsieur! he announced in a ridiculous accent. *An ice cream sundae pour mademoiselle!* I kept giggling.

We had another dinner, and another and another. He took me swimming in his hotel pool. We got massages on Sunday, and he walked me home from school on Monday. On Tuesday I went to one of the big department stores, a real Émile Zola place, and splurged on a pretty set of new silk underwear, in pale blue, for his last night. We spent it in his hotel bed, having red wine and baguettes with cheese for dinner, making out between bites.

I wasn't surprised when he called me the next week from New York to chat. And I still wasn't surprised when, a few weeks after that, I got to New York for a quick visit to see friends and he wanted to meet me that night. I picked out my vintage minidress carefully and put little rhinestone clips, which I'd bought by the dozen from French pharmacies, in my hair.

When I walked into the bar with my girlfriends, I saw him right away in the first room and ran up to hug him.

Hey, baby, he said. He didn't kiss me. *Can you lay low for a little? My fiancée is here.* I took a step backward like I'd been tased.

You have a fiancée? I said it almost like I was trying to understand it, not like I was trying to get him to confirm what he'd already told me. I almost muttered it to myself. I don't even think I was looking at him. A girl sidled up to him and ducked under his arm, leaning over the bar to order a drink. She turned around and nuzzled into him.

Sarah, meet Anna, my fiancée, he said. He sounded happy to introduce us, like he was connecting two people who might like each other and was pleased to be the matchmaker.

So nice to meet you! I said. I tried to be cheerful and not let on how shocked I was. She looked at me icily, or maybe I was imagining it. I wanted to say to her, *Your instincts are right! Your fiancée took me on ten dates last month, and asked me to sleep with him, and touched my boobs, and went down on me while I watched in the mirror over the armoire in his fancy hotel room.*

But I just smiled and backed away slowly. I wanted to tell her I hadn't known about her. Instead, I took another step back, bumping into my friend.

We gotta get out of here, I said. *The fucking guy from Paris is engaged.*

THAT'S JUST WHAT DATING had been like when I moved back to New York, for me and for all my friends, too—until I'd met Tom. It was so nice to feel like a relationship was solid and real, with a good person. It had been a relief to finally feel cared for. Of course, there were the random flirtatious texts; the occasional *You've never looked better* to an ex; or the relationships with women that weren't necessarily coy in content, but that he never mentioned to me, so that they felt like tiny lies of omission. But I was too head over heels to let myself focus on those small, common betrayals—which I considered standard male entitlements— or to count them as they added up over the years. My anxiety that I didn't deserve better kept me from telling him truthfully and forcefully just how much those communiqués hurt me. What I *didn't* say was that I'd leave him if they continued. I was too afraid to set that boundary.

By the time Guy was born, the dark voices in my head had burgeoned into a full-blown fear that if I said anything at all, the worst-case scenario would happen: by naming a worry, I'd guarantee its most catastrophic version. What if I said something to Tom about his stupid texts, and it caused him to leave me forever? What if we got into a fight, he stormed out of the house, had a heart attack, and died? I truly believed that I would speak my worst anxieties into existence through some sort of warped wish fulfillment. So, I stayed silent.

Now I couldn't stop asking myself: How different was Tom, really, from the engaged wolf? Was this association justified, or amplified by my unhinged state of mind? I was going from zero to sixty about absolutely everything, and I couldn't tell if lumping the two of them in the same camp–the Club of Men I Hate–was rational or some form of PTSD.

What's the experience like for you of playing with your baby? the doctor asked, jolting me out of my reverie.

I took a deep breath. I could either lie and tell her how amazing it was, or I could finally come clean. My current therapist had never asked me this exact question, but even if she had, I probably would have spoken in euphemisms and canned responses copied from other moms I knew. I was startled by how the doctor's questions felt so personal, like she was reading my brain instead of a form.

I make myself go into his nursery for fifteen minutes a couple of times a day, and I dread it so much that I put it off until it can't wait another second. Then I go in there and spend the whole time wanting to leave. My mind feels blank when I'm with the baby. My hands were trembling a little, and I put them in my lap.

I think you're in crisis mode, she said, like it was the simplest thing in the world. In fact, I was stunned by the ease with which she named distress. She moved the laptop over and folded her hands in front of her, clasped her slender fingers on the desk while she looked at me. *Have you told anyone else any of this? Your therapist, if you have one?*

Of course I have a therapist . . . I trailed off, thinking about how to explain my relationship with my therapist. *But I haven't said any of this, no. I guess I've thought about it in my head, but the kinds of questions they ask you at the ob-gyn's office and stuff just haven't really compelled authentic answers, or something. It's all like, "Are you happy? Circle one through ten." And I'm, like, no, but have I ever really been happy? And wouldn't it be the definition of insane to be happy when you're carrying the dead weight of an annoying husband and a baby you don't connect with, and the details of your life make you want to disappear?* I leaned my head against my fist, my elbow propped on the desk. *I may get divorced,* I explained. *But I think it could be for the best, and I'll be okay.* I was trying to make myself okay with this as an outcome, though I'm sure my voice didn't sound confident.

She shook her head. *No, no. You can't fight this alone. I don't care what your answers to the ob-gyn's questions are. Look, they work from a standardized scale, and that scale exists for a reason, and some people's symptoms cleave to it exactly. But this condition is not a one-size-fits-all thing. I think it's time for science to help you lift some of this anxiety and sadness off you.* She stood up and grabbed a blood pressure cuff from a little table behind her and walked around the desk to put it on me. *I just want to take some vitals before you get undressed in the other room,* she said.

Okay, I said, extending my arm.

I'm going to write you a prescription for a low dose of antidepressants, she said. *We can start with Zoloft. If you don't like how it feels, we can try another one. There's many, many options on the market.* She took out a piece of paper and a pen and started drawing a diagram. *I'm going to show you what they do to your brain, how they help.*

She finished her sketch, spinning it around toward me. She'd labeled the brain's synapses with tiny neurons going between them, like trains carrying cargo. It looked like an illustration in a high school biology textbook.

But you should talk to your therapist, because you're going to blow up your life if you stay angry. Rage is how we hide other, realer emotions. So, write down everything you are feeling. It's all valid. When you dissolve some of this anger, you can address it rationally. But let the medicine help you. I promise it's going to be really, really effective. I nodded. I decided to trust her because, honestly, it was my last-ditch effort before going to a psych ward. In therapy, I'd mostly ranted and complained about daily annoyances or talked about pop culture, or the ballet, keeping the worst bits of myself buried, afraid to share them, afraid to say I was hallucinating or that I hated my baby. To Augusta and Petunia, I tried to come clean, but certain things felt impossible to say. I decided to take the pills for a few months and see how I felt.

Go home and write down a list of things you haven't told your therapist, she advised. *Write down all the reasons you're angry. When you're done, start the pills. And then go to therapy and tell her everything. If she doesn't get it, find a new therapist. Call me anytime you need me, okay?* She ushered me into an exam room. *The nurse will be in shortly.*

IN MY TAXI BACK DOWNTOWN, I thought back to the Wolf. Months after I'd found out he was engaged, I was in the same bar with the same friends, very late, maybe three in the morning. I was back living in Manhattan and had started working in the art world. I went out every night, always looking for the next party. He saw me first, sitting on a sofa with a friend in the dark haze. It was swirling with the smoke of everyone's end-of-the-night cigarettes, and I could see their embers glowing, dotting the room.

Sarah, where have you been? I haven't seen you in forever, the Wolf said. He sat himself on the arm of my couch and looked down at me, as if nothing had ever happened. I looked up at him slowly, sipping my vodka soda through my straw, my lashes heavy. I felt my eyelids close.

Aren't you engaged? I said, doing my best impression of a bitch who takes no shit. He looked stricken.

I'm sorry, you're right. That was really messed up. He put his hands up to his face and pushed on his temples, wincing. I sipped more of my drink. *We were broken up when I was in Paris, but then she talked me into it when I got back, and I should have just been straight with you. But it's over now. Can we get out of here so I can apologize to you somewhere without cigarette smoke and loud music?*

I stood up, woozy from alcohol. I'd been drinking for hours, since ten or eleven o'clock. I couldn't remember if I'd done drugs or not. I walked outside with him, shivering a little in the early-morning air.

The doorman of the bar was standing at the entrance as we walked out. He was finishing a cigarette, waiting for his shift to end. He nodded at me. He was a Frenchman, and we chatted every time I came in. As Alex walked into the street to hail a cab, I saw him clock who I was leaving with, and he pulled me aside. *Il est un loup*, he said under his breath—a warning: *That man is a wolf.* I tittered. I could handle a wolf. I already knew him. I had already seen what I thought were his teeth. What was the worst he could do?

I got in the taxi. Even if I'd been afraid, I wouldn't have known how to back out of the plan, my fear of being impolite so deeply embedded that I couldn't imagine an excuse believable enough to recuse myself. "I changed my mind" didn't seem good enough. So, yes, I went willingly to his den.

From the minute I walked into his apartment, everything felt different. He seemed like a stranger. Or maybe I was too drunk, so the world was already upside down. It was just so dark in there; I couldn't get my bearings. Before I knew it, we were in a room at the back of the loft, my dress in a heap on the floor.

Keep your shoes on, he said. He pushed me onto the bed, and we started kissing, but his mouth was rough, and I couldn't tell if he was looking at me or not. There was no light to reflect off his pupils. I couldn't see into his eyes to know what was going on in his head. He flipped me onto my stomach, and I felt him push his dick into me, without asking. It made a noise, a squelch of air being forced out around it, which made me cringe, even though I knew it wasn't my fault.

No! I exclaimed. It came out seriously, not playful; not mistakable for a coquettish response. *I told you. I don't want that.* I moved forward on the bed to get away from him, but he grabbed my shoulder. He didn't say anything and thudded back into me twice, finishing quickly. I felt warmth on my lower back, and everything was silent for a minute. I didn't hear traffic or sirens or even his breath.

I crawled off the bed and found the bathroom, tracing my hand along the black walls, like I was lost in a cave, searching for flaxen thread to find my way out of the labyrinth. I was shaking as I wiped myself off with a hand towel. I felt so embarrassed, ashamed that I'd believed he liked me; ashamed that I'd come here despite the warning given to me. I went back to the bedroom area, fumbling around on the dark floor, and found my clothes somehow.

He got up as I dressed, leading me by my elbow to the door.

Call me sometime, he said, as if this was so normal that I should want more of it, and I couldn't believe what I was hearing. Was I supposed to accept that this was the way things were meant to be?

"MA'AM?" my Uber driver said suddenly, shaking me out of my memory. We'd pulled up to my apartment door, and instead of walking into a lonely little studio in last night's clothing, I was going upstairs to the home I shared with a husband and a baby. Thinking about the Wolf made me feel carsick, even though I don't get carsick, and I didn't want to bring that queasy energy into my house. It was enough to deal with my uneasy stalemate with Tom, like a thick fog in our bedroom. I reached to get my key out of my purse, and my fingers brushed the Zoloft prescription, crunched up like a useless receipt at the bottom of my bag. I considered walking to the drugstore to fill it but decided to go inside instead.

I'd looked at the drawing my doctor had sketched. I understood it intellectually, but it scared me. I didn't want to be a different person, to be changed by chemicals. I wanted to be myself and to have Tom know me so well and love me anyway, to understand all the reasons the traumas of my life had led me to where I was now.

If Augusta was listening to the thoughts rattling in my brain, she'd tell me that was unreasonable. *Think about it like this*, she'd say. *If Tom yelled at you all the time and got angry about random things you weren't even aware you were doing, and practically spit at you that he hated you so much, would you accept him saying, "Oops, too bad, it's just my trauma"?* And I knew fake Augusta was right. I didn't want to take the pills, but I did want to stop being such an asshole.

12

A for *Autonomy*

New York
September 2018

I'D MANAGED TO FIND THE RICHEST THERAPIST in Manhattan after dropping my first nice but ineffective one. It wasn't on purpose, but my new therapist had a summer house in Nantucket and a country home in Bedford. She also had the same short silvery hair and posh side profile as actress Dame Judi Dench—and an identical upper-crust accent: clipped and gentle, straight out of an old movie. It was like having a weekly story hour with someone who had just won a BAFTA. She wore loose, drapey clothing in solid neutrals from stores I did not know about. I would have loved to sit with her at the fictional dinner party I built in my mind.

After my GP had been so direct with me, I felt unsettled. And while the prescription for Zoloft she'd written remained crumpled at the bottom of my purse, something about her asking targeted questions—and not just reading the boilerplate list from the Edinburgh Postnatal Depression Scale, a test I'd been presented in the days after I'd given birth and again at subsequent checkups—had clicked. I was so used to filling out that asinine form that I could do it in my sleep. It was written as if someone imagined some uncomplicated, idealized form of postpartum depression, one that didn't relate to me:

In the past seven days, have you been able to laugh and see the funny side of things? Check the box that corresponds: As much as I always could, not quite so much now, definitely not so much, or not at all. Of course I had. Petunia made me laugh all the time. Sharon made me laugh. I wasn't a zombie. Laughing was one of the only pleasures I had left.

In the past seven days, have you felt scared or panicky for no very good reason? Check the box that corresponds: Not at all, hardly ever, sometimes, or very often. Who is to say what is a good reason to feel scared? I couldn't trust my husband's judgment. He was an imbecile half the time. No one thought of all the possible bad scenarios the way I did, because I was the one with maternal instincts. This question wasn't fair.

I have been so unhappy that I have been crying. Check the box that corresponds: Most of the time, quite often, not very often, or not at all. Well, yes. But I've been unhappy for rational reasons. Very sad, rational reasons. So wouldn't my crying be proof of my sanity, in fact?

THAT MY GP HAD DUG A LITTLE DEEPER had left me with a desire to open the locked and forbidden doorway in my mind—to find the crazy lady in the attic, even if, as I suspected, the lady was me. It made me want to keep talking, and I decided to start from scratch with a brand-new therapist. I didn't want to have to explain why I'd wasted a bunch of sessions with the old one by not coming clean.

So, tell me what's been going on, Dame Judi Dench asked a few weeks into our meetings.

Did I ever tell you about the Glamour Shots session I did in the hospital the day after I gave birth? I laughed and shifted on Judi's tasteful couch. *Sorry,* I said. *You probably never went to a mall in Middle America in the nineties. Glamour Shots was a chain of really cheesy photography studios.* Her office was bright and airy, more like a sitting room in a chic hotel than an office. *I'm not sure why I'm telling this story,* I said. I tucked my hair behind my ears, preparing myself for the small performance of sharing a tale in therapy. Dame Judi drew the blinds on her windows, which overlooked a grassy section of Madison Square Park. Normally no one could see in, but today there were window washers outside on their scaffolded elevator. She took a seat in the padded office chair across from me.

Go on, she said, a small smile on her face. *I do seem to remember something about big hair and eyeshadow that matched a pastel backdrop being quite in fashion.* Behind her a hanging fern waved in the light breeze of an air-conditioning vent.

These days, the day after you give birth, a photographer shows up in your hospital room to do a full-on photo shoot with you and your infant, I explained, *and then they send you the images by email, and you can buy them for exorbitant fees.* I waited, expecting her to say something. She just nodded. *It's sad,* I continued, *because all these women are so out of sorts, and it seemed a bit exploitative. Like, what are you going to do,* not *buy the photos?* She nodded again.

I wondered if the real Dame Judi Dench had ever had a conversation about hospital photography before. Then I wondered if this was what I'd really come here to talk about. *I look back at that day and remember how Tom had left me alone in the hospital room to walk and get us lunch, and he was gone for only maybe twenty minutes, but I was absolutely panicked. I was there alone, with this helpless infant in a little plastic bin, and I just stared at the little thing the entire time. I had to. He was my sole responsibility. Someone had to do it. I couldn't have left if I'd wanted to. And when I realized that, I felt incredibly trapped. Held captive. And I remember thinking I would rather die than be a captive.* Judi Dench smiled sympathetically, her chin at a regal level, eyes patient.

When you look at the pictures, are you thrown back into your feelings of "confinement," as you might say? she asked.

As if I ever tortured myself by looking at those hideous photos. Instead of saying that, I considered her question and how my immediate reflex was to respond with my signature delusional optimism. Remembering how nice it felt to open up to my GP, I forced myself to wipe the polite smile off my face and think about what she was really asking before I replied, instead of just telling her no and that everything was fine.

The pictures aren't something I like to revisit, I guess. I started off slowly. *Guy wasn't really a beautiful baby, you could say.* Her face was devoid of judgment as I continued.

He has all of my ugliest features. I laughed nervously. *I know what it's like to not measure up to the beauty standards I've always dreamed of meeting. It is even worse when your own child doesn't,* I said. *It feels like my fault. And it's hard to love something that looks like the worst parts of yourself. So, yah, I don't think I'd say I'm thrown back when I see those photos . . . it's more like those feelings never left. They just got worse and worse, and it made me feel stuck, as if I were bound and gagged half the time, and then I started getting angrier and angrier and sadder and sadder.* She looked up at me this time quite seriously, her pen poised above her notepad.

You know when you go to bed at night, and you walk through your house turning off lights? I went on. *Those photos make me want to do that to all the rooms in my brain: shut them down one by one, click the light switches and shutter the windows and double-lock the doors.* I watched her interpret what I'd just said, and I could see a flicker of recognition in her eyes.

You're very hard on yourself, you know, she said very kindly. *I believe you that your little chap was a funny-looking baby, but I'm not sure this is really about that. When else have those trapped feelings in your body been especially present? Aside from in the hospital?*

I sat there for a minute, then pulled my journal out of my purse and flipped through it, wondering if an entry would pop out. Sometimes when I was my angriest, most upset, and feral, I rage-wrote notes to myself. Sometimes the handwriting of my rants was so messy it looked like the hieroglyphs of some sort of protosapien, half monkey, half human, operating on raw and uncontrollable instinct.

Well . . . I hate playing with my kid. She nodded emphatically, though she didn't seem that fazed. *So, whenever I'm in his nursery.*

What else? she asked.

Have you seen The Exorcist? *Remember when her head spins around, and then she crab-walks across the floor, and it looks really unhuman? Right after she tells the priest his mom sucks cocks in hell? That is me at the ob-gyn now. My brain just starts powering down, and I feel that same trapped feeling.* She shook her head and pinched her lips tight. I could tell that her disapproval was not of me but of how she felt about my ob-gyn. We'd talked about it before. When I'd recounted Guy's birth to her in our first session, she'd been horrified.

Have you ever googled personal accounts of what it's like for women who have their amniotic sac broken after they've received drugs to be induced? she asked me now. I could tell she already knew what those results were and that she already knew my answer.

No, I haven't, I replied. I felt dumb; I hadn't even thought to. I'd been so convinced that my pain was my own overreaction that I hadn't even thought to compare it with anyone else's.

Your reaction was completely normal. Your doctor should have anticipated it and given you the option for pain relief. Even I can see that, and when I had my babies, we didn't have pain relief. That dreadful doctor, she finished, shaking her head.

I continued. *Sometimes when Tom wants to have sex with me, I find it a total imposition on my body. I cry afterward. I feel over-*

whelmingly sad, or sometimes angry, and I'm not sure why. Yet again she raised an eyebrow but didn't say anything. I found it so uncomfortable when she did this, just waiting for me to continue. If I didn't like her so much, I think I'd have found it infuriating. Some sort of Freudian-analysis-bullshit technique to get you to spill your guts. My eyes darted away from her, and yet again I remembered the prescription for the antidepressants, crumpled in my purse.

My brain decided to change the subject. *My GP told me she thinks I should go on a low dose of Zoloft. She thinks I have postpartum depression; she used the term* crisis. *I don't know if she's right, though. I don't know if I "count"–if it's bad enough, if I check enough of the boxes. So I'm leaning toward not filling the prescription. I wanted your advice. I guess I want to feel more in control of my feelings,* I continued, trying to give her enough time to jump in. *But a pill seems like sort of a fake way to do it. Like, if I chemically lobotomize myself, I'm not really fixing anything, I'm just taking away my ability to react to it.* She nodded again, and I shifted, pulling my skirt down my thighs. I wasn't sure what else to add.

I think you're right, she said, and I must have looked surprised at her forthright reaction, because she scrambled to clarify. *Not that antidepressants are "fake"–I think they can be very helpful and might even be helpful for you–but I do think it's important to figure out what is making you sad as well as treat your sadness. It's a mistake when someone only treats the sadness.* This was exactly what I meant, and I appreciated that she wasn't just trying to push drugs on me with no attention to the root cause. If I was going to go into all the dark rooms in my brain and unpack what was in them, I wanted to do it with someone who, when we were finished, would know how to close the door securely on the way out. It seemed like Dame Judi Dench could be this person.

Then what do I do now? I asked.

I hate to say this, but we are all out of time today, she said, nodding her chin over to the clock on her shelf, next to all her favorite books. *But think more about what we said today, about all those instances where your autonomy was taken from you. I think it would be good to examine that.*

OUTSIDE IT WAS SUNNY AND WARM, one of those late-fall days where leaves were still on the trees, but nothing was blooming to give me allergies. It was warm enough for bare legs, but I wasn't sweating. I didn't need to be home at any specific time, so I decided to hoof it back to SoHo, firing off a quick email to a client about a Jenny Holzer marble bench that they wanted to install outdoors, in Iowa. I wasn't sure if marble did well in extreme climates, so next I sent another email to a gallery assistant to see if they could do some research for me.

I picked up a bottle of iced tea at the shitty deli across the street, then walked down University Place, the short street that stretches the few blocks from Washington Square Park to Union Square, cutting through NYU. It always made me nostalgic to look in the windows of La Petite Coquette, the lingerie store where I'd worked for part of college. When I'd applied for a job, the owner had taken me outside to smoke a cigarette while she interviewed me. She popped her gum, looked at me sideways, and said, *How the fuck do I know you won't steal from me?*, blowing out smoke for effect. I told her I didn't have anyone to wear lingerie for, admitting to my own identity as constructed by the male gaze.

You're hired, she said, stubbing out the cigarette with her little black boot. *But don't ever let me catch you fucking taking my merchandise.*

I never bought lingerie now. I preferred big cotton panties from somewhere cheap and generic, like the Gap, so that when I got my period on them, as I did every month of my damn life, I didn't have to freak out about what they cost. I kept walking, winding under the arch of Washington Square, passing two cops on horseback. They were sitting smug and tall, domineering over the crowds, watching street performers at the big, round fountain in the middle of the park.

When my sister and I were kids, back in Indiana, we took horseback riding lessons at this barn called Grandview, which was neither grand nor had any sort of view. It was in the middle of flat suburbs and surrounded by track homes scattered with the few old oak trees that hadn't been cut down by rural development. I quit after the first time I fell off a horse, not because I was scared but because I finally had an excuse to stop something I found uncomfortable and boring; I was cold in the winter and hot in long jodhpurs all summer, and I left the barn so dusty and dirty that it gave me angry red zits on my forehead.

The owner of the place, a geriatric curmudgeon named Harry, used to stand at the side of the ring and watch the classes of young girls circle, tapping their crops lightly against the worn-in horses to get them to trot. Every so often he'd yell out a correction, such as *Heels down, Meghan!* or a piece of advice like *Get a bra, Ashley!* to some overdeveloped twelve-year-old with a little too much bounce. I remember that when my parents came in after class one day to talk about Deechie's desire to participate in competitions, he encouraged them to buy her a horse. *A horse is like a dildo*, he opined, with both of us kids sitting there. *You buy a girl a horse, and she won't need to go get pregnant at sixteen.*

A siren wailed as I crossed Houston, breaking my train of thought. I looked up at my old apartment on Mott Street. It used to be above an outdoor flea market that had since been replaced by a building housing an organic beauty supply store. I thought about how many cockroaches I probably ate in my sleep living in that shithole. They were everywhere. I'd see their shadows skittering in the night, illuminated by the traffic lights. I was incredibly lonely in that apartment, but at least my life had felt full of possibility and promise. I was a kid then. I knew I had so much ahead of me, so much happiness and companionship to find.

Tom was in the kitchen when I got home, scooping leftover fried rice into his mouth. Things were still reserved between us. He looked up at me as I watched a sticky clump fall off his spoon, and very quickly he wiped it into the sink with a sponge, leaving a trail of wet grease.

How was your day? he asked with a full mouth, shoving in the last bite. He scrambled to get a paper towel and finish cleaning as he chewed.

A mix. I sighed, dropping my bag onto the counter. He rinsed out his bowl and put it in the dishwasher.

For later, he said, popping a detergent pod into the little tray in the dishwasher's door. *So it's ready whenever, and you don't have to do it.* He smiled at me, hoping for a pat on the head, something Napoleon would do. I could practically feel the energy of his tail start to waggle at the thought of being called a *good boy*.

Thanks, I said. We smiled at each other a little bit, which felt sweet.

I'm home early because I wanted to give Guy a bath, Tom said, wiping the grin off his face. *I was going to do bedtime and books, too. But after, can I take you out to dinner? Make your day a little better?* His eyes were big and hopeful, and he reached out to touch my cheek with his hand.

We could do that, I said, trying to keep things positive. I dipped my chin as his hand caressed my neck. *Maybe sushi. I can call and book something for later.* I reached toward my bag on the counter to grab my phone, keeping my body where it was so that his hand would stay on me.

Awesome. Maybe after we could even . . . snuggle? I looked up to meet his gaze. I felt my heart fall and my chest get tight. My heart fluttered in a little burst, like I'd been running on a treadmill. I thought he was being nice, but really he just wanted to fuck. The thought made me sick, like I was just an object with a hole to him.

Oh, I said, *I don't know. We can't–I'm not ready–I'm not ready for that.* Fear crept through my body like a poison, and I felt myself shutting down. I put my phone back in my bag, walking to my bedroom alone. I heard him call my name, but I didn't respond.

BY THE NEXT WEEK, I'd walked by my neighborhood Duane Reade twenty times but never popped in to drop off the prescription for Zoloft at the pharmacy counter. I once even walked in to buy Cheetos and *still* didn't drop it off. I was held back by some internal inertia that told me antidepressants were some sort of cheating, like giving up, or not believing in my own ability to pull myself up by my bootstraps, which was the Indiana way. I'd been taught from day one that hard work and a healthy dose of gumption and discipline could fix anything, that cheating wasn't part of the ethics of midwestern success. No one I knew admitted to taking SSRIs, and I didn't know enough about them to understand who they were right for. I'd read the memoir *Prozac Nation,* and the protagonist seemed brilliant but absolutely batshit. Was taking meds admitting that I was as mentally ill as her? For some reason, while I had no problem popping a Percocet and chasing it with a glass of full-bodied red, I was unsure if I really wanted to make the commitment to take an antidepressant every single day, indefinitely. I couldn't ever remember to take vitamins, even the gummy candy kind.

One week later, as I walked into the therapist's office for another session, I noticed that the blinds were up, the window washers gone. The weather was a little chillier and the sun less bright, but the office was still filled with well-cared-for houseplants.

I hiked up my jeans before sitting on the couch. I thought about my hospital photos story from last week. I was never going to get better if all I could do was tell my therapist anecdotes about Glamour Shots. I needed to make myself focus on more pressing matters. I cleared my throat, wishing I'd worn stretchier pants, not jeans. I was uncomfortable, and they were digging into me.

I have been having these crazy nightmares that I haven't mentioned, I said. My voice came out tiny and belied the beginning of tears behind my eyes. *But I don't want to tell you the details, in case it makes them come true. I'm probably tempting fate by even saying this much. I'd never forgive myself if I made one of them come true.* This belief did sound a little unhinged now that I was saying it out loud. I shifted in my jeans, wondering if there was a subtle way to pull them out of my ass without her noticing.

That's very common, you know, she said, her beatific face shining with such compassion, as if she had been waiting for me to cop to this for months. *It's called "magical thinking," and it's when the mind believes that its rituals, compulsions, thoughts, or emotions have influence on the outside world. It's like thinking you can clap your hands to find a parking space. It's actually a sign that your brain is trying hard to quiet obsessive thoughts or make you well, but it can't.* She crossed her legs in her big office chair, and I fidgeted a little on the couch facing her. I really wished I was in my bed, in pajamas. I thought about how when I was a kid, someone had told me that I had to eat breakfast before I described my dreams to anyone or else they'd come true. I wondered if this was where this belief began or if it was one of the superstitions of childhood. *Step on a crack, break your mother's back.* How had magical thinking formed the plotline to the horror movie of my life? It was like a road map of thick, twisty vines, covering every moment of the past year.

I don't know if it's postpartum depression—I mean, it doesn't sound like any postpartum depression I've ever read about, so probably not. I paused, looking again into her kind eyes—not a hint of judgment in them. *I've done that Edinburgh Postnatal question-*

naire a jillion times, and it doesn't really make sense. I think maybe it was written by a bunch of dudes at the insurance companies who wanted to protect doctors from liability issues, and I don't think any of them had actually ever met a mother. I expected her to roll her eyes with me, but she didn't.

Actually, it was written by two women, I believe, though I don't know if they were mothers, said my therapist. *Why don't you tell me what doesn't resonate for you?*

I paused.

The questions just aren't . . . right. They don't ask the right things. I felt the words stick in my throat.

What would the right things be? she prodded.

One of my biggest symptoms, I think, was just being mad. So mad, so irritated, constantly. I am truly aggressively annoyed by Tom. Willing to throw away my marriage over how much his every move frustrates me. I hate him. Where is that on the list? Where does it say, "How badly do you want to murder your husband?" She nodded.

And then, of course, there was the whole not loving my baby. I wanted nothing to do with that little fucker. And sometimes now, when I explain that to people, they look at me like I'm horrible, but some women say, "Oh my God, I actually didn't love my kid for a while, either! It takes time! I've felt guilty for years about it, even though I love him to death now!" So that should probably be on there, too. She was taking notes, so I didn't stop.

I mean, even if they just asked, "Do you think your baby is cute?"—even just that would be an improvement. Because I thought my baby looked like a goat. And I don't even know if that was real or not. You know when mothers have full-on psychosis, they see the face of the devil in their baby and stuff? Maybe I had some diluted version of that, but I don't know. Feels worth asking. Judi kept taking her notes and nodding along.

The questionnaire could ask if you feel traumatized by giving birth or if you've had past trauma in your life. It could ask if you have a support system. Surely those things play into your mental state. But the worst is how they phrase the suicide question—it's unrealistic. It's as if they don't want anyone to be able to relate to it. It's as if they want people to read it and think, "Wow, suicidal thoughts are totally foreign and irrational and belong only in the minds of totally insane people," when, actually, it's not that out of the ordinary or that weird to want to give up. The test says, "Have you ever thought of harming yourself?" And it's, like, no, because that sounds messy and painful, and I'm lazy and pain averse. But do I want to exit my shit pile of a life that stretches out in all directions for eternity? Hell yes. I want to run and disappear and never come back. Does that count? I think it should. Yet that wasn't on the questionnaire.

I started crying a little, remembering the times I sat at my kitchen table, looking out my back window, wondering to myself the best way to disappear forever. It had been so glaringly lonely that I hadn't even realized how pitiful it was. I didn't want to jump out the window, but I wanted the window to swallow me whole. Anything to quiet the disorganized, chaotic jumble of thoughts.

Also, I don't want to have sex with my husband, and I'm worried about a million things all day, but maybe I've always been worried about a million things all day? I'm honestly unsure. I don't even really remember what I used to be like; I just know I'm not myself. And my doctor said I need antidepressants or I'm going to blow up my life, and I don't want to blow up my life. I hiccupped a sob, feeling myself getting wound up. She handed me a tissue, her lips in a pout, nodding her head. *Am I the only person seeing the world clearly? I ask myself that so many times a day. I meet other mothers who act like their births were miraculous, who love play-*

ing with their babies, and parenthood has brought more romance to their lives. She was still nodding, looking more like Judi Dench than ever.

When I think about my whole birth story, I feel so stupid that it traumatized me so much, because, on one level, nothing bad even happened. There was never a single moment where a nurse came rushing in, sounding an alarm bell. There are people who hemorrhage and almost die, and I am not one of them, but it was still so awful. And everything reminds me of it. When Tom tries to have sex with me, I think about all the other things that have gone in there and come out of there, and there's just no world where I could get turned on with those memories. She nodded like she was imagining everything I just said and it was painful for her. I felt like the room was spinning around me, keeping me pinned to the sofa with some sort of centripetal force, as if the rest of the world had frozen in time for a few minutes while I was in this office coming clean.

From what you told me, she said, *you went into true, definitive medical shock when they broke your water. That is a condition over which you had no control, and it likely colored everything else to come. Your doctor wasn't sensitive to your needs when it came to telling you what was happening, or administering pain control, or even telling you what was going to hurt. She negated your pain after, too. Didn't you tell me she acted like you were crazy for crying?*

I nodded. She had. The doctor had thrown her hands up in the air and said, *I barely touched you! I perform this all day, and it is not a big deal!* Judi Dench had reminded me of this before, of course, but every time she confirmed that my ob-gyn was indeed some sort of gaslighting asshole, it reassured me.

It is absolutely not strange that you had a reaction to that moment. Don't forget that, Sarah. I really want you to know that as a medical professional, she did not treat you respectfully, and it is completely justified that it has stuck with you.

I sat up very, very straight and steeled myself, clearing my throat. *When I think about her breaking my water, I have this other bad memory. It's been hard to talk about.* In fact, the thought of articulating it made me feel shaky.

Sarah, you are certainly not the first woman in a hospital bed to have bad memories. All doctors should approach all interventions as if the patient has experienced past trauma, no? Most patients have. She said it simply, like it was a given. She closed her notebook but kept a casual look on her face. I think she didn't want to scare me from continuing.

I decided to just tell her. I'd been thinking about this memory since the previous week, when she'd asked me about scenarios where I felt like I was held captive.

The flashback always starts with his smell, I said. *The Wolf, I call him. First, I can smell him, and then I feel his belly pressing into me. It was really warm–abnormally warm–like an animal.*

I closed my eyes and heard my therapist say, *Take a deep breath; there's absolutely no rush.* I inhaled slowly. I could feel my cheeks getting hot. I was embarrassed by the memory, embarrassed at having to say it out loud, but also remembering the mortification I'd experienced in the moment.

I feel the sheets of his bed underneath my fingers, like I'm crawling forward, and they feel really soft and clean, like they'd probably smell good. But before I can take in any details, I feel him grabbing my shoulder and yanking me back toward him and slamming into me. And then I feel this huge sense of–I don't know what the feeling is–I just want to escape my own body. Like I let him into my body, and I was just instantly filled with regret. What could I do? Scream? Who would hear me? What would I tell them? I'd gone there willingly. I'd been warned, and I still went.

I kept my eyes closed, trying to remember every feeling in my body. I still felt like it was something I could share only with the Wolf, even though we were nothing to each other.

When he came on my back, I was so mad. I had to go clean myself off, and it made me so mad that he thought he could treat my body like . . . like a garbage disposal. Like a trash can. And now I hate that feeling of any liquid on me that I'm not expecting. It makes me want to vomit and tear my skin off. I shuddered. I put my hands to my cheeks, and they felt feverish.

When that doctor broke my water in the hospital, when that liquid gushed all over me, it reminded me of that moment. And now, even after I have sex with Tom, I have these flashbacks, and I feel angry to the point of being deranged, but also horribly sad at the same time, totally devastated, like I could break into an ugly cry at any moment.

Strangely, while I was talking, I didn't feel like crying. I felt like the therapist wasn't there, and I was just taking layers and layers off my chest in an empty room, making more and more space around myself. The next deep breath I took felt much bigger than the last.

Sometimes when I'm holding Guy, I feel that same combination: angry and sad. In the taxi on the way home from the Wolf's, I felt like my insides had been ripped out—like I'd been emptied. And I feel empty when I look at my own baby, too. But also full of something horrible. I know it all sounds really stupid. None of what has happened to me is weird. I know girls who have been raped at the end of an alley in the dark by a stranger, left for dead behind a dumpster. I know people whose babies died during labor. My fucking sister's baby died during labor! I know what that looks like. I opened my eyes because I was now starting to cry, but I was too embarrassed to meet the therapist's eyes. I could feel them on me, but I didn't want to look up.

I feel like I failed at everything. I am not the strong person I thought I was. And when I tell any of this to Tom, he's going to realize how damaged and pathetic I am. He's going to be so grossed out by what other men did to me, because it wouldn't have happened if I had been smarter and stronger, you know? It's, like, only someone worthless would have been treated that shitty way. And if Tom finds any of this out, he's going to see the truth, which is that I must be worthless or it wouldn't have happened to me. None of it. The Wolf, the baby I can't love, none of it.

As I blew my nose into a tissue, the image of the Wolf saying goodbye to me at his door remained.

It really is crazy all the difficult things that come with having a vagina, Judi Dench said, almost like she was talking to herself. *It's hard for the female body to feel like a safe space when the colonialist masculine ideal of domination at the expense of all humanity is still so alive and well.* I sniffled some more. She truly had a way with words. *You're really brave for telling me this,* she finished softly.

I couldn't really think of anything to say, so I just nodded.

Is therapy going to . . . work? Ever? Am I ever going to get less sad? It's one thing after the next. Napoleon is getting old, and he's going to die, and then what if my mom dies? I will never be happy again, I choked out, holding my hands out to either side. She glanced off to the side, at her clock, and sighed.

Okay, Sarah, we are almost out of time. I think what I'm sensing from you is that you need some immediate relief. Why don't we expedite things. Start the antidepressants—you can always quit.

I was exhausted by what I'd told her already, wrung out by crying. All I could do was nod as I patted my face with a Kleenex.

I must tell you that what the Wolf did was criminal, she continued. *It's really a horrifying story, and it's horrifying that the doctor participated in the same sort of thing. It must be quite depleting. And if you want my opinion, I don't care what that Edinburgh Scale tells you. You have a massive and prolonged case of postpartum depression, likely compounded by some previous struggles—as most diagnoses are. Take care of yourself.*

Just like that, in the bizarre transaction that is therapy, the shift from intimacy to logistics, she was ushering me out the door. *Start the meds, and we will talk in a week.*

Still sniffling, I walked into the nearest CVS and dropped off my prescription.

13

The Walk

London
October 2018

I AWOKE IN A GIANT BED at Claridge's hotel and looked across the wide expanse of crisp, white sheets to Tom's side, which was empty. I rolled over to check my work email to make sure there were no art-world emergencies–like someone's Picasso delivery arriving late to their venture fund's office–then let myself lie there in the deep silence of an upholstered hotel room, darkened by brocade curtains and silk-covered walls. Normally, when I traveled with Tom, I accepted my role as his pinch-hitting secondary assistant, bringing him things he forgot up in the room, or having the concierge print shit out, or moving our dinner reservations. I was always changing my itinerary around his and waiting patiently for him to be ready for me, just in time for plans to shift and for me to be stuck by myself while he finished up whatever he was doing.

But this morning, I hoisted myself out of the mahogany four-poster and into the bathtub, which was shaped like an octagon, carved out of one piece of heavy marble. I don't care how fancy a hotel is, there is no cleaning solution that can make up for years of bathtub use, hundreds of strangers bathing and fucking, and rinsing off the fucking, all in the same tub. What else did people do in octagon-shaped bathtubs–all that hot water and room for eight different backs?

In my case, they cried, which I'd been doing since I woke up, sobbing my eyes out as if tears were a natural resource I could sell. Had I cried crude oil, I probably could have paid for our room by now, almost two hours later, alone time I'd been awarded as the beneficiary of Guy's jet lag. I could have paid for the tea party I was having later that day to celebrate Guy's first birthday, which was more for me than for him, a celebration not of his year of life but of my managing to keep him alive for a year. Or, more specifically, keeping Sharon alive, who kept Guy alive, for a year.

But my fixation on the fact that I would die someday, and that *my mom* would die, kept resurfacing like acid reflux. I couldn't stand the thought that if my mom died before I resolved my grudges with her, I'd never have the mom I wanted, and I would never become the mom I wanted to be. And even worse was the idea of my own death; that if I left Guy before I could become the mother I wanted to be for him–the mother I had mostly failed to be–I'd miss out on so much. I'd been on antidepressants for a few weeks, and hadn't expected to be this emotional while drugged, but this little tragedy all made total sense in my head.

Be happy, you have a healthy little one-year-old down the hall, I told myself, squeezing free body wash out of a little plastic bottle. It said "Gilchrist & Soames" on the bottom, which sounded so proper, some bespoke British Savile Row-suit soap, the exact product I imagined existed in stately old British hotels. I sudsed up the important parts, ran more water into the tub, rinsing everything. *Be happy you have him and can employ a wonderful woman to help you care for him,* I repeated over and over in my head.

We'd come to London because Tom had a gallery exhibition, coordinated with the annual art fair–an art-world trade show–in Hyde Park. Sharon had opted to stay home, suggesting I find a sitter through the hotel. *I hate rain, I hate fog, and this will be good bonding time for you*, she'd said. I knew Tom would be consumed by work, but my parents had flown in, so I figured they could help out if I got desperate.

Tom had been installing his show all morning, an immersive installation that replicated the bureaucratic process of getting a Swiss passport issued. It was a commentary on migration, borders, and the arbitrary decisions made by governments and the corporations that control them, and he'd been doing interviews for art press and meeting with collectors for days. Normally, I'd fly in the eve before the opening and busy myself at museums until he needed me, but last night he'd surprised me in the hotel room when we landed with a bottle of champagne and a hamper of snacks he'd picked up at the Harrods Food Hall. It was genuinely thoughtful, and I could tell he was trying hard to be sweet. There were already artgoers lined up outside the gallery to have their fake passports issued, but he'd snuck off to see me.

Be happy this is your life! Be happy that work and travel convene so easily that you get to be here with Tom for Guy's first birthday. Be happy you have a real reason to drink today, and people to do it with. I covered myself with a thick terry cloth robe and cinched the belt, slathering pink, powdery-smelling lotion out of a different tiny bottle onto my legs. Being clean always helped me feel less hysterical.

I slid into the slippers left on the bath mat and walked down the hallway of my room to a door, bolted open, that went into Guy's room. As my hand searched along the dark wall for a light switch, I thought about how my doctor had told me it would take several weeks for my antidepressants to kick in. But something about the thankfulness I was feeling, even though it was muddled by my tears and their accompanying waves of emotion—which I wasn't sure were gloomy, necessarily, though they were intense— felt already different and new.

During the depths of what I now thought of as my psychosis,

I'd forced myself to fill empty journal pages with gratitude lists. I'd scribble, in frantic ink, things like *Today I'm happy about buying flowers from the lady with the little stall on East 6th Street* and *One thing I was grateful for this morning was my sugary matcha with whole milk.* Sometimes I would even write these notes on my arm, pressing a Uniball into my flesh in tiny handwriting, little reminders that happiness still existed, somewhere. I was doing anything I could to find it, but I had to really think about it. The things I was reminding myself to be happy about today felt somehow more organic and essential. I wasn't pulling them from my brain by force, like a tapeworm I was yanking out inch by inch. They were easy to name. I *was* grateful that I was healthy. I was actually excited to be in London with my boy and my husband. I was also emotionally constricted, though, still consumed with a bunch of unresolved sad stuff. But I felt like my sadness, while deep, did not preclude me from also sticking my toes into the shallow waters of some kind of happiness, if that makes sense. For the first time in forever, I could experience a multitude of feelings, and feel them all, and handle it. If I had a bad thought, I could even articulate it or call Judi Dench about it. When I felt depression or anger pull me down into the seventh ring of hell, I didn't freeze up or go numb or pick a fight with Tom; instead, as much as I could, I tried to keep the lights on and look at what was behind the sadness or the rage.

Standing in Guy's room, I looked at my sleeping son and felt a peacefulness spread across me. I cocked my head to the side to study him, and as if he could hear my thoughts, his eyes opened slowly, a smile spreading on his face when he saw me, one little tooth hanging out of the top of his mouth.

For the past week or so, I'd found myself strangely drawn to his crib. Instead of popping into his room and seeing a black hole, I felt sort of sorry for the little toddler in there, and I actually wanted to check in and see how he was doing, and what he was up to. I'd been thinking about the German philosopher Martin

Heidegger's concept of *Geworfenheit*, which means *thrownness*. Heidegger wrote about how none of us choose to be here; how we are *thrown* into life. I'd done that to Guy–I'd decided for him that he would exist, and exist as my son. And while I thought it only fair that I find a way to be my own person and be a mother, something my own mother also seemed to always struggle with, I felt a growing understanding of how I hadn't appreciated Guy's circumstances more fully. He'd ended up here wanting only to be loved and cared for, and my own mental crisis had usurped his innocent need–a need *I'd* created.

Suddenly, peering into Guy's crib, I was overcome by a wave of something. It started in my chest, and as I felt it undulate outward toward my fingers, I grew warm, and my skin seemed to buzz, like a song I loved was pumping through a giant speaker and my cells knew every word of the verse. I had never experienced anything like it–it was as if the endings of all my nerves were deciding to be happy at once. I picked Guy up and held him in my arms, gazing at his cherubic face, and I actually laughed. Whatever I was feeling was so light. Was this just the meds hitting my system? Was it therapy *and* the meds? Did I want to hold my child?

We were still smiling at each other like idiots when the doorbell rang, and I remembered I'd told Petunia to come over and get ready with me. She was staying down the street, here to work the art fair booth for the gallery.

Look at my man, he's just gorgeous, isn't he? she said in her raspy voice when I swung open the heavy hotel door. She met Guy's lumpy grin with her own.

I think he should wear these red pants. What do you think? I picked up the little birthday outfit I'd bought for him. Red corduroys and shiny patent leather shoes and a smart cardigan. We were in London, and I wanted him to look like a little chap. I was worried the shoes might be a bit too Broadway, like he was learning how to tap dance, but Sharon had assured me he would look like a young Cary Grant in them. I handed P the clothes from his open suitcase. She looked at them lovingly.

I can't believe it's been a year. Is that why you've been crying? You look like shit. She laid Guy down on the bed to start dressing him, and he put a little black taxicab that the concierge had given him in his mouth. I reached to take it out gently and kissed his cheek. He smelled so nice, like French baby lotion.

Because you should be proud of him, P said. *I don't know shit about babies, but he's so cute.* She tugged his pants over his diaper, and I wondered why she was so natural at this. I looked at him smiling his goofy, mostly toothless, smile. I watched Petunia reach for his argyle socks and patent shoes.

When I was very little, before I could go to the mall with my friends and before she was overtaken by work, my mom would bring us twice a year to Keen's shoes. The store was a squat concrete building surrounded by its own parking lot, and there was a billboard out front, closer to the road, telling cars where to turn for children's shoes. Most of the time we just wore Keds, but at Keene's, we'd step onto the silver foot-measuring device, whose math I didn't understand, and I'd get fitted for one pair of black Mary Janes for the Christmas pageant or one pair of brown Mary Janes for school. The shoes Guy had on now were close to what I wore as a child, and I remembered being proud to show them off. I wondered what would go on in his head when we went downstairs for tea and he saw a bunch of adults at a table, waiting to see him in his little man outfit. Would he remember anything about this trip or this time? I remember once standing in the parking lot of Keene's, staring at a column, painted yellow and pale blue to match the facade of the store. I stared and stared at that column, the sky a brighter blue behind it. I told myself that if I could remember this insignificant moment forever, I could remember anything else I wanted to. I wondered if other kids played those sorts of internal games or self-competitions. I read once that some scientists believe dreams are your brain playing at night so that it won't get bored.

This was the daytime version of that, that feeling of living in your own head. Guy must live in his one-year-old head in some way, I thought, and I was glad to be able to experience this tiny moment, however insignificant. He didn't know a thing, not one thing. He came to us a tabula rasa. And now he could process words and phrases, say some garbled version of *I love you* back to us when we said it. When I made *That's what* she *said* jokes to Tom and he laughed, Guy would start laughing, too, even though he had no idea what was so funny. I marveled at the fact that he could suddenly interpret the world like a real little human. I hoped that his brain wasn't filled with memories of his mom being a crazy bitch. I hope I hadn't already fucked him up. I knew, of course, that he had been cared for even in my worst hours. He had a nanny and both his parents, and he had endless advantages. But until I'd gone to therapy and started antidepressants, I knew I'd been totally checked out. It wasn't just that I wasn't caring for Guy; I wasn't caring for myself, either. I wondered how that had impacted his earliest development and hoped he wasn't scarred.

PETUNIA STOOD GUY UP ON THE BED. *You're just gorgeous, Guy Sachs, just gorgeous!* She handed him to me. *So, what's going on with you? Are you going to do that thing again where you're so sad that you make me sad?*

I started my meds, I told her, putting Guy on my hip. He immediately reached into my robe and started trying to open it, just for something to do. I took his little paw off me and kissed it. *Maybe they aren't working right.*

She shrugged and said, *Or maybe you need to cry.*

I do feel a little different in a good way, I admitted. I bounced Guy and switched him to my other side. He was getting heavier every week, practically. *It's like I went from having constant PMS to having none. And I'm not crying because I hate my life. I'm crying because motherhood is like having no skin. Everything hurts.* I sniffled a little, then started crying again, but I laughed at myself at the same time. *I know, I know. I'm ridiculous. How do you even put up with me?*

I actually think this is progress, she said, then asked, *How's Tom?* She was looking at herself in the mirror, putting on lipstick. I blew my nose and considered her question.

I mean, it's not like I'm dying to tear his clothes off and ride him like he's never been ridden, but he's trying. I laughed again. *He organized champagne and food for me last night. He came home early to see me. That sort of thing. It adds up.* I turned to bring Guy back into my bedroom. *I'm gonna let him crawl around my floor while I get dressed*, I said over my shoulder. *Can you go to the restaurant and make sure the table looks pretty?* Petunia groaned begrudgingly as I walked out of the room and back down the short hallway connecting us. I heard the door shut behind me as P went downstairs.

Tom was there, changing into a suit, when we walked back into the other bedroom. *My loves*, he said, kissing my cheek. The smell of him close to me felt comforting, not repellent, and that in itself was nice. Once I'd admitted to Judi Dench that after I'd had Guy, I started to associate Tom with every bad man I'd ever met, we'd been trying everything under the sun to work on that. *Medical trauma in labor may have connected all these violations that have brought you harm, but you've explained to me how much you love Tom and all the wonderful things you see in him. The level of connection you have is rare. Let's remember that transference is a psychological bias, not an absolute*, she'd explained. *Let's not ruin your whole marriage because of it.* That had taken me a minute to understand. But I got it: my sexual assaults, from the pervasive and nameless ones to the more severe, like the Wolf, compounded with a medical trauma that felt eerily similar, had catalyzed a cross-wiring in my mind in which everything that had gone in and out of my body became jumbled into one pernicious lump. But that didn't mean my feelings were facts, and it didn't mean that I would always feel this way. In fact, Judi Dench was helping me to start separating the warp and weft of my memories and see each traumatic event as separate and distinct. We were teasing out and unspooling each thread of my story, and she promised me that eventually I'd be able to weave it back together into something more useful.

I placed Guy in Tom's arms. *Will you hold the birthday boy while I put on my outfit? Petunia just went down to check on the table.* I sniffled a little bit. It's not that I wanted Tom to notice I'd been crying for some sort of sympathy, but I wanted him to notice so that he could say something that would make me feel better. I hoped he would see my red eyes like Petunia had and ask me about it. For the first time in a long time, I wanted to talk to him about how I was feeling, because I thought his response might be helpful.

He kissed Guy on the head and put him on the bed, right in the middle, squeezed between the two big square shams. He handed him a rubber duck that the hotel had left in the room for him to play with in the tub. I slipped my pale pink dress over my head and pulled it down, opening my eyes the split second I could see Guy again from behind the fabric, which reached two inches below my crotch when yanked down properly, just where I liked my hem to sit, ever since I'd become fascinated by the 1960s trends I'd learned about in Kitty Leech's fashion history class my senior year. I didn't leave Guy out of sight for more than a second anymore, especially now that he was crawling like a demon and becoming more and more proficient at speed walking.

You look amazing, babe, Tom said, his eyes glued to me. I wasn't sure I believed him, but it felt nice to hear it. *This is your post-baby comeback tour, and you're killing it.* I think that was his version of telling me not to be sad. I could feel the corners of my mouth trying to smile, pulling into a half-grimace. *You okay?* he asked, tugging at his tie and smoothing his shirt. He walked a quick step over to me and pulled me hard into a hug. *You did it. Guy's one. You made him, and he's one.* At first, I stood there, letting him hold me, with no life in my arms, like a scarecrow. I felt myself start to cry again. Though my impulse was to hide the sadness that had flooded me all morning, I thought of something my therapist had said about magical thinking and how it was a fallacy to believe that just because I said something sad or scary out loud, it would come true. I had already lifted the veil of shame with her, so why not be honest with Tom about what I was really feeling?

I'm sad, I said. I heard my voice crack a little and stopped to make a pout face.

Oh, baby, whatsa matter? Tom wrapped his arms tighter around me.

I'm not sure, which I feel ridiculous saying, but I feel overwhelmed. I can't stop thinking about how horrible it would be if something bad happened to Guy, or to my mom, and I'm overloaded by thoughts of that. Plus, I didn't even have clotted cream yet today. He laughed gently and kissed my forehead. I stepped from his arms and threw myself on the bed, snuggling into Guy. I smelled his baby skin, mixed with plastic diaper smell, and broke into a real sob. *I just can't stop thinking about how if I d-i-e—I* spelled the word, not wanting Guy to understand—*no one will protect Guy.*

Tom looked confused and rubbed my back. *But you're not going to d-i-e for such a long time! And if you did, I'd take care of him, and so would Sharon and Deech and your mom.* He tried to reassure me, rubbing harder.

You don't understand, I choked out. *I think of everything that could possibly go wrong every step he takes, and no one else would be that vigilant. I made him, so I know him in a way no one else does. Does that make sense?* Tom was nodding along with me, like he knew I was right but didn't quite understand. *I know all the potential bad choices he could make. I know it in my soul. My cells made his feet, so I am the only person who could know if they are about to take a wrong step. And if I am not on this earth to worry about him, no one will be able to do it as well as I do it, and the thought of that is just so sad.* I buried my head in Guy's little lap, and he took two handfuls of my hair and pulled. I didn't even care. Tom let me cry a bit, working my hair out of Guy's clawlike grip.

But Sarah, nothing will ever end with you and Guy, Tom said softly. *It might change, things might look different, but your love will never end. Think of how hard you've been working to get to where you are, to be a good mom, and think about how much bigger your love is going to grow. You're infinite. I don't know how else to say it. You're infinite.*

I got up and patted my face, thinking about what my husband had said. *A good mom.* Was I? What *was* a good mom, even? I handed Guy some of the tissues by the bed to play with. I tossed one up in the air and watched him watch it float down.

Let's get ready, Tom continued. *People will be here soon for the party. Aren't you excited for that?*

I really do love clotted cream an unholy amount, so, yes, I guess I am excited for the party, I said.

While Tom finished knotting his tie, I walked back to the mirror and swiped on black liquid liner into two cat eyes. We caught each other in our reflections, and we both smiled, like two strangers caught checking each other out. *My eyes are so red it's horrible,* I said to his face in the mirror.

You look beautiful. Just tell people they were happy tears— because I think in some way, that's really what they are. It's a symbolic day. A big day. Let yourself have all the feelings, he said. We smiled at each other again, and this time I leaned over and kissed him quickly. *Why don't I go down to the restaurant and talk to our parents and stuff while you finish getting ready*, Tom suggested, *and then you can bring Guy down?* I took a deep breath and sighed my agreement.

I just need a minute up here. Will you make sure he has a high chair? He nodded at me as I walked around the room, picking up things to put in my purse and handing Guy every toy I stepped on to play with. I shoved a diaper into my bag. *Please?*

Of course, he said, propping open the door as he left. *Let's have fun today.* We smiled at each other again, and I felt my chest get warm as the door closed behind him. I swept a little powder around my face and put a lip balm in my purse.

You ready, Guy Sachs? I lifted him up and kissed the top of his head. *You want to take the elevator?* He repeated *Elevator* in his baby babble, though it sounded more like *Leh-leh-ler*. I slipped my feet into a pair of ballet flats. *Walk!* Guy insisted. I interpreted that as he wanted to walk down to the restaurant. I put down his little body, and he reached up for my hand as we walked out the door.

The minute we got into the hallway, Guy took off. The thud of his feet and the squeak of his diaper filled the formal, pale-green corridor. I chased after him, and we both laughed. I was shocked at how fast he could get going when he wanted to.

Guy, wait! Look! I grabbed his hand and swung his body up into my arms. Even though the walking was leaning him out, he still had his puffy baby tummy, and I felt it press against my body as I held him. *Look at this!* I pointed to a potted palm tree in a beautiful china urn. He pointed too.

Tree! he said. He looked at me with his toothy little grin and clapped his fat hands a few times. *Tree! Tree!* He giggled and clapped some more. The happiness on his face was so pure I couldn't believe it. I couldn't believe how proud it made me to see his big cheeks and bright eyes. I felt a tickle in my chest, and it wasn't a cough, it wasn't tears brewing–it was excitement or contentment, maybe. Was I happy being a mother? I put Guy back down to keep walking, a smile plastered on my face.

That's right, Guy! I said. When we got to the top of the stairs, he decided to sit. I sat next to him, just because I wanted to see what he was going to do next. Plus, I was getting sort of hot in my little dress. I was glad I'd decided not to wear tights, even though it was gray and chilly in London. Guy reached down and pulled a hair out of the carpet, holding it up proudly. He shrieked and started laughing. Hotels were too gross for me. I grabbed it from him, letting it fall behind me, and lifted him up. *You are Mommy's smartest friend, but that is nasty.* I kissed his plump cheek and kept walking. *We don't touch dirty things, little man.* When we got to the bottom of the flight, he started kicking his legs.

Down! Down! I set him down and watched for a second as he bolted from me, running away from the stairs to hide behind another potted palm. Even if I hadn't been able to see his body completely, I'd have known exactly where he was because he couldn't stop giggling. *Don't you know we are going downstairs for your party? Don't you want some cake?* He took off running again, and I chased after him.

I could feel my lower back start to sweat, and I thought about hiking up my dress to let some air in but was sure there were cameras in this hallway. Every time Guy passed a door, he said, *Door,* like he was informing me of some essential knowledge–except it sounded more like *Doh.* Somehow I spoke the language of Guy and knew what these cute attempts at English, these half-babbles, meant.

I picked Guy up again to carry him down the next flight of stairs. Then he got completely quiet, and I wondered if he was getting tired. As I rounded the corner to the last flight, where I could hear tinkling glasses and clattering silverware from the restaurant, I realized he was not sleepy, he was just focusing. Judging from the smell, his diaper needed a change. I thought about going upstairs, but then I thought about having to come all the way back down, when we were already late, and I could feel my hair getting poofier the hotter I got.

I laid him down on the floor and pulled out the diaper I'd shoved into my purse, along with the small travel pack of wipes I always kept with me. I felt my phone vibrate and decided not to check the time, so I wouldn't panic.

Late for your own first birthday, I said. He smiled at me. I smiled back, the biggest smile I'd felt in a long time.

I peeled down his pants and unsnapped the crotch of his small white onesie. *What did you eat, my little devil!* He chuckled again, like he knew something I didn't. I un-Velcroed each side of the diaper and gingerly lifted it away, setting it aside. I started getting to work with the wipes. One wipe, then two, then three–God, this was gross. I was concentrating on getting every little bit off my darling baby, out of every doughy crease. Suddenly I saw Guy mushing his hands together, and it didn't seem quite right. It was like he'd found some Play-Doh, but, somehow, he had shit in his hands and was mashing it between them and staring at it.

Mamma! He sounded amazed, as if he'd discovered something beautiful; as if he were passing a diamond back and forth, one hand to the other. Almost in slow motion, I looked down and realized the diaper had shifted. I'd put it too close to him, and he'd grabbed it. There was poop on his forehead. Was there poop on my forehead? My phone started vibrating again. I kept sweating.

Baby Guy, I said very, very seriously, *Mommy needs you to hold still, okay? Mommy needs you to freeze! Like a statue!*

Miraculously, he froze. *Stop!* he said, and I remembered playing that Red Light, Green Light game as a kid and loving it. Thank God someone had taught him how to stop. I wiped his hands as well as I could over and over until I was sure I'd gotten everything, and then I wiped them again. Next, I did his forehead and then another pass on the butt. I wrapped up everything inside the nasty diaper and Velcroed it back together. I was like a surgeon, or maybe the head of a bomb squad, detangling all the wires to stop some contraption from exploding. As I lifted up his legs to put the new diaper down, I remembered something a nurse from the hospital had told me long ago:

Whenever you clean a poopy diaper, make sure you clean the penis very well, because Guy is not circumcised, and if poop gets under the skin, he can get a very bad infection. Tom had opted not to circumcise Guy, and I'd left the decision up to him. Who was I to tell my baby he needed to have his penis skin removed? The only thing was, I had also told Tom that changing poopy blowout diapers and the requisite subsequent pee-pee cleaning were *his* purview. I think my exact words had been something like *I am the zombie version of myself, and if you think I'm going to spend the four operational brain cells I have left to learn how to clean a baby dick when you have two hands and considerable familiarity with phallus hygiene . . .* In summary, I hadn't dealt with this particular smiting for having disobeyed the covenant. The nurse had said something about pulling back the skin, and I know she'd shown me how, but I'd been a shell of myself. I couldn't take him down to his first birthday with shit under his foreskin, could I? How fast could an infection take hold?

I heard my phone vibrate again. Six missed calls, and we were already twenty minutes late. I could feel myself sweating more, my hair poofing up even higher off my head, sticking to the nape of my neck. I tried calling Sharon, but she didn't pick up. I googled *How to clean an uncircumcised penis.* I watched a YouTube video while Guy played with the pack of wipes, chewing on one end of it. He seemed perfectly happy to lie there on his back in Claridge's hallway. Amazingly, I wasn't crying, though I thought about calling my therapist and asking her if she knew what to do. I trusted her to take this seriously. Or maybe Augusta; she'd probably know. But then I heard footsteps on the padded carpet and looked up as a hotel guest walked up the stairs. She appeared to be quite a bit older than me. Certainly of or past childbearing age.

Excuse me, ma'am? She looked up, and I smiled really big. She smiled back. *Do you by chance know how to clean an uncircumcised penis?* I tried to sound as sweet as I could. I pointed at Guy. *Sorry, I just haven't seen one since this one time in college when, you know, it didn't look like this. In fact, I didn't even know he was uncircumcised, because, you know, it was*—she looked at me like I had seven heads—*hard. This one isn't . . . hard.* I said it even more quietly. I wasn't sure if she even heard. I shook my head and put my hands to my eyes, pressing hard for a second. *Anyway, I just watched a YouTube, but it said I need a Q-tip? Do you have a Q-tip by any chance?* I smiled at her one more time for good measure. *My room is six floors up, and I'm sweating—you know how it is.* She flashed the key card against her door and went inside, closing it quickly behind her.

I took it as a sign and decided to cut my losses. I pulled up Guy's pants, scooping him up along with the offending diaper, and rushed the final flight down to the restaurant, entering his first birthday holding a baby and a pile of shit in my hands.

THE RESTAURANT HAD ONE LONG TABLE at the back set up for a tea party for fourteen people. Our small area was sequestered from the rest of the place by a colonnade of elegant pillars, topped by lotus flower capitals. The walls were made of smooth ashlar, and mirrored obelisks framed the entrance. There were tiered, silver trays of perfect little white-bread sandwiches without crusts, and little pots of flowers, and green-and-white-striped teacups. I loved this hotel because it made me feel like I was starring in a Sherlock Holmes novel.

The black and gold smoking bar next to the restaurant, described as the Egyptian Fumoir, helped to prop up my fantasy. I expected to end my night there, and even though it was midafter-noon, I considered this tea party to be my night's commencement. I made eye contact with a server and smiled, signaling politely that I wanted to order something to drink. Guy was being oohed and aahed over, bouncing from lap to lap. Everything had turned out lovely.

In fact, it turned out better than expected. I'd gotten nicely champagne drunk. The in-laws had made friendly conversation with one another, mostly about Guy. No one had asked me any-thing annoying, like "When are you having a second kid?" Tom and I both had friends there, and we'd found time to sit next to each other and take a minute to watch everyone enjoying themselves. Guy had smashed the hell out of his cake.

Later that night, as Tom and I were lying in bed, I told him the whole shit-diaper story while he laughed.

What if I see that lady again? I asked him wide-eyed, laughing with my hands clasped over my mouth. *What if someone we know knows her, and I see her at a party? She probably thought I was deranged.* I pulled on the sheets, so they'd untangle between us, our legs intertwined.

The other part was nice, though, I told him, rolling onto my back. Tom put his arm around my belly. *I was so proud of Guy today, in a way I've never felt before. Of course, I knew that he knew all these words, but it was so cute to see him show off to me by using them. And when he put his little hand in my hand, it was like the whole world was right. He was happy and smiley and pleased, and I just couldn't believe it.* Tom put his hand on my forehead. *I never thought it could be like this. Also, I just realized that I wasn't even scared to walk him down the stairs! I didn't even think about it.* I didn't know where it was bubbling up from, but it felt absolutely wonderful to be this happy about my kid.

I'm so glad for you, babe; that's how it's supposed to be. Tom pushed my hair off my face. *I know it has been hard for both of us this past year. It's been hard for me to really connect with him, too, you know.* I felt a little twinge of defensiveness, but I let him continue. *He came to us as a stranger, and it's like any other relationship, right? It grows naturally, but it's not necessarily love at first sight.*

I nodded slowly, thinking about what he said. It was so hard to admit this. I was supposed to be his mother. I was supposed to love him the second he came out–and even before he came out, when he was just an idea of an idea. I was supposed to connect with him deeply while he was still in my body. That hadn't happened, but it was okay. Maybe it was happening now. I snuggled against Tom and put my head on his shoulder. I felt his beard prick my forehead, and I could smell his chest, the soap and skin.

Maybe every night we could say our favorite thing that Guy did that day? And make it a habit, I suggested. *What do you think?* I felt sort of silly and braced myself for Tom to say something non-committal, like *Yah, maybe.*

I think that's a great idea. We are learning to love him, and that's okay, my husband said. I could hear the smile in his voice as my eyes closed. My legs throbbed, they were so tired, and every limb felt heavy against the cool sheets. I could feel my jet lag kicking in. I wanted to respond that I didn't think it was normal for a mother to have to learn to love a child, but I was too tired to get into it just then. Plus, I thought, just before I fell asleep, maybe I had loved him a little bit all along.

Maybe I'd just been too scared to let myself feel it.

14

Mom Strikes Again

New York
Late October 2018

THE WAY GUY SLEPT WAS SO DEEP and heavy that it felt like his body became twice its normal weight. He slept with his mouth open, his wet, drool-covered chin pointed up at me, and I could smell his hot breath, lightly perfumed with baby bacteria, the tiniest bit stale. I liked the scent–it wasn't sour, barely human–and I timed my breathing to the opposite of his so I could inhale when he exhaled. Where his cheek and fat little hands met my chest was sticky, his skin so perfectly plump and clear. We flew home from London the whole way like this.

I felt like there were small fireworks going off somewhere in my body, somewhere in the distance. Not big bangs in my chest or loud explosions in my brain, just little sparks, dull gusts of some ancient maternal hormone traveling through my abdomen; tiny sparkles that felt like the euphoria of prescription painkillers, or the third sip of a first drink. There he was, there we were–finally. I looked at him dreamily. I wanted to memorize everything about his face, but it seemed to change as I was watching, like a slow kaleidoscope.

I thought back to the day my sister's baby died. *It's important,* the nurses had said, *very important to look at him, hold him, and celebrate his existence. It's important for healing and closure to know that he was here, and he will always be loved.* I thought about what that meant: "always be loved." Somewhere between Heathrow and JFK, as the ocean roiled dark and menacing beneath us, I realized that what I was feeling was just that: an infinite love that would never run its course. It might bruise, or have a weak season or two, but it wouldn't quit. It was baked into my body. I would always love Guy, and he would always be loved.

Why had it taken me so long to get here? I didn't want to feel shame or guilt about it, but I wanted to understand myself. Maybe I'd just been too scared to love him in case he was stolen from me. Maybe that fear was compounded by some sort of survivor's guilt or remorse over having a real, living baby I couldn't love when I'd witnessed the horror of my sister having a dead baby who had been deeply wanted and adored. Maybe my sexual trauma and my medical trauma had contributed. All mothers and their capacities to love and care are impacted by their specific pasts, so why are we expected to operate at some superhuman, supra-trauma level where our histories are erased the second we give birth? And while I forgave myself for my story, I wish I'd examined and understood it sooner. Guy hadn't asked to be affected by my own life's darknesses, after all.

Similarly, maybe there'd been some events in my mother's life that had made it hard for her to love me the way I wanted her to. I thought about what Judi Dench would say, and it was something like: *You felt unmothered, and as a consequence, you haven't been sure how to mother.* And she'd be partly right, but there was more to it. I didn't understand my mother's whole self–she remained opaque as a person–so how could I fully analyze her as a parent?

Moms are so unknowable, so filled with the secrets of their own lives. I knew my mom was afraid of heights, airplane turbulence, and cockroaches, and she said she was afraid of water, but I had memories of her swimming when I was a kid. She said she had naturally red hair, but hadn't I seen her dye it? She let people believe she spoke French, but I'd been to France with her and knew she could barely order a coffee. When did she start her period? Did she ever have boyfriends? Had she ever kissed a girl? Did she feel an intense, hormonal draw to me the minute I was born or had she hated me for a year?

Her laugh will be embedded in my brain forever. How she swallows loudly when she drinks water and how much that noise annoys me. No one can make me angrier–flip a switch in me that paralyzes my body with powerful white rage, as blinding and intense and fierce as my love for her. Every time the phone rings, in fact, a part of me twitches, worried it's the call informing me that something bad has happened to my mom.

I don't remember finding my pregnant mother on the floor of the bathroom when I was five, hemorrhaging blood with her arms wrapped around her big belly, my baby brother inside it. I don't remember calling 911 and saving her life. I remember only the words she says in her Texas accent, the story about when her parents left her asleep in the hot Galveston sun, letting blisters burn up and down her arms. I remember her teaching me how to draw the letter *R* as we waited for my dad to come home early from work; her taking me to the butcher shop, where the man behind the counter in his white apron would give me a slice of bologna; her walking arm in arm with me, *like French women do*; the impressions she does of my husband and her parents and our friends; the way she sets a table, and puts her soft hands on my cheeks when I'm sick, and says the word *sweetheart* when she means it.

And that version of my mother needed to be enough. Was it antidepressants, therapy, my hormones settling down, or simply the passing of time that allowed me to feel this way? Or a mix of all of it? I wasn't sure, but back in New York, I had barely a week before my mom was coming to visit, only two weeks after Guy's birthday party. *I just didn't get to spend enough time with him!* she explained. *And I have meetings I have to take, anyway.* I didn't respond by reminding her that in London, she'd decided to stay twenty-five minutes away from us despite my having told her a hundred times to book at Claridge's. And I didn't bring up that in New York, even though she stayed at a hotel roughly three blocks from my apartment, she often went entire days without coming over to see Guy. Once, she'd even told me she was leaving for the airport an entire day before she actually did, so that I wouldn't pester her about visiting him. I found out the truth only when my sister, Deech, accidentally told me that she was on the way to pick Mom up from the airport in Indiana–a day after I'd thought she'd returned home already.

This time she called me from her car as she was being driven into Manhattan. *When can I come see my Guy?* she asked, the fuzzy noise of highway traffic behind her. I imagined her crossing the bridge, talking to me on speakerphone while the driver listened. She probably sounded like a very doting grandmother. I was sitting in my office at the gallery, tearing through emails that had built up while I was away, trying to get it all done so that I could make it home to spend a few minutes with Guy before he went to bed. I pinned the phone between my ear and shoulder while I shuffled through the stack of mail on my desk, opening FedEx envelopes with slim exhibition catalogues in them and tossing invites to art openings into the trash.

He's napping right now, I said. Why did it seem like no one remembered the schedule but me? *He has been napping from eleven to one for over a year now. I'm in the office today, probably until five, when I go home to do bath. Do you want to come for bath? It's cute. You can sit on a chair and watch, don't worry. No one is gonna make you get your hair wet.* I thought about how happy Guy was to splash around in the water and how easily it soothed him. I needed some of that tranquilizer right now.

Perfect, she said, not seeming to notice my annoyance. *Will you take me somewhere for a martini after? Let's go to Baltha-*

zar, if you can get a booth. What time should I come over? It was as if she thought our whole world came to a halt the minute she landed.

At six, Mom. Bath is always at six. Guy goes to bed at seven. He sleeps seven to seven. Ever since he was three months old. So don't be late. I threw away all the empty envelopes and junk mail, then took a deep breath. I hated when I let my shitty, juvenile side come out. *Sorry I'm being snippy, I'm at the office trying to catch up on work. I love you, I'm glad you're here. Guy will be so excited to see you, and we will have martinis,* I promised. *Tom is probably going to work late, so it will just be you and me.*

Perfect, she said. *See you soon.*

AT SIX O'CLOCK I was on my knees filling our bathtub while Sharon played slot machines on her phone in the nursery.

Do you want bubbles, baby Guy? I asked my naked little boy, putting my hand on his soft butt. I could cup both cheeks in one hand and they felt like bouncy mushroom caps. He leaned over the tub and threw in his floating rubber toys, laughing as each one splashed. I squirted in some baby wash and watched as the thick rush of water from the faucet churned it into foam, my eyes darting back and forth to one of the screens of our keyless entry system, waiting for my mom to ring the doorbell.

Minutes ticked by, and Guy busied himself with his toys on the floor. I didn't want to leave him near the water to get my phone. In the CPR class given in the nursery unit at the hospital right after he was born, they'd warned us to throw away any buckets we had at home, all opportunities for drowning, which I'd never even thought of. I picked him up and carried him into the bedroom. He started crying and repeating, *Bath! Bath!*

Shhhh, baby, I know, you're gonna get your bath. I'm just waiting to see where my goddamn mother is. I jostled him on my hip as I grabbed my phone to call my mom. He got more agitated with every bounce.

No, Mamma, bath! His little voice broke into a cry. My phone screen said six fifteen, and my mother didn't pick up. I walked back into the bathroom with my phone and turned off the water, testing the temperature in the tub while Guy whimpered.

In, Mamma! In! I lowered his thrashing legs toward the water and patted off his tears. We had a policy of no phones in the bathroom during bath time, the rule I'd insisted on for my own peace of mind, but I wanted to know where the fuck my mom was. *We are starting bath*, I texted her.

Not gonna make it. See you at dinner, she replied. I flashed with anger. Before I could stop myself, my fingers flew into their own little tantrum:

You can break all the promises to me you want, but you can't break promises to Guy. We were waiting for you, and now his bath is going to be shorter than usual because we waited, and that makes him less easy to put down for bed. Next time I just won't invite you. I hit Send, then put my phone on a stack of towels and turned to focus on Guy, who was none the wiser. I hadn't lied: it was bizarre how tiny deviations from a baby's schedule could change his mood. My pediatrician had once told me that most problems could be solved with water: cranky babies are usually thirsty, or want something to splash around with, or need to calm down in a bath. It worked. It made his bedtime serene.

It didn't have the same effect on me, however. I walked into Balthazar a little huffy after having taken a quick shower and putting on a black leather skirt and cashmere sweater with a pair of kitten heels. It was only fifteen minutes, and my mom hadn't signed a contract that she'd be at bath at six, but what the fuck else was she doing, three blocks away? It incensed me. Yet I was also a little embarrassed by my inability to hide my chagrin. I thought about how one day I'd regret any bad word I ever said to her, any time I ever wasted being anything but glad to exist in her presence.

When I sat down at our regular booth, she was scanning her phone, her dark, heavy-framed glasses on. There was a martini in front of her, up with a lemon twist. The glass was still frosty.

There you are! She looked up, her giant smile flashing in her signature lip color. *How was bath?* She was doing her best Blanche DuBois from *A Streetcar Named Desire*.

It was great, Mom, but I'm mad that you said you were coming and then made us wait, and didn't pick up your phone, and then didn't even show–

Don't make Mamma drink alone, sweetheart, let's get you a martini. I get worried about you, getting all worked up like this.

I scooted roughly on the banquette, thighs squeaking against the leather as I slid myself back.

I'm not worked up! My voice did rise a bit, but only because I wanted her to pay attention to what I was saying. *I just want to be really clear: Can you please just not break promises to Guy? For both practical and emotional reasons. I really mean it. We want you in our life, but you can't be unreliable.* My voice cracked, and I couldn't make eye contact with her. I looked around wildly for a server.

You know . . . , she started, and I steeled myself against whatever excuse she was about to make, whatever admonishment of me. *I really do hear you.* My head shot up in surprise. She took a sip of her martini and handed it to me. I took a sip, too. It burned a little going down. *I've been thinking a lot about you. About how hard this past year was for you.* I side-eyed her again, wondering if this was some tactic to contextualize me as hysterical. This is exactly why I never told anyone how tough new motherhood was for me; I knew it could be used against me, the perfect evidence that I wasn't a good girl.

I remember how hard it was for me. And I am so mad at myself for not warning you and for not doing more for you. I really am.

She took another sip of the martini and so did I. I'd certainly felt the indignity of being a burden on her many times, but I guess I had never thought that it was maybe because she was struggling. I thought it was because she just didn't like me. And I'd certainly treated myself as if I was unlikable–or worse.

That's okay, I said. I almost felt bad for her, thinking about the pain of thirty years' worth of what I'd just experienced. *Plus, I think it's probably hard for you to remember that far back,* I added, tracing something imaginary on the paper on the tabletop. They didn't use white linens here, even though it was a really nice place.

No, no. I really should have warned you. I'm kicking myself. Did I ever tell you about when you were born, how much I hated your father afterward?

I couldn't believe what I was hearing. I had never even heard my parents have a fight. I always thought that all hetero marriages of a certain generation were like my parents', where the husband was oblivious to the wife's faults as long as she cooked dinner and got the kids to school on time. But maybe my mother got as frustrated with my dad as I got with Tom.

I signaled again for a server. *I just should have spilled to you about all of this. I don't know why I kept it all so secret. When I had you, I had absolutely no help. My parents didn't babysit, and your father's parents lived down south. A few weeks after you were born, my in-laws came to visit, and Daddy invited them over for cocktails.*

She called my dad *Daddy* because that's always what we called him as little kids, unless we were in trouble, when we had to call him *sir*.

My martini finally arrived, and I popped an olive in my mouth, chewing it without tasting.

So, I went into the bedroom while your grandmother and grandfather were oohing and aahing over you, and Daddy was fixing cocktails. And I figured I had about twenty minutes to my-self. I started cleaning the room up, organizing stacks of crap and folding laundry. The next thing I knew, your father was in there to check on me, and he acted like I'd abandoned him at the altar. He said, "What are you doing in here? My mother is out there!" Like his mother was the first lady. "You have to come entertain!" And I just wanted to shoot him dead. It was truly the first twenty min-utes I'd had in weeks where you'd been someone else's responsi-bility. And I remember thinking to myself, I will die if the rest of my life is me fighting my husband so that I can clean my house. My life has to be more than this. She leaned into her accent as she smacked both her hands down on the table. *More than thaaayis.*

Ugh, how did you not Lorena Bobbitt that fucker? I asked her. She laughed.

I didn't know it was an option, she said. *I guess I'm just not that creative.* I watched the choreography of white-aproned waiters setting steak frites on the tables of beautifully dressed gentlemen, refilling champagne glasses and pouring chocolate sauce over profiteroles. *Plus, it wasn't totally his fault. He didn't have any par-adigms for, you know, being a modern feminist husband. It took him time to get there.*

Do you ever wonder if you had some sort of postpartum de-pression? I asked. I wasn't sure if it was the need to get bread and butter into my system before I passed out, but the revelation that maybe all the memories of my mom's anger and irritability and exasperation with us could be chalked up to some form of depression made me feel lightheaded. Depression I could relate to, especially one stemming from a post-birth crisis of identity. I could envision Judi Dench's jaw dropping at this revelation.

Probably, my mom said, like she'd already thought of it. She was looking off into the restaurant, watching the well-timed ballet of the room. Somewhere a table broke into laughter.

I tell myself it's a rational reaction to something as insane as having a kid, I said. I'd felt so much anger toward my mom in my life; that she wasn't better at things, that she didn't seem to try. Simply accepting her as a flawed person had always seemed like it would be a catastrophe. I guess I'd been afraid that if I admitted she wasn't the selfless and perfect mother I craved, it might mean I'd have to accept the reality that I was never going to get everything I wanted from our relationship. But maybe accepting this was just part of growing the life cycle: leaving space for me to build my own bonds with the family I was creating and so on.

I watched my mom look up and smile, and I thought she was gazing into her own memories, about to say something profound. Instead, she lifted both her arms.

Tom Sachs! You come sit right next to me, handsome. Her grin was as big as I ever saw it as she reached up toward my husband.

Hi, baby. He pressed his forehead against mine. *I heard through the grapevine you were having dinner with your mom here, so I wanted to stop by to squeeze you.* He put his arm around my waist and pinched my hip. I felt my body get warm, like the early days, when I'd look into Tom's eyes and absolutely melt. I'd stopped putting him so high up on a pedestal. This was real love, the kind you had to work at; the kind you went to therapy for, and got on meds for if you needed them, and did nice things for each other, and chose your relationship over and over and over. I took another sip of martini.

Hi, Tommy. I smiled, a little shy in front of my mom. I scooted farther into the booth so that he could sit next to me. My mom shifted to the other side.

Tommy! she said, ten times as excited as me. *How's my favorite daddy?* When she wanted to pour it on, she did nothing better. I swear she shimmied a little as she said *daddy.*

I'd love a glass of Saint Emilion, Tom said to the server. *Aren't you two the picture of impropriety?* he said to me and my mom. *What have you been talking about? How was Guy's bath?*

My mom said nothing, looking at her phone. *Sorry.* She looked up. *Your father simply can't live without me.* She giggled and rolled her eyes at once, as if it were terribly annoying to be married to a man obsessed with her. Tom fumbled in his bag and pulled out a thin package, wrapped in aluminum foil. In Sharpie across the front, he'd written: *For Guy's mamma.*

What is it? I asked him, a little surprised. I hadn't anticipated him showing up, let alone arriving with gifts. Our anniversary was coming up, but not for several days. I pulled tentatively at the foil and saw a quarter of a photograph underneath, the bottom half of me in a hospital gown. Not something I necessarily wanted memorialized. *Is this a gift?*

I don't know, he said, his voice purposefully mysterious. *Why don't you open it and find out?* He nudged the package toward me. My mom was preoccupied with her phone. I tugged the aluminum foil open a little more, revealing a photo of the two of us in a hospital bed, both staring at Guy, passive in my arms. We looked shell-shocked.

Did you make me a zine? I asked. Tom was nodding like he'd gifted me pure gold. Somewhere behind us a glass dropped and shattered; a few people clapped. A rush of servers and busboys swept in to clean it up.

Oh my word, what's that? my mom asked breathily, pronouncing *that* like she was the antagonist of a Pat Conroy novel. She sipped her martini, and before I could answer her, she picked up her phone and started texting someone. I thought about Judi Dench's expression when I would tell her this story next week; how she'd purse her lips a little at my mom's erratic attention, and how she'd be glad that Tom had gone out of his way to spend a little time with me. *See?* she'd say. *He's trying.*

I looked so sullen in the cover photograph. In collaged typewriter script across my legs, it read, *My Beautiful, Poorly Behaved Wife.* Inside, there were ten photos of me that I had never seen before. In between each was another photograph, some examples of a mess I'd left. In one, there was a wet towel left on the bed. In another, a belt I borrowed from him and forgotten in a pile on the couch, with a pair of worn underwear. One page had a bag of dog shit that I'd picked up and left outside our apartment, unable to find a trash can between the site of the defecation and our door. At the very back was a love note, typed on a Hermes Baby typewriter, a wartime Swiss machine Tom had collected. *To my perfect queen, the best mother, most beautiful wife, the messiest and only one I'll ever love*, he wrote. The back cover was an image of Guy from his first birthday party. I could feel myself smiling as I looked at it.

So you'll always remember the last year, Tom said. *The contradiction and the pain and the mess and the beauty. I love you, Sarah Hoover. I know it's been hard, but you're an absolutely brilliant woman. I've been thinking about it since we got home from London, and I just finished this today.* He tapped the zine with his fingers. *I don't know where you're going exactly, but I know it's going to be profound. I'm so lucky I get to be on the ride with you.* Even my mom had put down her phone and was watching us as he put his hand behind my neck and kissed me, not as sloppy and wet as the first kisses we'd ever shared, but as deep and connected as I'd always wanted.

15

Phone Games

Saint Moritz and Honolulu
December 2018

NO MATTER THE SPLENDOR OF ANY HOTEL, when something disgusting happens in one of its rooms, the whole mise-en-scène is ruined. On our Caribbean honeymoon, I'd ordered room service and found an insect tail, articulated and crunchy, in my fried rice. In Los Angeles, during my bout of horrible postpartum depression brain fog, when everything seemed to move more slowly than usual, as if I were living underwater, I'd found a condom wedged between the night table and the wall, dried to a crisp and plastered to the wood like a curl of burned skin. In Fez, I'd had such a horrible period that I left every towel and sheet covered with either blood or chocolate. A night spent crying in the bath, my uterine lining sliding out in gelatinous sheets, made me so nauseated that I could barely eat for the rest of the trip.

As Christmas rolled around, a few months after Guy turned one, I geared up for another round of where-will-I-find-someone-else's-pubic-hair-in-this-strange-hotel-room? The art world shuttered its galleries for the holiday, emails stopped pouring into inboxes, and phones stopped ringing as we all took a collective two-week break. Yet somehow I found our family at one of the few places where commerce marched on: deep in Switzerland's Engadin valley, at the base of Mount Corviglia, overlooking the lake of Saint Moritz.

There is really no better place to have Christmas, Tom had said, explaining our plans to me one night over a late dinner at the kitchen table. I'd had a cocktail with work friends, and, as usual, he'd been in the studio, painting. *It will be so snowy and festive, and we can put Guy in the lederhosen we got as a baby gift.* He took a big bite of his take-out pad Thai. *We will be together somewhere cozy, most importantly. And you can ski.*

But Guy's too little to ski. He only learned how to walk about two months ago. I slurped up some of my own pad Thai and looked at my husband. *We have to think of him, too,* I said gently. I'd gotten much better at speaking to Tom calmly in recent months.

Ski school. How cute will that be, watching him bounce around like a little cartoon character in a colorful helmet? Like a little emoji. Tom smiled at me, and I smiled back in spite of myself.

You have to be potty-trained to go to ski school, babe. Tom laughed, and I smiled, picturing Guy's tiny body, his lisp, and small voice. It still blew my mind that Tom and I had a baby together, that he came out of my actual body and now could laugh and speak and cry real tears and clap his hands.

Well, we can ask Sharon if she's available, and he can hang out with her in the hotel. It has a really great pool, Tom said, like he'd already talked to Sharon about it. Like he'd already discussed her holiday plans. *I have a show opening the night before Christmas, and as soon as that's over, we can go somewhere else, just us.* I felt warm hearing the words *just us.* It sounded like a fantasy. *Somewhere tropical and romantic.* I thought about where that would be. Though it sounded impractical, I'd always wanted to go to Hawaii.

Should we come back to New York for a couple of days and then go to Honolulu? I suggested. I half expected Tom to change his mind, tell me how crazy far that was, and insist we go somewhere closer, or skip the trip altogether. *My jet lag has been fucking with my life for months; what's two to three more time zones?* I said, trying to convince him. Tom was nodding, excited already.

Yes . . . exactly, he said, munching on bean sprouts. *We can surf!*

OUR HOTEL IN SAINT MORITZ sat at the base of the mountain, a white fortress surrounded by pure, clean snow—so much snow that you couldn't see any evidence of the ground underneath, as if the whole building had been perched on a pillow. Inside, it was dark and dramatic: tapestries, carved timber, and shadowy stone fireplaces that all felt so frozen in time it was surprising to flip a switch and find electricity.

Guy and I would have breakfast together at whatever hour we woke up, usually alone in the main dining room, the vast windows looking out over a frozen lake and the mountain above it. Ponies practiced for polo on the ice below, and he loved to watch them and make horse noises. Sharon said she was too cold to leave her room. Tom was working around the clock, finishing his paintings that couldn't ship wet and had to be touched up on-site, so I'd take Guy on snowy walks, just the two of us. We were lawless. Receipts, Mickey Mouse ears, and plastic dinosaurs littered our floors; balloons floated, half deflated, around the suite. He was going to sleep with me after midnight and waking up with me at noon. We hadn't slept normal hours since we'd returned to New York from London two months before, the toll of our bounce from time zone to time zone, the exhaustion of following Tom to different countries.

I'd come home late, and Guy and Sharon would still be awake, making potions out of shampoo and soap in the minibar's ice bucket, or having a dance party, or drawing on the bathroom floor in chalk. I'd get Guy cleaned up, put him in a diaper and an overnight shirt. We'd pull heavy, expensive drapes closed over the big picture windows to make the room pitch-black and fall asleep with a Disney movie on low volume, all wound up in each other. I was always naked, even though Petunia had told me that by the time my son was two, I needed to start wearing clothes around him.

That new guy I'm dating, Hank, can remember his mom's nipples, she said painfully, *and now he claims he can't fuck a girl with small tits.* Meanwhile, I didn't even own nightgowns, let alone travel with them. In Saint Moritz, the snow muffled any noise we might have heard from the outside, and it was like sleeping inside a marshmallow. Even so, I fantasized about flying home earlier.

But it wasn't to be. Our flight home got delayed by a day, and we ended up staying a night in Milan to wait for the next one. I booked a hotel on my phone during the ride into town from the airport, and when we got there, it was a much more run-down version of a place we'd stayed years ago, the summer I turned twenty-four. There had been two Twombly paintings over the front desk, a gift from the artist. Now there were two faded squares where they'd once been, and the whole lobby smelled like thick, oily cologne.

What if you took Guy to the pool while I unpack some clothes for dinner? I said to Tom at check-in.

Part of me just wants to eat room service and hang out in bed, Tom said, resting his passport on the check-in desk. Sharon was sitting in a chair in the lobby with Guy on her lap, letting him watch her play the slot machine app. *But I feel like I haven't properly romanced you in months. I'm taking my hot wife to dinner.* He grabbed my hand and kissed it. *I'll exhaust our little hellion at the pool if you make a dinner reservation?* I nodded, thinking about what I wanted to eat. The concierge handed us our keys, hardly making eye contact. Every time he moved, I could smell the thick cologne wafting off him.

All those summers ago, we'd been upgraded to a beautiful suite in this hotel, a separate living room and everything. We'd had friends over for late-night Bolognese after the fancy three-star restaurant we'd gone to for my birthday had given us twelve courses of portions meant for birds, and the concierge had sent up a bottle of birthday champagne on the house.

This time the room was narrow and drab, the bedspread faded and old. The walls and silk headboard were yellow, and the lighting was yellow, and I didn't dare look in a mirror, just in case I was yellow. Instead, I unzipped my suitcase in front of the window, which had a view of nothing consequential. I pulled out a dress to wear for dinner. I had no clean underwear left, and the old trick of flipping some inside out never sat right with me. It's not the dirtiness I worried about but the smell, some sort of pubic-area oils awakened on already-worn fabric with a proximity to body heat. I was determined to spend some alone time with Tom somewhere with menus and old-fashioned waiters in tuxedos with white tea towels draped over their forearms. I would be going out to dinner with him, and I would not be wearing panties, and it would not be my fault if this resulted in a child-free, stress-relieving fuck session in a restaurant bathroom, something we'd absolutely never done but that the promise of going home together, to a quiet week in Hawaii, made me think was possible.

I pulled the throw pillows and comforter off the bed and put them in the closet. They grossed me out because I'd heard they weren't washed regularly between guests, and it was always one of the first things I did when I got to a hotel room. Then I climbed between the sheets and called downstairs to see if there was anywhere that would take a last-minute couple for a late and sexy dinner. The concierge put me on hold, and I drowned out the dinky music by imagining Tom's hand on my leg under the table later. It gave me the tiniest tickle in my middle, and there was something so nice about the feeling. It was like my passion for him had been frozen in a block of ice for so long and was just now starting to thaw. I'm not saying I wanted to rip his clothes off and have sex all night long, but the thought of our connection felt right to me. How fortunate that a delayed flight wasn't a catastrophe but a chance to have an unexpectedly beautiful night with my love. The hold music kept playing as I looked around the room.

I glanced at Tom's iPad when it lit up on the bedside table, casting a white glow on the list of stale minibar options. A text had come through, and I opened it immediately, killing time, noticing that it didn't also pop up on his iPhone, plugged in on the table next to it.

Call me, baby, it read. And then, immediately, *Are you home?* I was confused, like, my dumb ass sort of assumed someone had the wrong number for a minute. Or maybe the iPad was connected to someone else's phone, someone who worked with him. It didn't make any sense that this married man with a baby, who was taking his hot wife to dinner in Milan and who was working so hard to maintain a good relationship with her, who had made her a zine a few months before, and planned a beautiful Christmas trip, and who had just left the room to take their child swimming, would be called *baby* by someone who wasn't me.

As I was thinking about these things, another text came in. *I need to see you before you go to Hawaii.* The word *Hawaii* rattled around in my brain. It stunned me. My stomach dropped the same way it did on airplanes when we hit turbulence. I didn't need to read anything else, but of course I did. I read all of it, sitting in bed with that iPad, scrolling back months. The first exchange had been before Thanksgiving. In some sections, there were texts that seemed to be missing, as if he'd deleted them.

Who was this person? Had he told her he loved her? Had he told her the things he wanted to do to her body? Had he done them? I would never know unless I forced him to confess. But I did know that my husband, a father, told this woman she was hot, pretty, and sexy; all the things I worried I wasn't. It made my heart hurt. It made my face hot, my head heavy. It made tears start to gather behind my eyes.

• • •

I GOOGLED HER NUMBER and eventually found her—her LinkedIn and her name and then her Instagram, her best friend's Instagram, her mom's place of work, plus photographic evidence that I had a better butt. The only thing that might assuage the desperate anguish in my gut, I knew, would be incontrovertible, physical proof that I was *better than her*, a standard that one hour earlier I would have told you was arbitrary, made-up, patriarchal bullshit conditioning.

In some sort of badass and unprecedented trance, I screengrabbed the evidence, AirDropped it to myself, and deleted the images I'd taken before emptying the iPad trash. I remembered, just vaguely, my dad carrying me out to our driveway under the pale light of a big moon, me in a white flannel 1990s nightgown, to show me his newly installed car phone.

Now you can always reach me, he'd said, holding me at his waist. That cell phone number is tattooed inside my brain, and that feeling of connectivity and closeness it provided, like viscera. Now I was at the mercy of the same technology. Just as I was thinking about my father's kindness and dependability, I heard the mechanical whirring of the hotel room door unlocking, and I jumped. I knew the minute I saw Tom, carrying our son in his arms, both of them with wet hair and hotel robes on, that I was going to leave him. I just felt it. It was like someone slammed one of the pull-down gates on the back of a moving truck, the kind with the rope attached so that you can really yank down hard. It rammed shut right around the spot in my chest where I felt love for him.

The pool is super shitty, but your son doesn't care. He thinks he's Michael Phelps, Tom said as he waltzed into the room with Guy. He wasn't looking at me yet. I sat in the bed, on my throne, watching him, my chin up. He came and put Guy in my arms and kissed my forehead. His lips felt rough and cold against my skin, dry from the chlorine. *We missed you while we were gone, though. Did you get a dinner res?* I allowed his touch, not flinching, not reacting. I felt strangely calm, my heart beating so slowly it seemed unnatural. My hands felt as steady as a surgeon's.

I remembered a night early in our relationship when Tom had come to meet me out at the bar we all loved, our watering hole, which happened to be across the street from the house he was renting while he gutted his dream apartment, the one we'd move out of a few years later when I got pregnant. As I perched on his lap in the dark, smoky room, trying to support myself extra with my thigh muscles so he'd think I was light as a feather, he'd slipped a warm and confident hand under my shirt and pinched my nipple. I felt electrified, but my immediate thought was to show no response.

If he thinks I'm impenetrable, I thought, *he'll keep trying.* I thought it would demonstrate the ascetic denial of my desire, the same way men prioritize their own pleasure at the expense of women. He looked at his guy friend, across from us on a low leather couch, and laughed.

She's impossible, he joked. *She's so hot, and she gives me nothing.* I tried not to beam as I felt victory wash over me. I thought I had played the game right, demonstrated my strength and the need to be seduced all at once.

Pool, Mamma! Guy said. It sounded like *Poo*. I nodded at him. I wondered if my face looked peaceful, or tired, or completely disinterested, but Tom didn't seem to notice any change in me.

You are too grown up, little man. You are such a good swimmer, I said. He was naked under the pool towel, and I unwrapped him so he could get dry and warm under the comforter with me. His clammy skin met mine, and I reached for the remote to put on a kid's movie.

We're going to dinner at nine at Da Giacomo. I said it flatly, skimming the TV options for Guy at the same time. His little body was getting nice and warm against mine, and I kept my voice low and even so he wouldn't move. I could smell the pool water in his hair, mixed with his shampoo. *Why don't you shower with Guy while I finish getting dressed.* I kissed Guy's head and handed him back to Tom. They walked into the bathroom, and Tom still didn't seem to clock the shift in my energy.

In fact, I felt collected enough to take a piece of hotel stationery and a thick, clumsy pen off the table next to the bed and start making a list of every betrayal Tom committed that I could remember:

When we first got together, and he took me to a party where I heard he'd been out the night before with *Christine*, when he'd told me he'd been working.

The woman from his past who asked him if he wanted to meet up for a sex date, and he replied, simply, *It's complicated, but I can't.*

The way he held a woman's gaze in front of me once when I was pregnant, as if he found her ravishing.

So many other texts and emails I'd seen over time; little flirtations here and there that cut me sharply.

Every time I'd discover new evidence of his dalliances, part of me would blame myself. I'd think about how they must happen only because I wasn't beautiful or special enough to enrapture him, how it must be because I didn't match some culturally specified, made-up, and arbitrary beauty standard. I'd spent almost a decade thinking like that. Then, when I was at my lowest, suffering through my pregnancy and postpartum with a broken brain, I'd worried in all my *magical thinking* glory that if I mentioned how upsetting I found these exchanges, he might wake up to some deep-seated truth about me and flee the coop. Maybe it was true– maybe I wasn't good enough to captivate his attentions–or maybe it was false. That part didn't seem to matter anymore: what felt important was that people treat you how you let them, and I had to believe it was possible to be in a relationship that didn't include secret texting while I watched *Moana* for the five thousandth time.

Tom took Guy next door to Sharon to get his pajamas on, and he came back to the room so that we could get dressed. He locked the door between the rooms and pulled off his towel dramatically, draping it across the desk chair. He was naked underneath, and hard. He pulled back the sheets, my bare legs uncovered. He didn't notice the list and the pen next to me.

Should we do it before dinner? He laid down on the bed and slid his hands under my butt, cupping it, tucking his fingers delicately at my lower back. He kissed inside my legs, and I stared at him, feeling his beard tickle the top of my thighs.

Don't get turned on, I told myself. I talked to my own brain. *Don't react.* I felt something in myself closing down, like I was watching New York City's power grid shut off from the top of the Empire State Building, section by section.

Your pussy is ice cold, he said, pulling his head back. *What's wrong?* It felt right, to keep him on his toes, make him doubt his sexual power over me. I was sure that if I let myself be swept away by his touch, I'd feel overwhelmed and fragile, too caught up in the vortex of our intimacy to ever confront him.

I'm just not in the mood, I said. I reached over, grabbed my cell phone, and opened it, scrolling through Instagram. I still wasn't making eye contact with him; I couldn't have sex with him, but I wasn't ready for a fight, and I wasn't sure when I would be or what I would say. I knew I had to have some sort of prepared script, or I'd crumble, submitting to the easier path of permitting the status quo. My narrative wasn't quite ready yet; I needed time to craft my philippic. If my husband was going to give his sexual attention to other women, I felt more and more certain that it was no longer something I could consider important or central to our relationship, no longer something I would allow between us. But I was not ready to debate this with him.

Are you okay? he asked.

Fuck, I thought. *Am I doing this wrong? Am I giving him a reason to be mad at me instead of me being mad at him?* For a moment, I felt nervous that I was not playing my cards right, and I didn't know quite what to do. I thought about texting Petunia or Augusta for opinions and advice, but I'd never been able to share these stories with them. It hurt too much. It was too embarrassing, too shameful. Instead, I wanted to figure it out on my own. I wanted to count on myself for once. I was a fucking mother. I was raising a fucking son, a son who I wanted to grow up knowing that he was finally not a burden, not a hindrance or a barricade to the identity I wanted, but a joy to love. And I didn't know if I had the energy to provide that care while being drained by the demands of having a husband and receiving compromised attention in return.

I started thinking about my dad, and his relationship with my mom. He writes the woman love notes. I've never read what he writes to her, and she's never shared. She just opens the cards he hands her on her birthday or at their anniversary dinner or whatever, and then she looks at us kids misty-eyed, saying, *Your father is such a beautiful writer.* His cards and letters come in strangely masculine cursive, sturdy and thick. He writes only with a fancy pen, the kind with a nib that you have to fill with ink yourself. He learned that from his own mom, who kept her pens in a beautiful sterling silver box on her antique mahogany partners desk with a red leather top in the study of her house in Evansville, Indiana. She wrote in maroon ink, and I came to think of it as her color, because she also made cranberry sorbet at Thanksgiving that was tart and creamy, a flavor I will never forget even though she has been dead since I was eleven.

My dad writes his notes in navy blue and keeps his pots of ink at the top of his desk. I have never seen him look twice at another woman. I know that sort of love–committed and righteous–exists because of him. I used to think that this kind of old-fashioned love was so rare that I couldn't expect it. But I was struck now by the thought that I'd rather be alone forever than accept anything less. And I had to ask myself why on earth I'd chosen this man who did not put me at ease and nourish me. This man who was not consistent or dependable or truthful.

This wasn't the marriage I signed up for when I married Tom. Or, I take that back: maybe it was, but that felt like eons ago, another epoch, too hard to judge in retrospect. I'd been committed to therapy and antidepressants. I'd been trying as hard as possible to fix all the cracks in the foundation of my mental health, to clean up my side of the street and be the architect of my own home, building it to be as strong and solid as could be so that Tom and Guy could inhabit it with me. This work hadn't been easy, but I'd stuck with it. Meanwhile, Tom had leaned into old ways, all the while telling me he was on my team. At that moment, I felt bizarrely clear about what I wanted and how to get there, as if the synapses in my brain were firing up, a yellow brick road pointing in one direction: immediate divorce. I still was unconvinced that I was sufficiently pretty or special, I still hated my nose and my fucked-up ex-ballerina feet and the way my vagina looked post-baby; I couldn't imagine sex with anyone else but Tom, nor did I want to try, but what I did know–what I was sure of–was that I didn't need my damn *husband*, of all people, to make me feel even worse about myself. I didn't have time to fight those demons when my child was barely over a year old, more of a person than ever before. And I didn't need Tom for anything else, either, because there was nothing else he was giving me. I was merely his shadow, an afterthought of a shape that was always there. And instead of following him around, I suddenly saw a future for myself where I was fucking free.

16

The Confrontation

Honolulu
Late December 2018–Early January 2019

THE PLANE TO HAWAII WAS AN OLDER MODEL, relegated to American tourists headed to the tolerably exotic destination of Honolulu, its leather seats cracked and unable to recline properly, their gears caked with years of Pepsi residue. I'd gotten on it unsure of the right way to handle my relationship; I knew that I wanted it to end, but I was still afraid to say that out loud, scared to make it true. What words do you use to end a marriage? "I'm leaving you"? "I want a divorce"? "I hate you and want to cut off your dick"? I hadn't talked to anyone or run my decision by a therapist. I hadn't even told Sharon, who had stayed in New York and wasn't sitting right next to me. I knew if she'd been there, she would have gripped my hand on takeoff—we both hated flying, even more so on a shitty plane. I know she would have been on my side, but I hadn't developed the right words to explain to her or anyone else what was going on.

I turned to look at Tom next to me. His window shade was down, and he was sitting up very straight, writing in his little yellow notebook, the soft cover flopped open, but not to the point where I could read anything. His glasses were pushed up on his forehead, a quirk I used to think was so sexy because it made him look smart, like Indiana Jones. But now I just thought it made him look idiotic. Tom glanced up and met my eyes.

Hi, babe, he mouthed over the drone of the engine. He was acting like everything was normal, even though I knew it wasn't. He put his elbow on the console between our wide leather seats, shutting his notebook. I watched as he slowly pulled it under his arm.

Are you writing a love letter to your stupid girlfriend? The words just fell out of my mouth. They plopped out as my eyebrows shot halfway up my forehead, in an *I-know-and-I-won't-take-your-shit* type of look. I surprised myself with the force of my accusation.

Maybe it was the back-to-back twelve-hour flights, or the year and a half of postpartum misery, or the ten months of pregnancy before that, but at this moment, I had no energy to steamroll my attitude. I like to think some higher power came over me, maybe an ancestor–maybe my great-grandma Sadie, who'd moved to the United States from a ghetto in Poland in the early twentieth century and settled in the Bronx, where she'd *maybe* been a sex worker for some Mafia guys. By the time I met her, she was ancient, parked in a Jewish nursing home that smelled like antiseptic, piss, and chopped liver, and the force with which she offered me dried apricots distracted me from asking for confirmation of her story. But I like to think that on this airplane, Sadie was watching and wouldn't let me tolerate nonsense. The thought helped me stay calm–I was not the first woman to stand up to a man.

I didn't let my eyes look away from Tom.

Are you telling your little girlfriend what a piece-of-shit father you are? How you're teaching your kid to be disloyal and pathetic? He peered at me, wide-eyed, like a ten-year-old boy, and the weakness in his eyes emboldened me.

B-Babe– he sort of stuttered. His pupils dilated, a slight movement that I interpreted as fear. My eyebrows moved up again, this time more slowly and consciously. I knew their power, and I was not going to stop employing it.

I can read your mind, I continued. *Like a witch.* The drone of the engine soothed me a little bit. I knew that most likely no one else could hear us above it. I could see Tom trying very hard to not let any emotion show on his face. He was holding his jaw slack, like he didn't want any evidence of tension to appear. I wanted to admit that it wasn't just his mind–I could also read his texts and emails–but I kept that part to myself. *No use in lying to me,* I started, but my voice cracked a little, and I looked down at my hands. Blurting things out was easy, but the thought of having to delve into a fight about this suddenly seemed daunting. I felt the crease under my butt cheeks starting to sweat a little in the leggings I was wearing on the plane. A passenger walked down the aisle and slipped into the bathroom.

Tom opened his mouth but didn't say anything. He looked like one of those dogs who's had its vocal cords removed, barking but with no sound coming out. I could tell he was trying to formulate a thought or come up with some excuse or explanation. He scratched at his beard, one of his little tics when he's anxious. I figured that next he'd take a deep breath, and then he'd start trying to tell me that I was being crazy, or overreacting, or that I shouldn't have looked at his texts, if that's what I did, because, as I'd heard from ex-boyfriends–and from half the girls I knew who were endlessly fighting with their boyfriends about what was happening behind their locked phone screens–"If you look in anyone's texts, anywhere, you'll find *something* you don't like." There was some truth to that, sure. I mean, if Tom read my diary, or my group chats with Petunia and Augusta, he'd be confronted by some pretty cruel venting. I knew the ways in which people, myself included, could squirm to shirk accountability. But I was not going to let him off the hook for what I considered to be–at least for me, personally, in this moment–crossing a real line.

I'm going to get up and pee, I continued. *And when I come back, I'm going to move Guy into this seat, and take his, so I don't have to be so near you. I'm going to play nice in Hawaii, only be-cause we are meeting friends, and I won't ruin a trip for them. But when we get back, you're moving out, and I'm filing for divorce. I want you out of my life.*

It really did feel that easy. It felt like I was telling him my plans for the weekend or what activities we'd be doing on vacation. It all just tumbled out, like I was pulling clothes out of the dryer.

I unbuckled my seat belt as I watched him struggle for words. Something about watching him flounder made me feel light and happy, like I could float right up and fly next to the airplane all the way to Hawaii. It made me feel like I had the energy of a jet engine in my corner.

I have a vision for myself, I kept going, *I really do.* I was stand-ing over him now, long and tall in my leggings. He seemed for the first time like a little man or a garden gnome. This charismatic person, who for so long I'd put on a pedestal, was suddenly re-duced to a lawn ornament.

Guy and I are going to get a sweet little bungalow in LA, some-thing up in the trees with a view. I want the view that's sparkly, like those nighttime Ed Ruscha paintings—the ones he made when he'd fly himself home to Oklahoma in a little prop plane and paint the grid of Los Angeles after. Oh, and I want it to have a pool, just a small one, and some grass so I can do a workout outside, a place for Napoleon to pee in his old age. Two bedrooms would be nice. And we are going to go off and be happy, just us.

That part sounded a little complicated, the *"just us."* But I wanted Tom to feel left out. I wanted him to know that Guy and I were the cool kids, and we didn't need his popularity to win any contest.

A flight attendant wheeled past. *Anything else to drink?* she asked, her voice aggressively loud. She had a run in her tights, her skin showing through the beige hose.

You know what, ma'am? I would love a champagne, I said extra sweetly, my best midwestern politeness laid on thick. *You have absolutely perfect timing, because I'm celebrating a little something.* I didn't look back at Tom.

I took a swig of my champagne and saw the bathroom light flash green. Another sip and I'd downed the glass, then turned into the aisle, catching my balance on the seat. I tried to look solid and commanding as I strode to the toilet, opening the door gingerly and slipping inside. I slid the lock, the light brightened, and I stared at myself in the little mirror.

I could see my pores, and my skin was dry, my upper lip thinner than I'd ever seen it. My eyes, though, they were big and intense and the right distance apart, long lashes, and at least I had that.

No one knows if they are pretty or not, I guess. It's hard to be objective about your own beauty and your supposed worth because of it. At one point, I would have looked in this mirror and wondered how I measured up. Now, staring at my tired self, I didn't even care that much. Why should someone more attractive be more revered than the woman who made you a baby, who suffered to do so, who at times wanted to die by her own hands due to the intensity of that suffering? If I were ten times more beautiful, would his character still have gotten the better of him in the end?

I washed my hands with warm water and used the paper towel to open the bathroom door. As I walked back to my seat, the text messages echoed in my brain.

You're like my Angelina Jolie, he'd said in one. Did that make me Jennifer Aniston? I wondered.

Things are complicated at home, he'd sent. Weren't things complicated in everyone's home?

Delete these, baby, he'd written, with no trace of what the text must have referenced.

Who had the time and energy to lead a double life? Who even wanted something other than a happy family, especially once a baby was involved? The champagne had made me sleepy, not tipsy but tired, and I closed my eyes after I swapped a sleeping Guy into the middle seat, next to Tom, and strapped him in. When I woke up, we were landing in Honolulu, and Guy was sitting up next to me with some Legos in his lap.

Mamma? I leaned over to smell his head as Tom pushed up the window shade. When I saw blue water and the tops of palm trees outside, I felt so happy, so excited to be on a beach, relaxed and warm, until I remembered, quickly and like a slap, my predicament.

I pulled Guy from his seat into my arms, the weight and warmth of him a comfort. No matter what, I had him, my sweet little reminder that humans could be cheerful and gentle. I carried him off the plane as soon as the little bell indicated we could stand up. I didn't wait for Tom or look back to find him. I put my sleepy boy into his travel stroller, popping it open at the gate exit, and we walked grimly over to baggage claim. The airport was temperate, and I felt my hair getting a little fluffier and my skin relaxing in the humid air.

Why don't you go and get the rental car, install the car seat, and come back to get us, I said coldly to Tom. He tried to reach for my carry-on, and I flinched.

Want me to carry your bag, baby? he tried to ask me, as if I wanted any favors from him.

No, Tom. I want you to go get the rental car, install the car seat, and come back for us, like I just said. I stated this very quietly, scrolling through my phone. The loud screech of the luggage belt alarm went off three times, and it began to move. Guy started clapping. I smiled down at him and ruffled his hair while he watched two kids try to touch the suitcases as they came out, their parents pulling them back. Everyone seemed excited to be there, smiling and stripping off their sweatshirts, pulling their hair up into ponytails. I wondered if any of the wholesome tourists were also plotting their divorces.

Tom touched my elbow softly and leaned into my ear. I stood perfectly still and stiff against his hand.

Are you going to do this the whole time? His voice was pleading. *I'm worried if you treat me with this sort of disdain, we will never be able to recover.*

I turned to look right at him. *I have absolutely no interest in any sort of recovery,* I said. *It's honestly pathetic that you think I might.* We stared at each other for a second, and I saw his eyes get a little wet. *I will play nice in front of our friends, but don't, for a second, think I don't hate your fucking guts. Oh look! Our bags are here!* I said the last sentence cheerfully, high pitched and loud, to show Tom I could do it. *I will be the picture of familial happiness. But it will be an Oscar-winning performance! And no one will know but you! And you can suffer with that knowledge, like a sad, lonely, little dumbass.* I made my voice sound whiny, as if I was starting to cry, mocking him, patronizing him with the word *dumb.*

Sarah, you don't even know the whole story. I don't know what you saw, but I don't have a girlfriend. He paused and licked his lips, waiting for me to say something. I didn't. I tried to make it look like my eyes could bore right through him, burn laser holes into his face. *Sometimes people flirt, you know? So, yah, I said some things back, and I don't know what you saw, but I imagine it was the text about if she thought I was hot, but that one was just me being stupid, needing attention.* He was speeding up now, talking faster and faster. *I love you, and I love Guy, and I don't have a girlfriend, okay? I promise. I really don't, and I don't even want one. I only want you.*

You really are an idiot, you know. I had felt so controlled until now, but the fact that there was stuff I hadn't even seen yet hit me a little hard. *I saw a lot, but I didn't see that,* I said. *Way to dig your own hole even deeper.* I rolled my eyes, but more to hide that I was going to cry than anything else.

Oh, baby, he said, his voice breaking a little. *What have I done?*

I shook my head at him and looked away. Someone was waving at me from across the airport, and I blinked to get the tears out of my eyes.

There's Bill and Sierra, I said. *They're waving at us.* I watched our friends prance forward with their kid. Bill was carrying a net bag filled with plastic sand toys, and Sierra was pushing a giant suitcase with one hand and a stroller with the other. They were all smiling: big, beautiful, truly happy smiles, white teeth flashing far down the linoleum hallway. Up close, it was obvious they lived in California, with their lightly tanned arms, lean limbs, and all-American grins. Tom had been friends with Bill, a professional golfer, for years, and through him I'd met Sierra. Our lives were very different, and we didn't text or talk with tons of regularity, but we tried to meet up a couple of times a year in one of our cities, and they were our favorite people to travel with.

Yooooo! Bill shouted. Everyone seemed so excited and light, and it stung to see it, because I'd felt that way, too, just a few days ago. It was so clear in my memory, that feeling of thinking things were good and would only get better. That stupid, naive feeling.

Yaaaaay!!!! My New Year's crew! I put on a big smile and threw my arms up in the air, my two years as a cheerleader in high school finally put to good use. Bill and Sierra's little boy, towheaded and with giant saucer eyes, grabbed my leg and looked up at me with a big smile. *I missed you, sweet Henry!* I said to him as I bent down to pick him up. Guy looked curiously at me, another child in my arms, and he reached out, babbling a little. *Guy Sachs, say hi to your future husband! Or at least future best friend.* Sierra and I locked eyes and smiled.

Tom reached to wrap his arm around my waist, and I stepped out of the way, placing Henry back down next to Guy's stroller at just the right moment. *Give Henry a hug, Guy!* My son reached out to his new friend. When I stood up, Tom tried to do it again, but I linked arms with Sierra and started walking toward the airport exit, his palm slipping away from my lower back. *I can't wait to see this house*, I said. *I feel like rental pics are always a little better than the real thing, but at least we're right on the beach. Unless they photoshopped that too.* It could have looked like the Taj Mahal on the whitest sand against the bluest sea, but it wouldn't have made me hate Tom any less.

Sierra asked Bill if he'd get the rental car. *Take Tom too*, I said. And then: *Make sure both cars have car seats, forward facing, okay?* Sierra and I met eyes, and she rolled hers. *How much do you want to bet they forget that part*, she said.

As the men walked away, I thought about telling her what was going on with Tom. I didn't even really know how to explain it, though: I found some texts that led me to more texts? His small outburst a few minutes before had confused me about the details. Before I could come up with a way to explain it, she jumped in.

I brought mushrooms, she said. *Lots of them, in a container of baby formula so no one would search it. It's so unlike me, but I never really want to drink when I'm around the kids because I worry I won't wake up if something goes wrong in the night.* I nodded in complete agreement, even though for months and months after Guy was born, I'd been more than happy to get blitzed to hell every night and then pop a Xanax and sleep so deeply a fire alarm wouldn't have woken me up. I did not intend to do that on this family vacation.

Should we do them tonight? she asked.

Maybe a little bit before dinner, I said. *Like early enough that it will be out of our system by the time we go to sleep.* She nodded, keeping one eye on Guy and Henry, who were watching the suitcases go around the conveyor belt.

Should we tell the boys? she asked, but I could tell she didn't want to by the way she said it, with a sneaky little smile across her face, crinkling the freckles along her nose, the rest of her skin pristine, her eyes so big and doe-like it made her look like a teenager. She unclipped her shiny brown hair, and it came tumbling down across her shoulders. *What if we just . . . didn't?* she said, putting a handful of hair up to her mouth to cover her smirk.

LATER, alone in our bedroom at the house we'd rented, I pretended that Tom wasn't there. If he was in my way, I didn't say *Excuse me* or acknowledge him. When I went into the bathroom, I locked the door behind me. He wasn't welcome in my shower, that was for sure. I put a pillow in the middle of the bed; the line of demarcation. I dared him to cross it.

Stay on your side, or I'll make you get a hotel room, was all I said. He nodded somberly, trying to be on good behavior. I challenged myself to see how many days I could go without saying anything at all to him.

Sierra knocked on my door while Tom was showering and I was unpacking my stuff. She stuck her head in and whispered, *Eat this.* She handed me a flat, caramel-colored disc. *It's my grandmother's caramel. It's verrrrry special.* She winked.

Grandma sounds fun as hell, I said. *Should we send the husbands home and fly out Grandma for the week?* We cheersed our caramels together and started chewing. *Damn,* I said. *Grandma's a good cook.*

"Grandma" is a guy named Herb who lives at the beach near our house in California, doesn't seem to have ever used sunblock, and appears morally opposed to nail clippers. Want to go sit outside and look at the water?

I nodded and flipped my suitcase shut, grabbing a long-sleeve shirt from a drawer in case of mosquitos. I followed Sierra down the stairs and out onto the lanai, the covered porch on the back of our rental. It had big potted ferns hanging along it in a row, and it bordered a small, grassy patch, surrounded by squat, little palm trees. The area was big enough for two kids to play soccer, but not more than that. Past the grass was a wide stretch of sand, and the ocean beyond. We sat on the lanai in wooden chaises, where we could hear the rhythmic waves. I should have been so content. This was my dream locale, dream temperature, dream psychoactive substance, dream night. I would not let my nightmare excuse for a husband become a literal buzzkill.

By the time Bill and Tom put the kids to bed and came out to ask us what to order for dinner, we were both staring at the sky, talking about how we'd never go into outer space, even if we knew it was safe. When Tom walked up, I felt a sudden shift in myself, like a dark cloud had come over me, and I decided I really did hate him. It wasn't that my husband had loved another or had an affair, exactly; it was that he'd not loved me enough to take care of me properly. He had loved me but given his time and attention to a series of anonymous third parties, simply for the novelty and excitement and ego stroke of them not being me.

Hi, babe, he said. I kept staring up at the sky. *You two ready for dinner? Can I make you a cocktail?* I tried to ignore him, but he stood right in front of me, blocking my view. The moon was bright enough that I could fully see his expectant face, so eager and hopeful it made me want to smack him.

I searched for his eyes, attempting to give him one of my withering stares, but when I met his gaze, I saw fire in his pupils, and I thought that within the fire I could see the face of a red devil.

You guys okay? he asked. I leaned my head forward, as close to his face as possible without seeming like I wanted a kiss.

You have the devil in your hellish eyes, I said, then started laughing. Bill and Tom stared, and Sierra caught my giggles.

Are you guys on something? Bill asked. I ignored him. Sierra went to kiss him on the cheek. Maybe she was trying to distract him a little bit, to come to my rescue. I was busy staring at Tom, trying to parse out if I really did see a small devil face floating along in his pupils. I kept squinting and looking away and then back again to check, but it was there every time. A bearded, red man with horns, floating in the windows to Tom's soul.

The red devil lives in his stupid eyes, I said. Sierra's laugh slowed down, and she seemed a little confused at how intensely I was speaking. *Out, damn spot! Out, I say!* Everyone was quiet. Just the waves crashing and the buzzing of bugs in the trees.

Well, um, should we eat? Bill asked after a moment. *Why don't I go pick up some carryout?* We stood up at once. *I want to lie down*, I said. *Don't wake me up unless Guy needs me*, I said quietly to Tom. And to everyone else: *I'm so sorry; I'll be more fun tomorrow. Good night.*

When I went upstairs to bed, there was a letter on my pillow: pages and pages of apologies. It was written in a script almost impossible to read, rushed and sloping.

You're right, I've been in a flirtation, but it was just that. It was just a stupid distraction while you were so angry with me and so out of it. I ended it before Switzerland. I'm totally committed to you and to Guy. I will never, ever do this again. You can have the passwords to all my devices and read every text I ever send. I will go on antidepressants, go to couples therapy, see another therapist, buy you anything you want, become whatever you want me to become, hate myself forever, cut off my own dick, pour burning acid on my balls, castrate myself publicly.

Okay, he didn't write all that; I was on drugs. And it didn't matter. I couldn't trust a thing he'd ever said, and I had absolutely no basis for deciphering what was a truth and what was a lie from him. It was over, the whole thing, the whole relationship. There was an overwhelming amount of evidence to be upset about, and I couldn't imagine any road other than divorce.

THE NEXT MORNING, I was up early. The sky was still gray and misty, the sun not high enough to burn off the humidity yet. The ocean was very flat, and I could barely hear the waves. I slipped out of bed, put on a bikini and a button-up shirt, and went to the kitchen, a big room opening onto the lanai through long sliding doors. One door had a dining table in front of it, and the other side had a sofa and TV. There was the requisite papier-mâché blue marlin hanging over the television.

Bill was at the table with Henry, feeding him toast. Before they saw me, I watched them for a minute. Bill had poked holes in a piece of bread and was making faces at his son through it, like a bread mask, and Henry was giggling. I had never seen Tom like that with Guy, and I felt like he had no excuse. He wasn't plagued by hormone changes or deep depression or nightmares or brain fog or the weight of a jillion societal expectations. He hadn't had medical trauma that replicated sexual trauma. He hadn't had to beg me to be his partner in all of it. He wasn't lonely or alone.

Good morning. I tried to sound happy as I interrupted them. *How'd everybody sleep?*

I went over to give Henry's head a kiss. *Hi, darling boy. Where's your mommy?* I asked him, but really directing the question to Bill.

I'm letting her sleep in a little, he said. *We've been up since five, haven't we, Hen-hen?* He stuck his tongue out at Henry and got another ream of giggles.

I don't know how you do that, I said, sighing. *I hate getting up early. I can't function before seven.* I swapped places with Bill and started to make my own coffee. *Don't watch me, Bill, I like my coffee to taste like melted ice cream.* I dumped in a spoonful of sugar and opened the fridge to grab the fullest-fat milk I could find.

Naw, he said from behind me, *it's my favorite time. Everybody's so calm in the morning. We have our toast, and I put on cartoons super low, and we get silly, don't we, baby Henry?* He stuck his face over to his son and made kissy noises. Henry responded by planting a big, wet mouth on his dad, all drooly, with toast crumbs to boot. I knew what Bill meant. It was so special to get a little time alone, just me and Guy. *For real, though, kids are snuggly in the morning*, Bill said. He lifted Henry up and they went to the couch.

The TV was playing a cartoon movie I'd never seen; something about skeletons and death.

Kids movies have come a long way, I commented. *This is practically existentialist.*

Henry looked at me. *Essitentlist?* He tried to copy my words and gave me a big smile, proud of himself. We both looked over as fat toddler feet pitter-pattered down the hall.

Guyyyyy! everyone said at once, and Guy ran toward me with a big, drool-covered grin. He climbed up into my lap and nuzzled against me, warm and soft in his long pajamas, like a hot water bottle covered in gentle cotton. He smelled clean, no hint of morning breath. I felt calm with him on my body, like it was just the two of us, even in a room full of other people.

Then Tom entered the kitchen with thumping, heavy footsteps, and grunted a hello to everyone, eyes directed at the floor, like a gorilla, or maybe a bull. He headed straight for the coffeepot, dumped some into a mug he found next to the sink. I wondered if it was even clean as I heard him slurp loud enough to annoy me. He sat at the back side of the table with his little yellow notebook and started writing in it, flipping the soft cover back on itself. Guy went behind him and pushed at the screen door until it opened. He slid between the screen and the glass door, smushing his face so that his nose was pinched upward and his mouth pinned absurdly against the screen.

Daaaadaaaaa, he taunted, ending the word with a laugh he couldn't stop. Tom kept writing, and Guy giggled again. *Dada!* he said a little louder. Tom still didn't look up.

Tom, your son is speaking to you, I said a little sharply. I remembered the months when I didn't let Guy interrupt my own life, but I had an actual disease—an actual mental illness, that I had to treat with therapy and pharmaceuticals. I had made the kid, suffered through the process of that, and been so zapped by it as to be detached from him. I know I hadn't been easy to be around, but, still, Tom had no excuse. The only mental illness I could see him being diagnosed with was narcissism. There was nothing but selfishness keeping him from letting Guy's voice pull him to the surface. Nothing but selfishness that would convince him it was okay to have his little crushes, his little text flirtations, all while his wife was doing everything she could to become a mother. I remembered myself crying in therapy, deliberating over which antidepressant to take and if I should take them at all, and reading self-help books until late into the night. While I was trying to understand my predicament and change the way I was feeling, Tom was texting someone else. The temerity of that enraged me.

I clapped my hands to get Tom's attention, and I could feel Bill watch me from his spot on the couch, snuggled with Henry.

Sorry, sorry, I was writing, said Tom, snapping his head up. He turned around to Guy and smiled, guffawing a little when he saw him. *Awwww, Guy*, he said, a softness in his voice.

I heard Bill get up from the sofa. *Baby Guy, baby Henry, should we go for a walk on the beach? Should we go look for mermaids out there, or what?* I reached for a tube of kids' sunblock, one of about six on the kitchen counter. *Tom, you wanna go on a little boys' trip?* Bill asked as Tom scratched away at his paper. They both loved surfing and skateboarding, and they spent a lot of time doing that sort of shit together. I was happy for them to go off with the kids.

Not before I put this on your faces, my loves, I said. Guy came to me and tipped his chin up with his eyes closed as I squeezed lotion onto my fingers and started dabbing it delicately on his face. His skin was a perfectly smooth membrane–not a scratch, not a bump– and his eyelashes were so dark they looked almost like they were tinged blue against his cheeks. When I finished lotioning up the kids, I went out on the lanai to watch the dads play with them in the sand.

I couldn't hear everything they were saying or what they were talking about out there, but their laughter drifted over me, sprinkling me like a light rain. Bill did a cartwheel and landed so twisted on one ankle that I thought I'd have to call the paramedics, but just as I started to call out to see if he needed ice, Tom was mimicking him, and both little boys were doubled over, squealing at their dads. Then Bill was up, chasing them, waving his claws above his head like a tickle monster, while Tom jogged to grab a surfboard and drag it across the sand. He lifted the boys up one after another, showing them how to pose on it as if they were barreling under a wave at Pipeline. I wanted to keep Guy this pure and happy, this entertained by small delights, forever.

Sierra came out. *How are our four male children doing?* she asked, plopping down on a wicker chaise next to mine. *Has anyone broken a bone yet?*

It's really nice to see Tom trying with Guy, I said. *I think it's more about impressing Bill than anything, but I love watching it. I just wish he was like this more often.* I didn't say how sad it made me that he wasn't.

Sierra nodded. *Bill is a natural with kids,* she said carefully. *Maybe because he still is one. But, seriously, it's a slow build, you know? It takes them a while to get what it takes to be a dad. I mean, shit, it took me a while to figure out how to be a mom.* I nodded. I obviously knew what she meant, even though we'd never spoken about this so specifically, and I remembered the times I could barely even bring myself to try with my child. It took me longer than it took most people, it seemed–it took me until Guy could talk and walk and emote, far from being a little noodle of nothingness, to connect with parenting–so, yah, I understood.

I'm still figuring that one out, I replied. I had one eye on Sierra and one still watching the boys, making sure no one did anything too wild; ensuring that no child wandered off into the ocean alone. *But at least I want it. Tom doesn't even seem to want to be better at being a dad. If I'm being honest, it's not always fun for me, either, but I don't think Tom is even thinking about it. I think he's just selfish.*

Sierra put her hands up. *Well, that's his damn problem.* She dropped her palms onto her lap with a smack. *If he can't figure out how to experience the uncontaminated happiness of his own child, he doesn't deserve to know the magic. You can't fix him, and I do not recommend wasting your time trying. I've been there. We've all been there. You just have to do you,* she said, like it was so simple. I hadn't even told her about the texts, the vague emotional infidelities, and she was sort of saying what I was already feeling: there was nothing I could do to make Tom be the man I wanted him to be. I could only take care of myself.

EVERY NIGHT IN HAWAII, I got a letter on my pillow from Tom and threw it in my suitcase without reading it, making sure he saw it in there, unopened. We'd brush our teeth at the same sink, and I wouldn't make eye contact in the mirror. I'd fall asleep facing away from him. But in front of our friends, I'd laugh loudly at his jokes and ask if he wanted to share a salad as our appetizer. I'd faked enough emotion in my life that it wasn't such a challenge. Plus, I knew he was right there–I knew what he was up to. I had an eye on him.

It was different when we landed back at JFK. Walking toward the taxi line, I knew that if I sent him off on his own, I wouldn't be able to trace him. I wouldn't know if he was calling or texting another woman from some burner phone he bought at a shady deli in Times Square, begging her to come over. I didn't know if there were still shady delis in Times Square or if burner phones capable of sending texts even existed. But the thought of not knowing what bad behavior he was up to made me feel completely weak and sick, drained of the ability to keep my head above water.

Kiss Guy goodbye and get your own car, I said before I could change my mind. If it were a song, the bass would have dropped. *We can talk this week with a therapist present. You can't sleep at home, though.* He looked exhausted and ragged, his skin slack around his mouth, his greasy forehead furrowed. But I also thought he was maybe faking it.

Seriously?

It's late, I said. *I need to get Guy to bed. And you probably have to get to a hotel room so you can call some girl from a pay phone and invite her over.* I adjusted my carry-on bag on my shoulder and peered into the stroller to make sure Guy wasn't listening. He was so little, but I worried that any anger in our voices would do something horrible to his development, like impact the way his synapses were growing, or that our harsh words might make his brain shrink away from us.

Sarah, I have no interest in anyone but you. I'm not lying. He looked at the floor and took a breath. *I will never, ever again engage with any woman like that. Even if you and I never speak, ever again, I've learned my lesson. It was disrespectful to you, and shitty, and I'm deeply sorry.* The taxi dispatcher waved at me then to get into the first car.

Bye, Tom. Kiss your son, I said impatiently. He helped me convert the stroller into a car seat and snap Guy in. Tom kissed his cheeks slowly. *Okay, Tom, good night. I'm closing the door now.* I pressed the button for the van door to shut automatically. Tom stood there, on the other side of the window, staring at me. I shook my head as we pulled away, and looked down at Guy, who was already asleep.

WHEN I WALKED INTO OUR APARTMENT, it was so clean and quiet. We hadn't been home in more than two weeks, and it was like the house itself had a vacation. Nothing was out of place; there was no laundry on the stairs waiting to be taken up, no bottles drying next to the sink. It wasn't sad–I was used to being home without Tom. In fact, I spent most of my nights home without him, while he worked late–or, rather, while he did God knows what while he *said* he was working late. I found it peaceful to be home without him. I didn't have to worry about what he'd want to eat, and I didn't have to help him unpack or remind him where to put the clothes that needed to be dry-cleaned. I didn't have to apologize for my blow-dryer making noise, which he hated, or for watching reality TV, which Tom forbade around him because it *impeded his intuitive creative process.*

I had to think only about me, and my little son, who felt like an extension of me. It was as if I'd blown a big, shiny bubble and put it around me, and around Guy, and around our house, and it was just us in there, and it was always sunny and warm, and there was always something to celebrate. We ordered pancakes for breakfast and shared an ice cream after dinner. We watched cartoons together, and I came up with arts and crafts projects that wouldn't make too much of a mess or take more than ten minutes, which was Guy's attention span. We went to the park with Sharon. Life was lovely.

FOR THE NEXT FEW WEEKS, I kept Tom on ice. He slept in his studio and came home to give Guy a bath every night, which Sharon would supervise, while I'd sit in another room with the door shut. I told him I needed a complete break for a while. He respected my wishes, hoping, I think, that every day we stayed married, the less likely I was to file for divorce. To distract myself, I signed up for a writing class with Petunia, and afterward, we'd go out for pizza and wine and talk about books and politics. I started running again, just twenty or thirty minutes in the morning, and thought about maybe training for a half marathon, just to see if I could do it. I started writing, first just in my journal, but then I had the idea to turn some of my rants into personal essays, and I'd been staying up until two in the morning writing about everything from my birth experiences to my depression to the condition of crying after sex, which I learned was called postcoital dysphoria and had first been written about in ancient Greek philosophy. I bought ballet tickets, and I'd go alone to matinees while Guy was at nursery school. I wrote to a ballet company I loved and asked if it had a board I could join, and I started going to meetings. When I sat there, surrounded by people I didn't really know who loved dance and music as much as I did, racking my brain for ideas that could help the company fundraise or get it more press, I didn't think about Tom at all. Instead, I felt focused and excited.

ONE MORNING, Sharon knocked on the door to my bedroom, which she'd done only once before, when Guy was sick. *Sarah Hoover*, she said loudly, without opening the door. I was sitting up in bed, writing furiously. I'd had a crazy dream about being on some horrible dude's yacht, and I was scrambling to get an idea for a short story on the page. *Come in, Sharon; you don't have to knock*, I said.

Um, I don't know what kind of weird shit you get into up here. She opened the door slowly and stuck her head in.

What's up? I asked her.

We gotta talk, because I love Guy to death, but I think it's time for me to take another job, so here's your notice. Bye, bitch! She started laughing, and I couldn't tell if she was joking or not.

Wait? You're ditching us? Are you firing me? I threw off my covers and swung my legs over the edge.

Honestly, I like working with babies. Guy is not a baby anymore. He's a big boy. You *are still a baby–a very pathetic one–but that's a different conversation.* She fluttered a hand at me while she laughed at her own joke. *I stayed to make sure Guy would be okay with you, because these last few weeks, without Tom in the house and all that . . . but when it's time to go, it's time to go.* She mimed a goodbye kiss and a princess wave to me. *Make another baby, and I'll come back.* She said it so nonchalantly that it stopped me from speaking for a second.

Whew, this is a lot. I exhaled. *But I'm somehow okay with what I'm hearing? Like, I'm not scared?* I was thinking out loud. I took a second.

I woulda killed myself without your help, I told her gratefully. *Thank you for everything, especially for not judging me when I was at my worst.* I threw my arms around her and remembered the first night Sharon came, the first hug I gave her. It seemed like a million years ago.

Call me the next time you're pregnant, she said.

LIFE CHANGED A LITTLE when Sharon moved out two weeks later, especially before I found another nanny. In the mornings, I'd get up with Guy. He slept in my bed every night, but we'd go down, and I'd make tea and get him a bottle of warm milk, and then we'd go to his nursery, where he'd play quietly with building blocks on his carpeted floor while I journaled from the little twin bed in there. Augusta encouraged me to sign him up for a bunch of morning classes on top of his nursery school sessions, and I'd work from home while he was in them, or coordinate with Tom, via short and aloof texts, for him to pick Guy up so that I could spend a day at the office or time running errands or at the gym. Bill had been right, though: our mornings together were so quiet and sweet, especially the days that Guy climbed back into bed with me and watched cartoons on his iPad. Sometimes we'd make toast and try different combinations of peanut butter, cinnamon, and jam. Other times I'd read him books. It was mostly just us, and it was fun.

. . .

WHEN DID YOU LAST TALK TO TOM? Petunia asked one evening over a bottle of red wine that I knew would later give both of us headaches. Augusta nodded, sipping from her glass. We were at our favorite pizza place on Mott Street, where no matter how many times we went and how well we tipped, they never remembered us. It was one of the New York City restaurants that had clearly been devoted to at least two different types of cuisine in the past. The stained-glass skylight gave it the vibe of an Irish pub, while the dark-brown built-in banquettes made it look like a German beer hall. Only the big pizza oven in the middle alluded to the current menu.

Petunia wasn't making eye contact, and I could sense she had something to tell me. My stomach dropped a little because I imagined her saying she'd seen Tom out on a date, or kissing some young, hot barista, or maybe with his arms wrapped around a bartender or a waitress who worked in Dimes Square.

I don't know. I mean, we text pretty much every day, I replied with a shrug, waiting for her to jump in with some story that I knew would make my heart hurt. *We mostly just discuss logistics. He comes home every night to do bath time and puts Guy to sleep, and I just hide in our bedroom until he leaves.* My voice was speeding up. I wondered, if I just kept talking, would I never have to hear about the supermodel Tom had moved on with?

Look, she said. She still wasn't making eye contact with me, which probably meant this was worse than I even imagined. Could he have gotten someone pregnant? It had been only, like, three weeks, right? I tried to do the math. My eyes darted over to Augusta, who was avoiding the conversation by cutting her pizza with a fork and knife. It felt obvious that she already knew what was coming.

Can you eat that pizza with your hands like a normal person, please? I said to her, giving myself a beat before getting Petunia's bad news. *Sorry,* I said quickly. *I'm kind of on edge.* Augusta smiled at me, but I sensed pity in it, like these were about to be my last moments of innocence.

I saw Tom at the CVS on Houston, Petunia began, *which I never really go to, but I needed condoms, and they have the best selection.* I waited for her to say that Tom was buying condoms too, or even worse, Plan B, or a pregnancy test.

I bumped into him. He was holding, like, six bags of beef jerky, which is just . . . some pathetic bachelor shit. I grimaced. I would never let that crap in our house. *Sarah, when he saw me, he burst into tears.*

I knew it. He was embarrassed, caught buying lube and condoms and Plan B and pregnancy tests. Just as I'd suspected.

He's lost, like, ten pounds. He cried so hard he couldn't really talk at one point, and I was just like, "Sir, I'm here for Magnums, not a therapy session." She was looking at me now, her hand clasped around the stem of her wineglass. *You're probably mad that I spoke to him, but the man was crying at a CVS, Sarah. He was CRYING.*

I took a deep breath.

You know how many times he's made me cry, P? Do you guys have any idea? I haven't even told you half of it, but you'd have told me to leave him years ago if I had. I looked at them to see if they had an inkling of what I was going to say next.

There has always been the looming shadow of some other in this relationship, and it was always some woman. A text flirtation, an ex-girlfriend visiting town—and I was always left wondering if I was being overly sensitive and childish, if this was just what modern love looked like. I always told myself that marriage is hard, it's complicated. Half the women I know complain about the off-color interactions their husbands have, or the porn they watch, or some other stupid behaviors that feel not quite . . . the actions of a man totally devoted. And he comes home to me at night; shouldn't that be enough? But you know what? It hurt me. It confirmed all my worst fears about myself. I paused to choose my words carefully. *I thought if I told you two, you'd either hate him or judge me for not leaving him. I was afraid if I left him, that I'd never find someone else, that I wasn't good enough to ever find anyone else, and that I'd always be alone or I'd have to move back to Indiana. I was afraid that this was the best it would ever get for me. And you know what? I refuse to continue like that anymore.* I pushed away my plate in defiance and looked at Augusta. She leaned forward with her arms across her lap, her heavy blonde hair in a clean line right below her collarbone. Her face was concentrated.

What do you think? I asked her. She'd tolerated all sorts of crap in her own dating life, which I'd been around to witness, but the stakes were different now that we had kids, which she had to understand. I pulled the plate toward me again. There was still pizza on there.

Augusta pulled her lips into her mouth, looking up at the ceiling, as if she was really contemplating. *First of all, Tom is not your boyfriend. He is the father of your son.* Her voice was very soft, like she was expecting me to pounce.

Genetically speaking only, I spat. She ignored me.

I think if you want to make the relationship work, you can, she continued, swirling the wine in her glass. Her dress fell off one of her small shoulders as she swirled. She was forever finding a way to look like a beautiful damsel in distress, without having to try. *Most men need some sort of training. I've done it—half the married women you know have done it. We've found ways to make our husbands see the world through a woman's eyes. Some of them don't get it, and they stay immature. But Tom wants to be better for you! He knows what he did wrong. He wants to change.* She tossed her hair behind her shoulder defiantly with a shake of her head. *You're telling me you've never had to change a thing about your behavior to grow up in some way, to make something work?*

What both of you aren't understanding is that I don't just want to "make something work." I want to be in a relationship because it's a choice that I can stand behind. I don't want to waste more energy on "training" a grown-up. I cannot continue in a relationship that makes me feel bad about myself. I won't do it. I felt something pass between Petunia and Augusta, some glance or look, and Petunia opened her mouth, but then Augusta jumped in.

I have been around for your whole relationship, and you're right. There have been some shady moments. We both agree. Petunia nodded along, and Augusta pulled her lip gloss out of her purse, applying it to lips that looked a little bigger than the last time I saw her, a thought I filed away to discuss later. *It's not like we haven't noticed.*

I thought you should take a hit out on him until I saw him in person, Petunia said. Augusta flashed her a look that read *Take a back seat.* She dabbed her mouth with her napkin, wiping off the extra gobs of shiny gloss, then placed it back on her lap carefully and slipped the tube in her purse.

I'm just saying, Augusta continued, *he really is remorseful. He wants to be better, be the best husband and father he can be. And you should at least hear him out. Not for him, not for you, but for Guy. He's Guy's father.* She said this slowly and quietly. *You have one final conversation, and then you can make a real decision in good conscience. He really only sent some texts.*

I feel like you both are trying to convince me to stay married. No one refuted this, so I continued. *I know you love the institution of marriage, Augusta. I know it really means a lot to you, and I respect that—for you.* Augusta had a six-hundred-person wedding down in the Delta: a full church ceremony and a cake taller than a grown man at the reception. She'd looked like a beautiful, perfect debutante doily. *But I don't think that a happy and healthy child requires some Disney-bullshit family unit. What's best for Guy is me being my peak self. Do you think it's better that I suffer just so*

Guy can have a daddy at home? I tossed back the rest of my red wine. I was already getting a headache, but I figured the gesture looked dramatic. I reached for the bottle to give myself a refill, but it was empty. Augusta signaled the waiter, one of her delicate, manicured little fingers going up politely. *I know that I was detached and depressed for the whole first year of Guy's life. I'm trying to forgive myself for that, but I had severe, untreated postpartum depression. I'm trying to make up for it. And I think that's what being a mom sort of means. It's just years of fucking things up with your kids and then spending the rest of your life learning how to love them to make up for it. And I want to do that. But I will not spend another second suffering to love a man who couldn't even be fully by my side during my hardest year. A man whose idea of the best he could do was sexting some other person.*

The server appeared next to me just then and started uncorking another bottle. It was probably a bad idea, but I accepted his pour.

Speaking of the hardest year of your life . . . Augusta said, nodding at Petunia as if they were about to launch into a choreographed tap dance or an intervention by flash mob. I half expected Petunia to stand up and count out a *five, six, seven, eight!* Instead, she leaned toward me.

You're not gonna like this, and Augusta is probably scared to say it, but, look, you were no angel during that year. Some of what you're complaining about here was actually you being nuts. You were either acting like you were the happiest person on earth or you were unhinged and talking to yourself, pretty much all the time. We could deal with it because we got to get rid of you after a few hours. But you were a tyrant. You were off your rocker. You acted like every single thing that went wrong in your life, every mild inconvenience, was organized purposefully to fuck with you. You cried more than once about being stuck in traffic, at rush hour, going crosstown. You cried in my office for an entire lunch because your mom hung up the phone too abruptly, even though she always hangs up abruptly. You would freak out on Tom on the daily about coffee rings on the counter.

I felt my blood pressure shoot up at the mention of coffee rings.

He did leave coffee rings on the counter, though! I defended myself.

WE KNOW, they said in unison.

Tom is annoying, Petunia continued. *He's flawed. He has done dumb things, and they aren't necessarily forgivable. He's a messy human–like any human is, to be fair–but your communication skills and your troubleshooting strategy have not made it easy for anyone. I would also suggest that some of what you hated about him was invented by whatever the fuck crazy shit was bouncing around your brain.*

I refuse to buy into this narrative that because I was fed up with Tom and demanded more of him, I somehow deserve his disrespectful ass. Because that is what we call victim blaming. Was I just drunk? What they were proposing seemed insane. I shuddered at the idea of being expected to shoulder the burden of male fuckups, especially at a time when I had been so broken and sad. Why hadn't my husband noticed the depths of my suffering and tried to get me help? I felt like I had been one hair away from being hospitalized. But maybe my outsized reactions read to him as marital discord instead of what they were, which was mental illness. He needed to clean up his side of the street, but I'd hidden my true state from everyone–including myself–to my own detriment. I guess I couldn't blame Tom for that. I could tell him it hurt me and see if we could agree to new boundaries, though.

Sarah, we aren't saying it is your fault, Augusta added, her cheeks red from the wine. *We're just saying that this isn't as cut-and-dried as you're making it out to be. First of all, he didn't actually cheat. He flirted a bunch. It was dumb, and he should never disrespect you. But have you asked him why? Have you asked him why he wasn't the husband or father you expected? You should spend a little time investigating the gray area before you go filing for divorce. This could be a good opportunity to redefine the relationship you really want. There are reasons you fell in love with Tom, and I'm not sure those have changed.*

I knew they were partially right because I had that pit in my stomach that told me what they were saying was too true to ignore. Tom hadn't morphed into some new person. Somewhere inside there was still the brilliant, strange, generous artist I'd first felt that sublime *unfolding* with. The thing that had really changed, in fact, was me, and maybe I owed him an explanation of that before I moved on. I'd morphed into a whole other being when I became pregnant, then again when Guy was born, and even a third time when I'd realized, only recently, the extent of my postpartum depression–a phenomenon I was just processing–a chemical catastrophe in my brain. Judi Dench had last said to me, *Don't rush to any decisions*, and maybe she and my girlfriends were right. I could talk this through with Tom before I decided what to do next. I could see if he could become the person I wanted him to be, and I could also try to become a better version of myself.

I nodded at them as the server cleared our plates, putting down three spoons and a crème brûlée. *Courtesy of the kitchen,* he said. I guess all we had to do for someone to be nice to us here was order three bottles of their most expensive red wine and talk about the failings of my husband until closing. I watched Petunia crack the sugary top with the side of her spoon and scoop a layer of it into her mouth.

I CALLED TOM on the way home from dinner. He picked up after half a ring.

Is everything okay? Is Guy okay? He sounded panicked. I'd never listed him as my emergency contact because he never picked up his phone. Hearing his voice was comforting, even though the memories of his unreliability made my chest tighten.

Petunia told me she saw you, and I had just enough wine that she talked me into calling you. I was a little drunker than I thought, and I wasn't sure what I was supposed to be saying. I walked up to my door and put my key in, then sat on the stairs in my lobby. I didn't want to get in the elevator and get cut off. I let myself sit for a minute in awkward silence.

I miss you so much, he stammered. *Please give me one last chance. I've been in therapy twice a week for the last month.* I watched another tenant clack her way through the lobby in her Manolos, then press for the elevator.

What am I supposed to do with that fact, Tom? You've been in therapy since you were seven. This is New York.

Please let me take you away for three days, with absolutely no expectation, just alone time, just us. And when we get back, we can either go our separate ways or not, but I just want three days together to state my case, no distractions. He blurted it all out so fast that it took me a minute to process. I was silent, looking at the keychain in my hand. One of the keys on it was for Tom's studio, and I realized I could just go down there anytime and spy on him at work if I really wanted to. I can't believe I had never thought of that. I could just go down there and see what he was doing. *I will take you somewhere warm and special, okay?* I thought of Guy, laughing on the beach in Hawaii, calling his dad's name, clinging to him in the pool.

Fine, I said. *Even though three days of good behavior on a trip is not exactly meaningful. It's not real life. And I won't be fucking you.* I could hear exhaling on the other end of the phone. I wondered what he was wearing and where he was sitting, what his days had looked like these last few weeks. I stood up on the stairs to walk to the elevator.

What could Tom ever say or do on this trip to make himself redeemable? I thought. He'd spent so much time blindly proceeding through his days, making art with his ego intact as mine fractured, my brain a casualty of a pregnancy and a motherhood that didn't seem to factor into Tom's daily life. I mean, sure, I hadn't been confined to my bed, silently weeping every day, all day, refusing to leave my room, but hadn't the rapid cycling through tears and the disorganized thinking, partying, and rage been a major hint to him that I needed real help? Was my jumble of symptoms so strange and difficult to interpret? Did he never stop to ask himself why I was so damn angry? Granted, it was challenging and likely confusing to navigate the symphonic swell of my moods, but was his solution just to hide in his studio all day and hope it would all blow over? Maybe the vicissitudes of fatherhood had been traumatic for him, too. Not just the constant care of another human but also my sharp decline. I hadn't been able to diagnose myself, after all, so why should I have expected anyone else to do what I couldn't?

I hear you. And I'm so grateful. Seriously, Sarah, I'm so grateful. Just be ready on Friday at eight a.m. With a passport and a bikini. I already asked my parents, and they'll come in and take care of Guy, and make sure Napoleon is okay, too. The poor dog was so old at this point that I lived in constant worry I'd come home to find him in rigor mortis.

Fine, I said. I tried to make my voice emotionless, but inside I felt shaky. He had hurt my feelings so much. When I recalled the texts I'd read and revisited the images I'd AirDropped from that hotel in Europe, my face still got hot and my breath seized. When I thought about how lonely my last months had been, I could only say to myself, *I will never allow myself to hide how I feel for fear of repercussions, whatever they may be. I will just say whatever is on my mind, magical thinking be damned.*

After we got off the phone, I spent some time thinking about how it wasn't just Tom who had been complicit or contributed to the success of a patriarchy bigger than both of us. I'd been a mean girl before, I'd snubbed women with whom I caught Tom flirting, as if it was their fault or as if it would somehow teach *him* a lesson. I'd laughed at bad-boy behavior from peers and been entertained by their brazenness. I'd been in strange awe of men who were promiscuous. I'd revered artists, writers, filmmakers, photographers well known for their misogyny. In fact, I'd probably even considered, on some level, their misogyny to be *why* they were good at their art—as if the ability to dehumanize women was a necessary side characteristic to inspire creativity. A true genius needed—*deserved*—muses, I rationalized. A real artist had to be willing to make selfish decisions to prioritize his work. What would Picasso have been without his passion? What would he have painted if not the women?

As much as I always wanted Tom to be the dream husband, a potential I saw within him, I also really, really wanted to unlearn a lot of the cultural conditioning that had led me to allow his behaviors to go unchecked, to tolerate the daily grievances for the sake of keeping the marriage intact, as so many women around me had done in their own relationships—a fact I held up as proof that things would never be different for any of us. This conditioning had allowed the voice in my head to convince me that I didn't deserve better, that I would invite chaos if I spoke up. Muses were silent, after all, something I could no longer be. And while I knew that I'd have to continue to advocate for myself for the rest of my life, it was now Tom's turn to do his own work if we were going to be together. He had a lot of figuring out to do—a lot of his own conditioning to interrogate. Maybe there was no such thing as a dream husband or a dream house or a dream baby, only this: the promise to try to be your best, a dedication to evolving, and a belief that demanding the kind of care and boundaries needed in a marriage was a right and necessary part of being in a happy relationship.

. . .

CUBA WAS HOT AS HELL. It was like I'd never really seen sun or felt tropical heat before; that's how intense it felt to be on a Caribbean island, but in a dense, real city. I loved it, from the moment we landed and got into a pale-blue taxi with streamers attached to the side-view mirrors, the driver in a fedora. The beautiful old squares sat between big stone government buildings and dilapidated, classical apartment blocks, some missing roofs in parts, flowering vines falling into their crevices. When their big, wooden shutters were open, you could see rows of white linens hung inside high-ceilinged spaces. They looked like the ghosts of dancers haunting their former ballrooms.

Waiting in line to get into the National Museum of Fine Arts, I watched a mom standing in front of us with her baby strapped to her. It made me miss that heaviness. It made me miss the experiences I never got to have. I was nostalgic for the false promise and connection with my newborn that I'd expected and never felt. Now I just had to live with the knowledge that there were so many intimacies I'd missed. But I was ready now, and that's what mattered. I missed Guy. Havana was so pretty, but a trip where I couldn't experience the world through Guy's eyes felt wasted.

And as we chased Ernest Hemingway's ghost through bars, old bookstores filled with revolutionary texts, fruit markets, and coffee shops serving syrupy espresso shots with heavy cream and smooth sugar, I realized how much work Tom had put into planning our trip. There were no ATMs, and hotels didn't take credit cards. He'd planned every dinner, every activity, every meal, and brought exactly the money we'd needed in his carry-on. He'd contacted artists to tour their studios and mapped out a trip outside Havana to a local beach, without any access to a cell phone network or Wi-Fi, neither of which would work on our phones anyway. On our final night, he led me into the Cuban National Theatre and surprised me with tickets to the ballet. The bartenders hand-muddled mojitos at intermission.

Afterward, on a massive restaurant terrace overlooking the old city, I let Tom sit next to me on the banquette. His eyes were a little misty, but we were both smiling.

So, what has your life been like the last month? he asked. He couldn't quite look at me straight, as if he were a little shy.

It's been really, really nice, I said. I didn't want to lie; I saw no reason to. *We've found a little pattern to our days, and it's been really sweet. God gives you what you can handle, I guess. We made such an easy baby.* I looked over and up at Tom, who couldn't hold back his smile. I think he was encouraged by my use of *we.*

And what about you? he prompted me again. He was totally asking me if I'd been hooking up with anyone, and I kind of loved the small show of jealousy.

Actually, I've been writing. Tom raised his eyebrows. *Yah, I know, I mean, I've never thought of myself as any kind of writer, and maybe I'm not, but I decided to take this writing class with Petunia. It was so fun to be in it with her, but I really like the writing. I think I want to do more of it. Like, professionally.* I hadn't said that to anyone yet.

I've always thought of you as an artist, he said. *You just needed to pick a medium, some way to share your brilliant and hilarious view of the world.* He actually *had* always told me that. He'd been calling me his orchid for at least a decade at this point, his *flower that would bloom over and over.* He had always believed I would find my calling, again and again. He had seen in me what I had never really seen in myself.

I shook my head at him, looking down at the table. *You did always tell me that. But you also made me question myself so much.* I crossed my arms and didn't look at him. *You were unfaithful to me–unfaithful to the concept of us–and it made me doubt my intu-*

ition. *When I called you out on things I was sure were wrong, you convinced me I was the one who was wrong for being bothered by them. And you told me I was beautiful and amazing, but then had other priorities, like these stupid flirtations—as if I wasn't enough. If I was so great, why did you choose other people over me? Who can become themself in conditions like that?*

Thinking about this would have made me mad a month before, but now it just made me sad. So much time and energy wasted. He put his head in his hands, and I thought he was crying, which felt unfair to me. I didn't want to have to manage his emotions when I had at long last learned to manage mine.

It was both, baby, he said finally. *I promise you: it was both. I was a scumbag, and you are my love. I had all these behaviors left over from when I was single, these stupid, selfish ways to feed my ego. I wasn't putting you first, and I should have. I didn't see how destructive it would be to continue to act like I was a lone wolf—until it was too late.* He lifted his head but kept his eyes closed. I realized he was just focusing, trying hard to say the perfect thing.

Our family is so important to me. I wasn't prepared for a love like this. For my connection to you and Guy. I didn't realize how much you were suffering. I swear, I thought you were just really mad at me the whole time, and I hate myself for that. I hate myself for not knowing it was more than just coffee rings and a love of parties, for not digging deeper into the root cause. I didn't realize how I was contributing to it all, and I will spend the rest of my life fixing this if I have to. You deserve the chance to reclaim your personhood, Sarah, and I want to be the person who helps you do that. I remember when it happened for me, and I want it for you.

Look, I told him, considering a last sip of rum. *When we get back, I don't care if you come home to the apartment. I'll figure out my life either way.* He looked confused, like he wasn't sure if this was good news or bad. He sipped his drink and winced. *I abso-lutely do not trust you. We need therapy. I need time. I'm not even saying we're staying together. I'm just saying, if you come back, you need to know that things are going to be very different. At least for a long while.* He was nodding along as if I were explaining how to follow a map to buried treasure. *You do not have the right to ask for anything from me. I want to be selfish right now. I deserve to be my own focus.* He kept nodding.

Your emotions can't be my burden. You can't ask me to listen to your problems or help you brainstorm. I don't want to be a muse or a nurse or a therapist. I want to spend that energy on myself. Tom took out his little yellow notebook and a pen, and I almost laughed.

And don't plan on me spending time with anyone or at any party where I don't really, really want to be. I won't be making sure your clothes are clean. I won't check that we have coffee beans—I don't even drink coffee at home! Don't ask me what's for dinner. Get your own medicine when you have a cold. I tapped the table with my fist after every line, and his head followed my hand up and down. *Consider it retribution for the ten years we've been to-gether. I gave you everything, and now I'm done. I know this has been a tough year, and I am sorry for that. I'm reflecting on it and taking responsibility for my part in everything. But I'm going to give only to myself and to Guy. And my writing, whatever that turns into. Maybe I'll leave my gallery job . . . I just want to write and be with my kid.* He nodded, which I didn't expect; I thought he was going to be defensive or tell me why this plan wouldn't work. He didn't. *I want us both to take this chance to learn how to be better versions of ourselves.*

I deserve this, he said. *I said I'd do anything to win you back, and I will absolutely do all of this. I am grateful for the chance to grow and do better. It will be my privilege to do it, I swear. Not only that, but I think you should fold this into your work. Write about me, about this, about us, if you want. I believe in you as an artist, and while I'm ashamed of what happened, you own your story. This is what artists do: they tell their truth, and sometimes it's at the expense of their own pride or the egos of other people.* He looked me right in my eyes. *I love you no matter what, and I am unfazed by your demands.*

17

The End
Is Just the Beginning

New York and Los Angeles
April 2021

WHILE GUY WATCHED A VIDEO on his iPad of a grown man squealing like a cartoon character, I tiptoed into our big white bathroom so that I could pee on a stick in private. Through the half-closed door, I could hear the video, an aquarium visit, the man announcing the colors of each fish in a squeaky voice. I googled this guy once, and he had made a name for himself doing scat porn in the early 2000s. He decided to reinvent himself by making little shows on YouTube for children, and he'd earned millions more doing that than he ever had shitting on grown adults. Kids were obsessed with him.

I hit the electric blinds so that the neighbors across the street couldn't watch me on the toilet. For a while after we'd moved in, I thought they couldn't see me. A chance meeting with one of them in a hotel bar steered me straight.

I think I live across from you, she'd said. *You have a little boy who you're potty training, right? And you live on the top floor?* I'd been relieved she hadn't asked why my husband spent so much time on the toilet, a question I also had.

Guy was now three, graduating from diapers to small, striped underpants that bagged around his skinny thighs. Once the shades had darkened the room, I sat down with my unpackaged test. I peed with my hand shoved down between my legs, stick held at an angle, then set the test on the counter, trying to keep it parallel so that none of the urine would drip. I didn't dare guess the outcome. Instead, I stared at myself in the mirror over my sink.

Two years had passed since I let Tom back into our house. Guy was in preschool. Sharon had worked with another family for a while and then with another friend of mine who had a baby. We texted and called every month or so, and she came to see Guy on his birthdays. Tom had gone to therapy; we'd gone to couples therapy and even sex therapy. We spent many hours in the glow of a tabletop Noguchi lamp, analyzing our relationship, a psychological conductor facing us in her midcentury office chair.

So, tell me why we're here, we'd been asked in the first couples therapy appointment. The psychiatrist was dressed in a gamine pantsuit and seemed charmingly neurotic, like an Annie Hall–type character. I thought again that a dinner party with all my doctors in one place would be amazingly chic.

I'll go first, I said. I took a breath, giving myself a few seconds to gather my words. *A delightful fact I learned recently from a children's book is that some cats have a parasite in their poop that turns mice into zombies. If the parasite gets into the little mice brains, it causes them to lose their fear of cats and become attracted to cat pee, and then, of course, the cats attack the mice, and the parasite goes back into their stomachs to live.* The therapist's pen hovered over her Moleskine notebook, hesitant. *After I had a baby, I felt like a parasite moved into my brain, is my point. It was like I was some helpless rodent. Someone else had the controls.* She scribbled down something, as if she suddenly understood what I'd been getting at.

And whatever or whoever that thing was, it turned on a part of my brain that was insufferably angry. So angry I couldn't see straight most days. I couldn't function. But you know what's even weirder than cat poop parasites? She did not look up and try to guess, so I continued. I'm not convinced that whatever took over my executive functioning was even totally wrong per se, because there really is a lot of messed-up stuff about being a woman. Especially one who has had a baby. I had reasons to be mad. The problem is, my brain was incapable of being anything else. I was stuck in this spiral of feelings, and more than anything, I hated this dude right here. He seemed like the root cause of everything. I cocked my head at my husband. Sorry. Thought I'd give you the Wikipedia summary. Thank God for meds, right? I tried to keep a slight sense of humor about how out of my mind I'd been for so long, but the therapist just smiled at me, like it wasn't really that funny.

Tom adjusted his legs next to me on the couch. There was an awkward therapy pause, and her eyes shifted over to him. I thought she was about to say something predictable, such as And how did that make you feel? But instead, she turned to Tom and said, And why didn't you get her help? Sounds like she truly needed partnership. Part of me wanted to clap or give her a high five. I was about to burst out with a Thank you, but Tom started talking.

A really long time ago, I told Sarah to be more of a bitch. I meant that she should stand up for herself more out in the world. But when she was pregnant, and after, it was like that finally kicked in, but only toward me. I just thought she didn't want to be with me anymore, he said with a downcast laugh. I never thought that she had postpartum depression or anything like that. I just thought she hated me. He glanced at the therapist, who nodded at him. The afternoon sun shone saffron across his face. It wasn't like she was sending clear and decipherable signals for help. It's not like she cried all day and started cutting herself and listening to the Jesus and Mary Chain. But, yah, you're right, I should have done something. A lot of things. I fucked up very, very badly, in many ways. I looked at him, and when our eyes met, I actually didn't feel mad; I felt solidarity. Like we were doing something good for both of us. Unfolding together. *Sarah, I know I keep saying this, but I'm utterly committed to sitting on this couch for as long as it takes. I am so sorry.*

Marriage is so complicated, I said. *Part of me wants him to suffer forever and possibly die lonely, but I also realize I scapegoated him for a lot of rage I had about other things, things I was scared to face—or didn't even know to face—before I became a mom. I know I was pretty intolerable.*

Tom put his hand on mine, and we intertwined fingers. I looked at my lap. *We knew postpartum depression would be a possibility,* he said. *But no one told us what that really looked like. The form it would take. There's this checklist the doctor gave me . . . I don't remember the name—*

The Edinburgh Postnatal Depression Scale, the therapist and I said in unison.

Yah, that, Tom agreed. *It just didn't totally seem to apply.*

I TOOK MY TWEEZERS OUT OF A DRAWER and considered performing an exorcism on my eyebrows. Just then, the two-minute alarm I'd set on my phone pinged.

When I looked down at the second positive pregnancy test of my life, my sister was the first person I texted. The message flew from my fingertips like I was a medium between the cell sac of that inchoate baby and the world. I barely thought about what I was typing.

I sent her a photo of the positive symbol. I felt no fear as I spelled out the words: *Deech! I'm fucking pregnant!* Just excitement. Bubbles in my chest. Since one of my legs was falling asleep a little bit, I thought about standing up and getting in the shower, but I didn't move from the toilet. I watched the three dots of her typing.

I'm so happy for you, Sarah. It's gonna be different this time, okay? She'd been brave enough to get pregnant again, and she now had a headstrong, hilarious, and beautiful little girl. I felt tears behind my eyes, but I wasn't sad; my brain was racing, scanning the list of who I could tell, and when. I didn't want to jinx myself by sharing the news too early, but it felt like my news to share. This was my do-over: a chance to have everything feel right. I stood up and shook out my legs. In the mirror above my sink, I could see the shape of a toilet seat imprinted into my butt cheeks in red.

I sent the same picture to Tom, and he called me right away.

I am so, so happy, baby, he said before I could even say hello. He was practically screaming. I could hear from the light echo that he was hiding in his bathroom at work. *I'm going to be totally different, and we know now—we know how to do it better.* I turned on the shower to let the hot water run and peered behind myself into the bedroom. Guy was on my bed, still entranced by his iPad. I could hear the faint squawks of his YouTube hero, the shitter, who was now visiting a boatyard.

I feel so happy, I told Tom. I meant it. I couldn't really think about anything aside from how glad I felt. The shower door was all steamed up, and I wiped it with my hand, revealing my reflection. I had a smile on my face; a small, self-satisfied grin. I stumbled over my left leg, still numb from sitting for so long. I put one hand under the hot water, which jiggled my brain back to reality. *Look, next week is Guy's spring break*, I thought out loud, switching into logistical mom mode. *Why don't I take him to Chateau? He can swim, I can relax, and you can get some work done in New York. Then when I'm back, we can tell him about the new baby together.*

If I was eight weeks pregnant now, I'd be ten when we got back, and I could tell him a week or two early. The thought of getting to spend time in our old bungalow, just us, made small, crackling crystals form in my chest; little, tight sparkles of happiness. I thought about soaking in the news that I had a little baby inside me and how hard it would be to keep the secret from Guy, even if he couldn't quite understand it.

You should absolutely go, Tom said, which I expected. *Maybe I'll come at the end of the week, but you should go, either way. Luxuriate in this moment. Write about it. We get to do it again.* His voice was buzzing, a sort of low, pleasant vibration. I pulled a towel off the shelf, hanging it on the hook outside the shower for when I was done. I felt light and exhilarated, no fear. I knew what to expect this time and what to do if my depression returned. I knew that at the end of all of it, I'd get a version of my Guy.

Afterward, hair still wet, I decided to make dinner by plating fancy Thai delivery and pulling together a salad. It was like I was already nesting: a warm, domestic contentment settling in my bones. As Tom walked into the kitchen a few hours later, I was spooning dressing over a big bowl of greens. He sat on the bench to take off his sneakers before coming over to kiss me.

Guess what! he said, looking up at me. *I called my parents and told them our good news.* My jaw dropped, and I stared at him, slowly resting my big serving spoons against the edge of the wooden bowl in front of me.

What good news? I asked, hoping he meant something else. I picked the spoons back up, tossing the lettuce, trying to seem nonchalant.

THE news, he said. *The baby.* I thought about hurling the bowl at him. It didn't feel like his news to tell.

Why the fuck would you tell them? I asked. I could feel a tentacle of the old panic start to strangle me. *You didn't even ask me if you could tell them. You know how superstitious I get. I don't want a million people to know yet.*

No, no, babe, he tried to reassure me. *Everything is going to be wonderful. You'll see.*

• • •

A WEEK LATER, while on the plane to California, I got an email from the new ob-gyn I'd found: *The embryo is not viable*, it said. I looked over at Guy, asleep in his chair next to me, completely still, his skin like a melted scoop of vanilla ice cream. We hit a few bumps of turbulence, which always terrified me. I looked back at my phone as a distraction. *I tried to call you, but it went straight to voicemail. You'll start bleeding soon if you haven't already. Your hormone levels are off, which shows me there is something catastrophically wrong. Consider it a blessing.* I read that line a second time before continuing. *The embryo wouldn't progress well.* I wasn't shocked, actually. I'd sensed it, or maybe more accurately I'd feared it, and now it had come true, a possibility I guess I'd prepared myself for with superstition. Tom had told his parents I was pregnant with our second child, after all, before I even told my own mother, or Guy, and now I'd lost the embryo.

I got off the plane in Los Angeles and watched the rows of scraggly palm trees as we drove from the airport to West Hollywood back to the Chateau. Pulling in seemed like a time warp. That hotel had seen things: It had survived earthquakes and riots and picket lines, rock star mischief and starlets' secrets. My terrible postpartum depression three years ago. Guy falling off his pool chair. As we entered the bungalow, I inhaled its familiar smell, the evidence of fifty years of partying painted in layers on the walls. I decided to text my mom.

I just got to LA with Guy, and I'm miscarrying :(. I sent it before I could read it over because I knew if I dwelled on the words, I might not share them. My mom called me right away.

I'll take the first flight I can get and meet you, she said, her voice hushed. *Tell the front desk to hold a room for me for a few nights, and I'll be there tomorrow or the next day.* My mother can be very levelheaded in an emergency, not that this was one. No one was dying, except the little embryo, of course, but that had already happened. I grabbed my bottle of water and took a chug, forcing my swallow muscles to work against the lump in my throat. This baby would never know how excited I had been because it would never know how I tried to save it simply by wanting it badly. It would never feel my love.

LATER, I ordered room service for me and Guy, and gave him his bath, filling the old, cracked tub with extra bubbles to give him something to play with. Then I tucked him into my bed with his gray scrap of a blanket and a bottle. He was out in ten minutes, the time change from New York working in my favor. I went to the living room to finish my martini with olives, hoping it would help quiet my brain. I thought about taking some notes in my journal, but I could only find a pencil, which I hated.

The martini I'd ordered wasn't doing much for me, and writing wasn't possible, so I thought I'd try a massage, and the hotel concierge could only get a male masseuse to show up so late.

I felt like I was cheating. I opened all the doors in the living room so I could see the moon, even though it gets so cold at night in LA. After the vodka and two measly olives smacked me right in my empty stomach, I wanted fresh air, and goose bumps, and the slightly miserable feeling of being weighed down by a wet towel made of breeze and massage oil. I wanted to hear cars rushing up Sunset Boulevard, taking those long, soft curves toward the edge of Western civilization in pale zooms in the distance. I wanted to smell night-blooming jasmine and see a coyote or something. Against the heavy, foggy darkness, I wanted to feel like the masseuse was a butcher, carving apart my sinew with velvety strokes, exposing my warmth to something brutal.

I'd been scared to get massages when I was first pregnant with Guy, imagining some masseuse accidentally pushing on a pressure point and causing a spontaneous miscarriage. Now that I was having a real miscarriage, expelling an embryo I'd been so happy to grow, I craved ferocious kneading, something to mimic the torment of not getting what I wanted from my own body. I'd done so much work to get here: I'd faced my traumas and my demons and my flaws, not to make them go away but to know them so well that they couldn't scare me. I said them out loud and wrote about them and shared them with people who asked. I'd even published some articles about it all. I felt that it was the only way to grow into a good mamma for Guy. And I was convinced it would help me get pregnant again.

With my face down and a soft Brian Eno soundtrack emanating from my iPhone, I let myself imagine another baby, another pregnancy, and how I'd insist on comfort and care. First, I'd interview all my doctors, and I'd tell them what happened to me. *I'm a survivor of physical and emotional sexual violence,* I'd say, looking them right in the eye. *No more than any other woman, but no less, either.* I'd analyze whether their faces divulged skepticism. *Even though my doctor did nothing "wrong," according to the medical-industry standards, my sexual trauma was triggered by the way I was treated when I was giving birth.* I'd wait to see if they cocked their heads or nodded along. *So, here's what I require: I need a doctor who is willing to take the time to educate me about everything they intend to do. I need a doctor who asks and receives enthusiastic consent before touching me or changing their touch. I need a doctor who provides me with a word that means they will stop what they are doing, and another word that means they will take their hands out of, or off of, my body immediately. I need accurate descriptions of the pain level I can expect and how long that pain will last. I need my doctor to be prepared to acknowledge and treat my pain differently if it does not match the description they gave.* I'd pause then, just briefly, to make sure they weren't leaping to any sort of self-defense.

Also, I will not put my feet in stirrups. I will insert my own speculum. I may need my doctor to hold my hand. If I cry, I may need my doctor to be kind to me. I need a doctor who understands that the trauma of my past lives in my cells, even though I've processed it intellectually. I can describe it without getting upset, but sometimes when I'm touched, my body can't help but react. I need a doctor whose every move reflects that understanding. I'd expect them to take notes on all of this.

Also, I will have a doula, something every pregnant person should have free access to, which every good doctor should welcome and encourage, in an effort to increase the birthing person's safety and comfort. I imagined a smart, empathetic doctor nodding her head and saying *Absolutely!* and it made me smile a bit in the pillowed face cradle. Then I thought about a doctor laughing at me or telling me he wouldn't be able to do any of what I asked for, and instead of feeling sad, I felt emboldened. I decided then and there: I will not stop talking about this until the end of time–trauma-informed care must be taught in medical schools as a baseline for the standard of care that every patient deserves.

I SLEPT DEEPLY and wildly after my massage, as if I were dreaming on mushrooms, drowning in surreal storylines. And then I awoke the next morning, dragging myself up, and saw blood on my sheets–not a lot–just a few soft pink and brown spots. I'd known it was coming, and now it was here. There was something spooky about it, being practically alone, miscarrying at this old, haunted hotel, after paying another man to touch me late at night.

The morning walk to the pool was easy as always. Across my little lawn and onto a rock path, down a flight of stairs surrounded by bamboo; if you peered between the stalks, you could see the employee changing rooms and rest area, with its plain outdoor umbrellas, so drab compared to the blue-and-white-striped ones, with their Regency-style pagoda peaks. I saw a hummingbird on the way, not even afraid of me: he just hovered. Only a few hours before, I'd seen a small bobcat in my yard, and we'd locked eyes. He looked hungry. I, on the other hand, had no appetite; I wanted my iced coffee, hoping it would make me shit, debloat me, and deflate me with everything going on down there, the dead baby trying to flush itself out.

No one was ever down at the pool when I first arrived, but around eleven, people started trickling in. My bungalow, the little house where I'd spent so much time the last few years, was right above it; if the sun was hitting right, I could see who was there.

I called my mom when I got to my chair. She picked up after one ring. *I'm in a really critical meeting. Are you doing okay? Can I call you back?* She was, I would say, an efficient phone user.

When do you land? I asked. *I just called to get an idea of your timing, so I can tell the concierge, and book dinner for us and stuff.* I found that focusing on logistics was the best way to get answers out of her.

I couldn't get a flight for a few days; there simply weren't any— well, there were lots, but not any that worked for my schedule, and I'm so sorry about that, sweetie. Travel is just so complicated. I rolled my eyes.

She switched into her maternal voice, the one she'd used when I was a little kid and I was sick from an ear infection or strep throat and I'd cry in her lap, extra upset that I'd have to drink that pink antibiotic mixture.

But I can't wait to see you and my Guy, and I'll be there just as soon as I can, okay? Just give me a couple–three days. Let's say until Friday. Have you started bleeding? I thought about telling her everything. Miscarriages are really gross: the stuff pouring out of me was intense. But before I could explain it all, she made her goodbyes. *Sweetheart, I've got to finish up with what I'm doing here. It's critical.* She hung up without waiting for me to complete the word *bye.*

. . .

SO MANY TIMES, I'd been here at this pool; listless, stagnant, escaping something; in need of mothering and tortured by not getting it. In need of being a mother and tortured by not knowing how. But that's not how I felt on this trip. This time I felt patient with my own brain. I let myself think calmly, writing down all that I was feeling, working on my book, relying on Guy for stillness. At night, I'd drag him from his crib into my room, and then I'd go back for his blankie and his baba and his Big Bird. With just a comforter and a sheet, we'd have to snuggle deeply to stay warm during the witching hours, all part of my master plan to get more of his cells inside my body where I could watch after them, hold on to them, keep him with me every second of every day for the rest of my existence. I stared at him while he slept, trying to memorize his ever-shifting face.

My littlest love. Why had it taken so long to know that's what you were to me? I thought to myself while I looked at the thin lids covering his big eyes. I couldn't blame any single thing: not my mother, not the shock of my sister's baby dying, not the depressions I'd felt over the years of my life and not known that's what they were, not Tom's emotional absence, nor my inability to demand more from him as a partner. I couldn't condemn my own immaturity or the hormones or the rupture with my past identity. It wasn't solely that I didn't relish being a mom. It was the whole recipe, all mixed together, a thick stew. I buried my face in the back of Guy's head as I drifted off to sleep.

I'VE NEVER BEEN IN LA in August when it was so cloudy; normally that's reserved for February and June. *June Gloom*, they call it, but it burns off by lunch. These clouds were just sitting, not moving anywhere, framing Hollywood's alabaster castle in all its beauty, adorned with its myriad turrets and terraces. There was not a bit of breeze, and the air was thick and sticky. Ninety degrees. A plastic dinosaur sat at the bottom of the pool, which one of the guests had taken to stirring with the cleaning net like a big pot of soup. A thin layer of oily sunscreen and tiny, dry, brown specks–some sort of dead plant detritus or seed–was floating across the surface so evenly that if you went for a dip, you came out with a skin of it on you, not that I ever really swam; only visiting French women actually swam in this pool, for the most part. They were the only ones to get their hair wet. They wore conservative bathing suits, sometimes even one-pieces, even if they were young, and they smoked in the sun while the water evaporated from their skin.

Guy came over to me after the playgroup I'd signed him up for let out. He was naked, shiny with sunblock, and he ran across the hot bricks into my arms. His legs were getting so long, no longer a baby but still with a sweet, lisping voice.

We made cupcakes today. I brought one for you, Mamma. His babysitter, the cousin of the babysitter of one of my Los Angeles mom friends, trailed behind him, languid in the heat.

Did you get your work done? she asked. I nodded while Guy climbed into my lap. I was editing a proposal for my memoir, and it didn't feel like work at all. It felt like the only choice for me, to tell my story to anyone who wanted to read it. Even this, even this part of my story, the resolved part where I don't hate Tom and I don't hate my life, and the little soul that died was hardly alive to begin with.

After all, how many people can say they've bled into a diaper beside the same pool where Marilyn Monroe once sunned herself, just down from the bungalow where John Belushi was injected with a speedball a little too big and a little too strong? How many people can say they've bled into a diaper here *twice*? It wasn't so long ago that I was staring at this same lemon tree, watching the lemons fall off every so often and for some reason fizz when they hit the water, crying behind my heart-shaped glasses because I had ruined my life by becoming a mother.

Years ago, Tom took me to New Orleans as a surprise for my birthday. I was so mad at him because he didn't plan anything, not a single reservation for dinner, nothing but a room in a bed-and-breakfast. He handed me a bunch of printed-out emails on the plane.

Here's what Mary and Frank suggested, he said, showing me pages of recommendations from the two people he knew who grew up there, dropping them on my tray table with the smug pride of a man who really thought he'd done something great. Which is how we ended up fighting at a twenty-four-hour diner, the kind with a bucket and a ladle next to the grill top, filled with melted butter to pour over two a.m. grits. Our waitress popped her gum and wore the same cat eyeliner as I did.

As I walked back to our hotel in the rain, crying, I heard piano music and stopped, and I peeked in the window of a sweet little town house on a corner with cherry print curtains. Women and men were dancing in a circle, dressed in poodle skirts and twin sets, with a pianist playing old-fashioned music. The sign said *No dancing unless you've paid for the breakfast club, 5 cents.* I still think they were all spirits, sent to break me out of my spell, because the rest of the trip was lovely. One of those trips I still think about, where I really felt the energy of the city's strange history. It's where I realized: I do my best in haunted places.

This time, this trip to this haunted hotel, my second baby couldn't make it. Instead of my body betraying me as it did when I gave birth, denying me any ability to love or be loved or be happy for my firstborn, my body became smart. My brain knew something I didn't, and it made the decision for me that this little sac of cells had to go.

Now I'm staring at a pool I'm not allowed to swim in, doctor's orders, with a bikini top on and my nightgown pulled down to my waist. When I put my legs up on my chaise, the people in the hotel could probably see that I was wearing a diaper, or my big bloody crotch stain, depending on the day, if they happened to be looking out of the windows down at the pool. A miscarriage is so much blood. Gelatinous, creamy, chunky blood. You can feel it drip out, hot and thick, like a clock ticking into your underpants. My baby was the size of an orange seed. Earlier, I thought I saw him, the outline of a tiny baby, in the muck. I tried to grab him and look at him up close, but he was more slippery than I thought, less sticky, and he fell into the toilet before I could squeeze away the slime around him. I felt sad for him then, alone in there. I would have preferred to give him a burial instead of this Viking funeral, pushed out to sea, off to a merman's death. He's really gone now.

ONE NIGHT I TOOK A VICODIN and went to Dan Tana's for martinis with a friend from college. We sat outside, which was so quiet, and people-watched while the taciturn waiters in thin tuxedos, shiny at the elbows, shuffled around with their trays piled with chicken parm and mediocre pasta, industrial tomato sauce, and clumpy, pre-grated cheese. I didn't want to feel the cramps, and I didn't want to feel sad. I sat peacefully, a little introspective, watching my old friend eat the crispy potatoes and onions over her steak. I made a toast to my little dead seed, and she cringed.

To my loser embryo who couldn't get his shit together. Cheers. I thought I was being funny; why couldn't I make jokes about my own dead baby? I should have been allowed to make jokes about my own dead baby. I'd always remember the time he leaked out of me slowly over the course of so many days, ruining all the underwear I'd brought with me to LA and staining the pool towels, too, so why not commemorate it with a stupid toast? Those towels had looked so white in the bright, pristine California sunshine, until I showed up and let my dead baby ruin it all.

After dinner, I considered trying to masturbate, but when I walked into my bungalow, Guy was still awake. He was naked, dirty, and unbathed, stirring hotel ice in a big bucket with a serving spoon from the kitchen, talking about *secret potions*. I said goodbye to his babysitter, washed him off and made him a bottle, and rubbed his back until he fell asleep, which was right before I fell asleep. I'd had a martini at dinner, then some red wine when I got back to my room—some leftover Brunello that tasted like water. I accidentally gulped the last sip with all the debris in it, and it knocked me out. I fell asleep before I could try to touch myself quietly in the bathroom, thinking about Tom's eyes, but it's nice to have feelings down there about a man I once wasn't sure I'd ever feel safe touching again. A man I now missed.

When I was here after Guy was born, there was nothing the ghosts could do to save me. We were equally forsaken. I was only technically alive. I spent my days at this pool drunk and high, hating my life, knowing I should be more grateful, knowing I should be kissing the ground every second in thanks, but numb to my eyeballs instead. It was silent here, empty during the week, aside from the birds and the traffic right below me on Sunset, right where Helmut Newton's heart stopped working, causing him to crash his car and die in a fiery, dramatic, dazzling death. I wanted to crash a car, too. I didn't want a fiery death like Helmut because I didn't want anyone to know I'd gone. I just wanted to slip away, quietly, without any attention or fanfare; no sirens, no parade of emergency vehicles announcing my untimely demise, no helicopters hovering above the scene.

I'm not depressed, I'd thought then, hiding behind my sunglasses and sipping sweet tea through a paper straw, like liquid candy, my hydration between those acrylic pool glasses filled with wine. *I'm just realizing the world for what it is. Anyone who doesn't see what I see is deluding themselves.*

At the time, I didn't know that this wasn't the whole story. Because depression is a symptom, not the problem itself. The problem is the grief and rage under the depression; the worms under the rock. And a symptom of depression is thinking there will never be a solution. My problems had mostly been avoidable, which is what bothers me the most: I could have prevented a lot of my suffering if I'd been in therapy, had earlier access to medication, and had an ob-gyn who practiced trauma-informed care. And now I could never get that time back. Not with Guy and not with myself.

At five o'clock I had my hair blow-dried in my bedroom. I sat in a low, midcentury chair while the stylist negotiated with the electricity, the outlets, and systems as old as my seat. *The fuse blows if I turn the lights on*, I said to her, *so do you mind if I just keep the curtains open?* I slid back the sheer drape to reveal a long sliding door, and light poured in, bouncing off the white sheets.

When Guy was born, and I was under the thick smog of depression, I'd have to lock Napoleon outside because he would bark at blow-dryers, as well as the sound of martini shakers in the bar where I'd take him before dinner. I'd spend an hour smoothing my hair to the top of my waist, ends split and fraying, but I liked that. Everything else was rich, so my hair could be trashy, evidence of my Indiana roots—more approachable than a coif that would make me look older, anyway, and the effort of staying as young and pretty as possible was the only mask I had to hide the misery of new motherhood.

I'd toss on the biggest faux fur, something candy-colored and shaggy; minidress underneath, baubles on baubles, rhinestones everywhere they should and shouldn't go, all perched on the highest platforms; rainbow sprinkles and Chanel bags; Hello Kitties and whipped cream on a Britney Spears sundae; off to a party in the hills above us. The owners of these houses never had kids, or if they did, you wouldn't see them. At one sparkling glass ranch, the much younger wife of an octogenarian eyed me across the room, looking me up and down.

Since then, three years had passed. I'd taken many trips back to this LA bungalow, with and without Tom, but the irony of being here without him while miscarrying was not lost on me. My dog was dead. The little orange-seed baby was dead, and I was counting on that embryo. More love to add to the world, more security that Guy would be loved, more assurance that if something bad happened, one of them would call for me; that my love would double, and then it would be able to fix anything on this planet. I was making Guy a sibling. An ally against me and their father. I wanted to see them hug and play pretend, babbling together. I wanted to see them grow up to be close, their bond a kind of safety against the passing of time.

But instead he died, that little thing. His essence hung in the smog. When I heard screams in the distance or sirens from down the hill, it made sense. This is the place, after all, where you find wild bobcats in your yard in the morning, savagely hungry looks in their eyes. This is the place where the air is so dry and desperate that no amount of lotion keeps your legs creamy or your hair from feeling like straw, where little pieces of you flake off.

TWO DAYS AFTER WE CHECKED IN, Guy started seeing ghosts in our bungalow. *The man is looking right at you*, he said, dragging me to the door and pointing to our yard. *He's so mean; so, so mean, Mamma! He has a beard and no hands.* I looked up photos of Belushi with a beard, but Guy didn't seem to recognize him. *Look at them, Mamma*, he said a few days later. *Josh and James and Ted, they are having a party, and it is so loud.*

We stayed up so late together, I guess the ghost party gave him an extra boost of energy. We watched movies until midnight, then slept until eleven. We ordered donuts every day practically, except on the weekends, when the hotel made us chocolate chip pancakes for breakfast. We wandered the main building, where they kept the lights off inside on most of the floors. It was spooky at night, and Guy continued to tell me he saw ghosts over there, too.

There's so many of them, everywhere, Mamma, but they stay outside, Guy told me in his toddler babble. For the last week, he'd been going on and on about ghosts, half intelligible and sometimes mostly to himself, when his babysitter said, *You know he's not lying, right? He really is seeing this stuff.*

He's not the only one who saw shit there. When I was at the pool, chatting with a makeup artist I knew from New York, she told me that her daughter Eleanor used to see something otherworldly in bungalow 1 as a kid, and the French film director staying in bungalow 2–the one who wore long sleeves and baked on the hottest days–looked over and agreed, admitting, *I feel them.* Next to him an aging male dancer languished, and I thought I saw Hilton Als. I walked across the hot pool bricks and thought about the callused bottoms of my feet, my ballet injuries, the shame of ugly pointe-shoe toes made worse by pool water and hot bricks and bad hotel pedicures.

When my mom didn't arrive down at the pool as planned, I called her to see if she wanted to come over for a coffee. I was sitting at a table, my journal and a pen in my lap. There was an ashtray next to me, overflowing, and I considered moving it so I wouldn't have to hear her complain about the smell when she got here.

Your call woke me, she said, her voice thick with sleep. *This time change always gets me.* I was quiet for a second, trying to figure out how she could have had time to land, get to the hotel, and already take a nap. She seemed to know what my brain was contemplating.

I flew in last night; got a last-minute ticket on an earlier plane, she explained quickly. *I knew you'd want to be out with your friends,* she said with practiced sincerity in her voice that I thought was surely a performance. *I didn't want to bother you. And by the way,*

I canceled the res you made at Chateau; I'm down the street at the Tower, anyway. I know how you like your space. The statement felt like an accusation.

My space? I asked, feeling a little irked. *I thought the whole point of the trip was to be with us.* I felt myself start to unravel a little, unsure of how to interpret what she was saying.

Oh, I'll still see you, silly! she said. *But you know the martinis here are much, much better. And they know me so well. All the cute valet boys remember my name.* I started to sigh, but then I thought about Guy. He'd be so happy to see her after his playgroup.

Okey dokey, Mamma, I said with a little laugh, mostly to myself. *Whatever works. I'll just be glad to see you.* The Tower was only two blocks away, and fighting over a two-block walk seemed futile. I wanted to look back on these days and think that I honored my lost, little embryo and my existing, beautiful boy by choosing to let this annoying shit go. *Should we meet somewhere amazing for lunch?* I asked, looking forward to a good meal.

You pick. I'm feeling particularly selfless, considering your condition, she said. *I guess not sushi. And not some place with ridiculous vegan salads. And nowhere that uses garlic too liberally in case one of these valets tries to kiss me, ha ha. But other than that, you pick. And please note this fine example of maternal altruism.* My mother's ability to mock herself was one of her finest qualities. *And how are you feeling?* she asked more sincerely. I was about to launch into the gory details: Day one there were chunks, I had to sit over the toilet and let it pour out. Yesterday I downgraded from diapers to pads, and today I made the decision to give up and just stain my bikini bottoms without worrying.

Better, was all I said, deciding on efficiency. I could feel my allotted time on the call waning.

Good! Text me where to meet you for lunch. I have to go make some calls. And she was off again.

There's a big, blown-up, glossy photograph in my parents'

house of the two of them on their wedding day. My mother is beaming next to my dad, who shines with his own happiness, his eyes wet. Her hair is straight at the top but grows wide with curls as it nears her chin, as if she stepped out of a Warhol painting from the seventies. She wears a long-sleeve, loose dress in lace. *Mollie Parnis designed it, and she was a big deal at the time*, she used to tell me with a laugh when I criticized it.

She is a beautiful woman with full lips and sparkling eyes. Hers is a real beauty, not frigid or alien but humane and warm, and filled with a youthful energy. Our energy is what connects us. And I'm not referring to the fact that the lady went into labor with me in a Jazzercise class—I'm talking about a love of life and celebration that permeates our choices. It's how I know she'll be awake when I text her with an idea at midnight. It's how I know she'll never retire, and always listen to the youngest person in the room, and play pop music in the car, and travel wherever I ask her to meet me. And when I think about the times I can remember that she didn't have that energy—that she was angry, sad, or mean, that vitality leaving her gorgeous face—I have to admit that life might have chipped away at her exuberance the same way it chipped away at mine. For all I know, she could have been sexually assaulted a million different ways, splintered by patriarchy, harmed by a doctor in labor. She might have had postpartum depression and never recovered. And I realize that to understand my relationship to that gorgeous movie-star bride, to understand the times she wasn't her best self for me, I had to process that everything about her—every misstep that ever made me mad or hurt or disappointed—had nothing to do with my value or worth.

I'd felt unparented in my life, but it wasn't because I wasn't parent-able. I'd felt unloved, but it wasn't because I was unlovable. I felt like a burden at times, but it wasn't because I was an albatross. Holding these grudges was doing nothing but damaging the shared energy I felt with my mom, and I needed her connection.

Our cells live in each other's bodies, after all. Maybe that's why it feels like we can read each other's minds and why I constantly, forever, want more from her. A fetus will leach calcium from the mother's bones if it isn't fed enough via umbilical cord. We are parasites to our mothers to begin with, dependent on them for existence and for connection. But at some point, to move the life cycle forward, a mother can no longer be her child's host. And to make myself a better mother, I needed the space I was spending on criticizing her choices. I needed to fill it up with love and acceptance, for Guy and for all the future little guys.

MAYBE THE GHOSTS were keeping me buoyed, but it was probably the three years of two kinds of therapy and almost leaving my husband and then deciding what marriage needed to be for us; what motherhood needed to be for me; and how best to manage the worries and the fears that caused the most anguish. How best to manage the extreme condition of merely existing as a woman in even the best of scenarios.

I was finally okay with all of it, even sitting with myself. After all, this time I was here as a real mother. Last time I had a baby with me, but I wasn't a mother yet. This time, finally, I was living for my son's bright eyes, and his sticky fat feet, his skinny chest with the blue veins, his mushroom-cap butt cheeks, his jagged baby teeth, his soft curls, the baby duck hair on his lower back, his doughy little thighs, his laugh when the tickle monster came, the way he clung to me in the swimming pool, teeth chattering but refusing to get out, his pout when something I said made him sad, his tangled eyelashes.

Are you sweet? I asked him.

I'm not sweet, I'm Guy! We laughed.

One morning he turned to me and said, *Mamma, I'm happy to be here.* He had no idea.

While the burden of a mother is to hold humanity's pain and fear as our own, chasing our children around filled with worry and anxiety, it is also to be depicted as weak and hysterical for our distress and vigilance. Husbands, clasping beer cans around a grill, laugh about how nervous their wives are, how overbearing.

Babe, he's going to be fine, Tom reassured me, sensing my panic every time Guy climbed too high or went near the edge of something. I thought that creating a sibling, a partner for my baby, could do some of this job for me; could make sure that after I left, someone else would love him the way I did. It broke my heart that one day Guy would live on this earth without me to watch out for him, and I wanted to make him someone to replace me, an impossible task.

Just then, a picture of Tom and me kissing flashed on my phone screen, and my stomach fluttered a little bit. I found it unbelievable that we'd managed to get to a place where I got excited when he called me. I remembered feeling absolutely hopeless, resigned to the fact that our relationship was over, and thought about all the work it had taken us both to recover from that. Sure, a huge part of it was stuff he'd had to do, but the most important adjustment had come from me: I now fully believed I didn't need Tom to survive. I was who I was with or without him, and I was proud of that person. She didn't need anyone else's support to be her truest self.

I could, instead, have hated him forever. I could have divorced him. I could have measured my own self-worth as a reflection of how he treated me, and I could have lumped him in with every man who had ever wronged me. I could have clung to the belief that the only thing separating him, and all men, from the Wolf was a matter of degrees. Now I was glad to say I saw all men, all people, as unique entities capable of their own special brands of shitty and loving behaviors.

Hi, my love, I'm at the pool. My mom arrived, got in last night but didn't tell me. And moved to a different hotel. I let myself sigh, and I heard him chuckle at that.

It's always something with her, he said, and I could hear the smile in his voice. *Should I come out on Monday, stay a few days, and then fly home with you?* he asked. *Would that make life easier or harder?* We'd become much kinder to each other, after all the therapy; we'd chosen to make emotional generosity a habit. It made it easier to be nice when we wanted to murder each other over things like toilet paper.

I told him not to stress. *We'd love to see you, but really, we're good. I've bled on every surface at this hotel, but I'm doing all right, you know? All I need in this world is my world. You, Guy, my writing. And, okay, yes, I admit it, my mom.* We both laughed a little.

She is . . . seductive, he reasoned.

She is, and she's fun, and can be really, really funny, and a million other good things, but I'm sort of just too focused on Guy to waste energy being frustrated by her faults—or anyone's, I explained, flipping over on my lounge chair and putting on a hat—my endless battle against the melasma that decorated my face during pregnancy and never went away.

Yah, exactly, said Tom. *Priorities, you know?*

I HUNG UP WITH TOM and scrolled mindlessly through my phone for a minute, and then put it down, watching two dragonflies chase each other over a cloud of pink bougainvillea hanging off the tile structure that housed the pool filter. I flipped open my journal and dated the page.

I thought about the spider sculptures that Louise Bourgeois made at the end of her long life. Some of them were more than thirty feet tall and weighed almost ten thousand pounds. I'd driven to visit one once in Spain, and from afar it looked like an alien creature. Up close, it was even more menacing. Not only was it a feat of engineering, balancing on its spindly legs as if it were as strong and alive as a real spider, needing no buttressing underneath, but it also had no eyes. Nothing about it was friendly. From below, you could see its egg sac, the cage of its ribs, even the part that spins the web. She'd named them each *Maman.*

The French-born artist wrote about her own mother as patient, neat, and useful; she correlated her to a spider–an indispensable woman who could mend and stitch and watch over everything. A spider has eight legs, after all, four more limbs with which to *do*, more chances than most other creatures to multitask. A spider also has eight eyes with which to be watchful; all aspects of the maternal ideal. Yet the sculpture's appearance was grotesque and scary; its formal relationship to mothering was incongruous. But I guess that's just it: being a mother *is* grotesque and scary, at the same time that it's monumental. It is both a dark underbelly and a great gift of human existence.

Yet no one had described the full breadth to me. My pre-birth care did not map transparent discussions about the potential emotional difficulties of my upcoming experience, nor did it describe a range of acceptable ways to be a parent and to react to parenthood. No one told me–and certainly no doctor told me–that even the most normal, standard, and easy pregnancy, birth, or parenthood situation could be traumatic and churn up past trauma, that fear and derailment after such a transformative experience could actually be considered a rational response.

LATER THAT MORNING, my mom showed up at the pool. I heard her before I even saw her, because as she came down the path from the main hotel, she sang sympathies to me in her exaggerated drawl across the potted succulents and patchworked ferns.

My poor baby! Come hug your maaammmaaa! I rolled my eyes

and hauled myself up off a towel. The rusty-brown patch I left behind was smaller than it had been the day before.

I'm here, Mom. I waved at her, putting down a fresh towel, since I knew she'd say something critical about my decision to free-bleed. It was gross, but certainly grosser things had touched the towels at Chateau Marmont.

Sweetheart, she said as she hugged me. She smelled like she always did: a little like hair bleach and brewed coffee, and powdery, like expensive face products. *Let's talk.* She ushered me to sit back on my chair and took out her cell phone, spending a full two minutes typing on it before looking at me and smiling. *I'm so sorry that this has happened to you. It's a fluke. I just know it. You are just like me, in every way, and you're going to get pregnant again, just like I did after my first. So don't think this is going to be your norm.* Her icy gray eyes looked right at me, and I could tell she was not full of it. Her attention was usually short-lived, so I spoke quickly.

Mom, I said. I sat up, and I could feel her glance at my distended belly. *I don't know if it's a fluke or not, I guess. I'm sad, but also I'm still processing everything, and I just want to focus on Guy. And on myself. I don't want to try to control the future.* She nodded like she was listening, one hand rubbing her leg as she pondered.

I think that's really smart, Sarah. Let's talk about what you can control, how about that? She smiled, her bright lipstick stretching across her full lips. I really wish I'd inherited those.

I think I'm going to write a book. I went back to look at all my journals from the last couple of years, and I know it's crazy to think anyone would want to read my shit, and I know I'm probably too old to suddenly decide to try to be a writer, but I'm putting together a propos–

A book! That's so exciting. I sort of thought you should, after the articles you wrote. Will you do a press tour? She whipped out her cell phone like a cowgirl reaching into her holster. *Should we celebrate? Where should I book dinner? Who all knows about this?* Her fingers hovered, awaiting my instructions.

Honestly, no one. I mean a few people–a few of my best friends, and Tom–but I don't even know if it's going to happen. I flipped my sunglasses down on my face, afraid I was going to tear up, and I didn't want her to think I was sad.

Baby girl, I didn't start my first restaurant until I was almost forty. You need to kick that impostor bullshit to the curb. Put all that energy toward writing this book and being your damn self. That's the only thing that ever made me happy, she said with finality, clapping her hands together and standing up. *Well, and you children, of course. I mean, some days. Mostly once you'd moved out.* She looked at her phone again. *Oh shoot, it's my office. I knew this would happen. Let's save lunch for tomorrow and just meet at dinner later. I have to take this call.* She picked up the phone abruptly. *It's critical,* she mouthed at me, and flashed me a peace sign, followed by a pantomime of calling me later. I could hear her bossing someone around as she walked down the path, her figure tessellated by verdant plants until she disappeared.

Green palms fluttered against the brightest blue sky. Guy slept in our bungalow. Some things in California looked especially dusty, but the sky stayed sharp, as if I were seeing it with a different set of eyes. I loved the palm trees with all the leaves, not the royal kind but the Jurassic ones, with prehistoric, spiky fronds that you could hear slide against one another when the breeze blew through. LA had its own music. In New York, I could hear strange echoes, snippets of conversations from blocks away, someone shouting curse words, fighting with a stranger, the city sharing its secrets, everyone in it together. LA air went right through me, holding me in place in front of this icy pool with the pregnant lemon tree, reminding me that I might be alone now, but I wasn't lonely anymore.

. . .

WHAT I WANTED TO SHOUT after my mother as I watched her leave me–that I was sorry for all the worst parts of myself, for all the times I was horrible; that I'd be sorry every second for the rest of my life; that I forgave her for her faults, because I understood them; that I empathized–didn't come out in time, but I felt that maybe, somehow, she knew already.

In geology, a *mother lode* is the central and principal vein of an ore or mineral, the place where the largest amount of gold or silver in a particular area can be found. There's a mother lode of gold in California that stretches 120 miles north to south and three miles wide, and its discovery started the California gold rush of the mid 1800s, which in turn redirected the technologies and advancements of the American empire for the rest of the century. Colloquially, the use of the word refers to the real or imagined origin of something that exists in great abundance: *the mother lode of treasure found in King Tut's tomb.* But in that moment, I thought about what the word, in any of its spellings, meant to me–how the load of being a mother can be almost unbearable, how I'd barely made it through. How searingly painful it had been to shoulder all the burdens of birthing a child in even the best of circumstances. How much the experience had diverted my life–how there'd been so much to learn from it.

The forgiveness I craved from my mother had to equal the forgiveness I was willing to give to her, and I hoped that one day I could expect the same grace from Guy. There might be a time when he'd think he hated me, filled with teenage angst or a resentment I couldn't foresee, and I could only pray that one day he'd understand what I'd gone through, and would appreciate my limits. This potent cycle of absolution is what makes us human and is what makes human life worth it. And while the heaviness of carrying on this chain can be brutal, it's what rescues us from the inevitable sorrow of losing one another, because it renders the most essential part of us–our complex and immutable love–everlasting.

I got up off my chair and looked out at the streets of West Hollywood splayed beneath me, radiating away from the canyons, whose crevices are always the color of dark iced tea. I stretched and yawned, grabbed my journal, and took the stone steps back to the bungalow two at a time, my bare feet skimming them gently. *Back to Guy,* I thought. *Back to my happy little boy. What a lucky place to be.*

Acknowledgments

Thank you to my editor, Samantha Weiner, and to Elizabeth Breeden, Michael Holmes, Clare Maurer, Gina Navaroli, Tom Spain, Desiree Vecchio, and everyone else at Simon Element–especially Doris Cooper.

Thank you to the best literary agent, Sabrina Taitz, and to WME's finest, Rachel Liebenthal. You are agents for good and also good agents–and real friends.

Thank you to Andrew Dunlap, without whom it wouldn't have happened.

Thank you to the rest of my WME team: Ty Anania, Laura Bonner, Cashen Conroy, Hilary Michael Zaitz, and Matilda Forbes Watson.

Thank you to my earliest supporters and their unwavering vision: Andy McNicol and Brooke Drabkin, Brad Weston, Jessica Rovins, Leah Trouwborst, and the legendarily elegant Shelley Wanger.

Thank you to Paul Bogaards, Kate Downen, Stephanie Hauer, and everyone at Bogaards Public Relations.

Thank you to Beowulf Sheehan, Quinn Murphy, and Karla Serrano.

Because I judge every book by its cover and never know who creates that magic, thank you to John Gall.

Thank you to my very generous readers: Stephanie Danler, Mark Guiducci, Chloe Malle, Samira Nasr, Katie O'Donnell, Mike

Quinn, Meghan Riley, Chloe Schama, Noor Tagouri, Cece Thompson, and Harley Viera-Newton.

Thank you to Emily Stone.

Thank you to Erika Bloom, Lois Braverman, Jess Castro, Pempa Dolma, Casha Gobin, Dr. Nerissa Guballa, Viktoria Harkot, Julia Jacob, Victoria Leanna White, Shalom Melchizedek, Beth Nicely, Dr. Sonal Parr, Marie Pavillard, Terry Richmond, Sabita Shrestha, Stephanie Tillman, Rian Tompkins, Fiona True, and Dr. Julie Von.

To my family: David, Erica, Mary and Mario, Rachael, and Susie.

To my beloved, Tommy.

To my most wonderful father, John.

To Guy, to Fred: the little great loves of my life.

And mostly to Martha, with whom it all starts and ends.